Social Work and
Human Services Best Practice

Social Work and
Human Services Best Practice

Editors

Wing Hong Chui

Jill Wilson

THE FEDERATION PRESS
2006

Published in Sydney by

The Federation Press
    PO Box 45, Annandale, NSW, 2038
    71 John Street, Leichhardt, NSW, 2040
    Telephone (02) 9552 2200 Fax (02) 9552 1681
    E-mail: info@federationpress.com.au
    Website: http://www.federationpress.com.au

National Library of Australia Cataloguing-in-Publication
    Chui, Wing Hong
    Social work and human services best practice

    Includes index.
    ISBN 1 86287 599 5   (*from January 2007*: 978 1 86287 599 9)

    1. Social work administration – Australia. 2. Human services – Australia – Management.
    I. Wilson, Jill. II. Title.

361.30680994

Text printed on
100% recycled paper

Typeset by The Federation Press, Leichhardt, NSW.
    Printed by Ligare Pty Ltd, Riverwood, NSW.

Preface and Acknowledgements

No one denies that working in social work and human service organisations is challenging and demanding. Practitioners and managers alike are subjected to harsh criticism and increasingly required to justify their work, and, amidst critical public scrutiny, prove their effectiveness with explicit evidence. While we are expected to do more with less given the pressure on public expenditure, service users' demands on, and expectations of, the welfare provision continue to rise. In these circumstances, practitioners must grapple with the problem of working in a cost-effective manner under resource constraints, whilst pursuing their commitment to respond creatively to varied agendas that arise from the conflicting demands of service users, taxpayers and other stakeholders. The book attempts to provide insight into what is (and is not) the best practice to work with service users or clients across a range of fields of practice.

More specifically, the primary aim of the book is to look at the best practice models, frameworks and approaches in relation to different fields of social work and human service practice. Our aim has also been to produce a cutting edge volume which advances theories, practice and research relating to contemporary social work and human services in Australia. Various key topic areas in social work and human services include child protection, youth justice, adult corrections, ageing, disability, mental health, healthcare, refugees, Indigenous issues, and working in remote and rural communities. Indeed, these topic areas or themes for each chapter have been identified following consultation with students, social workers, human service professionals, co-ordinators of the Undergraduate studies of Social Work and Human Services, and academics in Australia. While we do not intend to give a definite statement on what is and what is not 'best' practice, we want this book to serve as the basis for discussion, debate and research on the issues covered.

The book symbolises the concerted efforts of practitioners, academics and researchers to examine controversial topics with a view to identifying and promoting effective social work and human service practice. As a result, it offers practical help to students in social work and human services, and provides information to training officers, managers and practitioners in these fields. It is thus a comprehensive and user-friendly text that covers various key topic areas in social work and human services, and draws on an extensive store of current expertise in the field in Australia.

Last, but not least, both editors would like to thank all the contributors for their willingness to play a part in writing this book and for their quality work. In addition, we would like to thank a number of renowned scholars and practitioners across the world who reviewed the earlier drafts of the chapters and provided us with extensive comments on how to improve the content and the quality of each chapter. They are (in alphabetical order): Professor Iris Chi at the University of Southern California; Mr Steve Corporal at the University of Queensland; Paul Davis at the North Somerset Housing and Social Services; Mr Colin Farlow at the University of Exeter; Dr Gai Harrison at the University of Plymouth; Dr Mark Hughes at the University of New South Wales; Mr Gordon Jack at Durham University; Professor Mike Nellis at the University of Strathclyde; Professor Nigel Parton at the University of Huddersfield; Dr Richard Pugh at Keele University; Dr Mark Sherry at the University of Toledo, and Mr Paul Stepney at the University of Wolverhampton. It should be emphasised that we alone are responsible for what follows.

Wing Hong Chui
Jill Wilson
June 2006

Contents

Notes on Contributors

Bindi Bennett

Bindi Bennett is a Kamilaroi woman who graduated from her Bachelor of Social Work in 1997. She has worked as a social worker in the areas of child and adolescent mental health, school social work, youth work and community development. She has also worked as a Lecturer at the School of Social Work and in the Djurawang program at Charles Sturt University, Wagga Wagga. She has published in the area of domestic violence and Indigenous communities and has co-researched, presented and published with Joanna Zubrzycki about Aboriginal social work. She is an active member of her own Indigenous community as well as the local Indigenous community in which she currently works.

Robert Bland

Robert Bland is a Professor of Social Work at the University of Tasmania. He completed his undergraduate and postgraduate studies at the University of Queensland and worked for many years for Queensland Health. He has extensive experience as a social worker, administrator, teacher and researcher in the area of mental health. His research interests include the spirituality of mental health, housing, and families and mental illness. He is a life member of Association of Relatives and Friends of the Mentally Ill (ARAFMI).

Helen Cameron

Dr Helen Cameron has a psychology and education background. She is a Senior Lecturer in the School of Social Work and Social Policy at the University of South Australia. She has worked collaboratively with the South Australian Department for Correctional Services in developing training packages for correctional workers and she has presented conference papers and has published in the area of correctional rehabilitation. Her primary areas of teaching are in counselling and interviewing skills and in conflict management. A major theme in her research activities concerns the life-chances of disadvantaged people. She currently holds responsibility for Australian Research Council funded research grant, focused on the experiences of families from disadvantaged backgrounds.

Lesley Chenoweth

Lesley Chenoweth is a Professor of Social Work at Griffith University and has more than 30 years experience as a social work practitioner and academic, 20 of these in the disability area. Her current research interests span disability issues, human services and rural communities. Lesley has conducted research on disability policy analysis, deinstitutionalisation, families, violence and abuse, and delivering human services to people in rural communities. She is a regular consultant to government and community organisations and has served on numerous boards and committees for disability, legal and family welfare agencies. Lesley is a regular invited speaker at conferences both in Australia and overseas.

Wing Hong Chui

Dr Wing Hong Chui is a Senior Lecturer in the School of Social Science and the Program Director of Bachelor of Social Science at the University of Queensland. Before this, he held lecturing positions in the Department of Social Work and Probation Studies at the University of Exeter, UK, in the School of Social Work and Social Policy at the University of Queensland, and in the School of Law at the City University of Hong Kong. His areas of interest include youth studies, criminology and criminal justice, social work, and migration studies. He has published articles in *British Journal of Social Work, International Social Work, Journal of Social Work Practice, Howard Journal of Criminal Justice, European Journal of Criminology* and *Australian and New Zealand Journal of Criminology*. He is the co-editor of two books, *Moving Probation Forward: Evidence, Arguments and Practice* (2003, Pearson Education) and *Experiences of Transnational Chinese Migrants in the Asia-Pacific* (2006, Nova Science).

Ros Darracott

Ros Darracott is based in Charleville, South West Queensland and has lived and worked in the region for the past 12 years, with prior experience in the Riverina. Her practice has involved providing generalist, generic services across large regional areas and the management of a broad variety of social care programs, including disability, child protection and family counselling services delivered across South West Queensland. Her Masters research explored the application of grief and loss frameworks to working with primary producers and she has a current interest in domain location and its implication for practice.

Bob Lonne

Dr Bob Lonne is a Senior Lecturer with the School of Social Work and Applied Human Sciences at the University of Queensland. He has extensive practice, managerial and research experience of rural social care, particularly in the fields of statutory child protection and welfare, and juvenile justice and has published and presented widely on these. His doctoral research examined factors affecting the work stress and staff retention of rural and remote social workers. He is currently researching the application of the concept of domain location for rural social care practitioners.

Jennifer Martin

Dr Jennifer Martin is an Associate Professor in social work at RMIT University. Her main areas of research and teaching are cross-cultural practice, critical theory, mental health and conflict resolution, and mediation. She is the author of *An Ordinary Life in China, Malaysia and Australia* (2003, Ginninderra Press), a story of the experiences of an 'ordinary' immigrant to Australia. She has conducted research with the Chinese Communities of Melbourne on health and welfare issues. She was invited by the Mekong River Commission to conduct a workshop on Conflict Resolution and Prevention in the Mekong River Basin. Over 50 representatives from countries that rely on the Mekong River for their livelihood attended this workshop. She is particularly sensitive to issues of racism, discrimination and social exclusion on both a personal and political level.

Noel Renouf

Dr Noel Renouf is a Chief Social Worker at NorthWestern Mental Health Service in Victoria and a Senior Lecturer in Social Work at La Trobe University. Noel has extensive experience in the areas of professional development of social work staff, and is a leading Australian academic in the area of connecting theory and practice in mental health. Robert Bland and he have collaborated in research and teaching, contributing extensively to the knowledge base for social work practice in Australia.

Deborah Setterlund

Dr Deborah Setterlund is a Senior Lecturer, School of Social Work and Applied Human Sciences, at the University of Queensland. Her research focuses on the outcomes of social work practice and the translation of research into practice. A large area of current research considers the implications of legislative changes for older people, particularly in relation to the management of their assets, the experiences of carers and older people in sharing asset management, and theorising around financial abuse of older people. She teaches in the areas of social work practice generally, social work with older people, group work and case management.

Sandy Taylor

Dr Sandra Taylor currently holds the position of Associate Professor in Social Work at Central Queensland University. She has worked for many years as a social worker in a variety of hospitals and community health settings, primarily in New South Wales and Tasmania. She co-ordinated Huntington's Disease and Predictive Genetic Testing services in Northern Tasmania for 10 years and has maintained a strong research and professional interest in issues affecting individuals and families with inherited conditions and disorders. She also maintains interests in professional social work and clinical issues in healthcare, Australian healthcare policy, preventative healthcare and cross-disciplinary education and practice. She is currently involved in several research projects, including a nationally funded study of genetic discrimination.

Cheryl Tilse

Dr Cheryl Tilse, a Senior Lecturer in the School of Social Work and Applied Human Sciences at the University of Queensland, teaches research methods, knowledge and practice and working in human service organisations. She is committed to research that informs ageing policy and practice primarily in the areas of asset management, financial abuse, substitute decision-making and the legal needs of older people, housing options for low income older people, enhancing communication and participation in residential care and the impact of user charges in aged care.

Chris Trotter

Associate Professor Chris Trotter has been appointed to Monash University Social Work Department in 1991 after working for 15 years in management and direct practice positions in the child protection, juvenile justice and community corrections. He has undertaken more than 10 research projects and more than 50 publications during the past decade focused primarily on working with involuntary clients. He has two commercial books *Working with Involuntary Clients* (Allen and Unwin/Sage with German translation by Edition pro-Menta) and *Helping Abused Children and their Families* (Allen and Unwin/Sage). He has developed a worldwide reputation for his work on pro-social modelling and has undertaken consultancies in Australia, Austria, United Kingdom and Ireland, Singapore and New Zealand to assist probation services and child protection agencies to implement pro-social modelling. The Cognitive Centre in the UK has published and widely distributed his training manuals on effective practice in corrections and in work with families.

Jill Wilson

Associate Professor Jill Wilson is Head of the School of Social Work and Applied Human Sciences at the University of Queensland. She teaches in field work and social work practice and researches in the areas of substitute decision-making, aged care, the management of older people's assets and the financial abuse of older people. Her research has a strong practice focus and looks at the intersection of policy and practice. She is interested in how social work education can promote a stronger interest in students in the contribution older people make to the community and explore effective ways of working with older people in their families, communities and residential services.

Joanna Zubrzycki

Dr Joanna Zubrzycki is a first generation Polish-Australian woman who graduated from her Bachelor of Social Work (Hons) in 1986. She has worked as a social worker in the areas of child and adolescent mental health, disability services, equal employment opportunity policy, brain injury rehabilitation and adolescent parenting. She is currently a Senior Lecturer in the School of Social Work (ACT) at the Australian Catholic University. She has conducted research and published in the areas of rural social work, parenting and social work, the use of self in practice, Aboriginal social work, cross-cultural practice and the construction of personal and professional boundaries.

Chapter 1

Looking for the 'Best' in Practice: An Introduction

Jill Wilson and Wing Hong Chui

This book looks at the best practice models, frameworks and approaches in relation to a wide range of specialised practice areas or fields. This chapter provides an outline of what is meant by 'best practice' and a framework for understanding areas of practice, commonly referred to as fields. It then examines some of the current challenges for practitioners concerned to offer individuals, communities and policy makers the most accountable and effective practice options. In the final section, we set out the structure of the book by highlighting the central messages our contributors want to convey.

Best Practice

'Best practice' is a generic, broad term that is linked to practice which achieves social work goals and outcomes. Defining what the 'best' is in this endeavour is often a major debate in its own right. According to Thompson (2000: 128), 'the notion of "good practice" is linked to (1) our conception of what social work [and human services] is and what it is for … and (2) our value base which … is not a simple or straightforward matter'. In this collection the focus of social work is taken to be the inter-action of individuals with the many social processes and relationships by which individuals and social structures are produced and reproduced – the social arrangements of which they are a part (O'Connor, Wilson and Setterlund, 2003). Practitioners focus on these interactions with the goal of promoting 'the development of equitable relationships and the develop-ment of individual's power and control over their own lives' (O'Connor et al, 2003: 5). These goals suggest what should be assessed, the type of knowledge that should be applied to the understanding that is developed, where intervention should be targeted, what intervention is trying to achieve and benchmarks against which practice can be evaluated. Most social work authors take a particular perspective which impacts on what they see as 'best' in setting goals for practice, in understanding the issues, identifying the nature of change and the skills and knowledge this will require, in involving individuals, families, groups, communities and in assisting practitioners to articulate what they know from practice and what they bring to practice. What is seen as 'best' will drive any evaluation of practice.

It is important to consider the question of best for whom? A number of studies over many years have consistently found that people who use social work services (often when they have little choice in the matter) value warmth and perceived power to help (for example, Biestek, 1961; Polansky, 1971; Rees and Wallace, 1982; Oldfield, 1983; Thompson, 2000), and open, non-controlling relationships (for example, O'Connor, 1989; Howe, 2000). Best practice needs to take this evidence into account.

From the perspective of using critical theory as an interpretive framework, Ferguson (2003) explicitly defines 'best practice' as being 'solution-focused in that it attempts to be strategic in terms of identifying ways of working that offer positive resources to professionals in guiding their work, but in a manner that which takes full account of issues of power, inequalities and constraint, as well a creativity in how skilful social intervention makes a difference' (p 1009). Ferguson points out that 'best practice' designates the integration of these different aspects within the realties of what is currently possible (2003: 1009).

Within the literature there are two broad approaches to what contributes to best practice: evidence-based and reflective practice.

Evidence-based practice has its roots in healthcare. It aims to use knowledge generated by scientific research to improve the likelihood of obtaining desired outcomes. It challenged authority-based practice which is characterised by making decisions based on the individual worker's opinions rather than the available knowledge (Gambrill, 2003: 3). The approach has come to be associated with the outcomes of practice measured by statistical measures of significance (Macdonald and Sheldon, 1992; Sheldon, 2001). Sheldon and Chilvers (2000) urge the practitioners to make use of current best evidence in making decisions and delivering treatment programs, and outline the underpinnings of evidence-based social care, namely conscientiousness, explicitness and judiciousness. Conscientiousness refers to 'ethical obligations to clients, not least among which is to try to keep up to date on research which helps us understand the nature and development of personal and social problems, and to keep abreast of studies on the effectiveness of particular interventions which *might* ameliorate this' (Sheldon and Chilvers, 2000: 5, italics original). Explicitness refers to the 'open and contractual' working relationship between practitioners and clients. Judiciousness implies 'the exercise of sound, prudent, sensible' judgment (Sheldon and Chilvers, 2000: 7). Webb (2001) notes that it is supposed that evidence-based practice, within the scientific paradigm, will give 'a more effective and economically accountable means of social work practice' (p 60). This approach has been critiqued as devaluing professional practice and as a managerialist device for rationing service provision. Healy (2005: 99) also notes that it does not provide ways of sifting through often contradictory research findings.

In contrast, the reflective tradition of knowledge development and use developed initially by Schon (1983, 1995) is made up by knowledge in action – the process of developing knowledge in practice, rather than applying theories – and reflection in action – developing and refining knowledge in practice to create new ways of understanding and responding to practice issues. This tradition values the flexibility to respond, on the one hand to the complexity of the issues people using human services often face, and on the other, to the uniqueness of each situation. Healy (2005) notes a core strength of the approach is that 'it recognises and indeed values, social work practitioners as active creators and users of theory and other forms of knowledge' (pp 100-101). Nevertheless these strengths can also be seen as its limitations in terms of being accountable to others for what is done, in being able to build on the knowledge of others and indeed in teaching emerging practitioners.

An understanding of best practice is also linked to a coherent understanding of what is effective in practice. Ferguson (2003) suggests that what is seen as best practice is not necessarily the same as best value. This understanding is seen in terms of both applying knowledge and skills to practice and developing knowledge and skills from practice. These two broad approaches are seen to complement and be necessary to each other. Drury-Hudson (1997) offers a model of knowledge of social work that is divided into five main overlapping knowledge forms: theoretical, empirical, procedural, practice wisdom and personal knowledge. In broad terms the first three can be seen as knowledge largely applied to practice, and the last two to knowledge developed from practice. Drury-Hudson (1997) suggests that theoretical knowledge, which provides the frames of reference used to organise phenomena, provides a link between empirical knowledge, gained from research, and procedural knowledge linked to relevant legislation and agency policies and between personal knowledge gained from our backgrounds and practice wisdom gained from social work experiences. In the context of applying knowledge to practice, best practice has also been linked to practice competencies (for example, O'Hagan, 1996), and to practise that is outcome-based (for example, Schalock, 1995; Milner and O'Byrne, 1998).

Much of the literature concludes that social workers rely more on practice wisdom, organisational and legal protocols and a value framework than on a conscious application of knowledge gained from research or codified theories (Drury-Hudson, 1997). Munro (2002: 43) suggests that rather than arguing for the virtues of one form of knowledge over another, both forms are seen as important. They form an analytic-intuitive continuum, with different stages of the assessment and intervention processes relying on different areas of knowledge.

These approaches all stress the importance of articulating knowledge, skills and values relevant to identifying a purpose, articulating what might achieve that purpose, carrying out those actions and evaluating outcomes against the purpose of a piece of practice. Best practice is linked to a conscious approach to knowledge use and its development, a purpose that is responsive to the needs of the most disadvantaged and skills and an awareness of the constraints and opportunities in the contemporary service environment, an area we return to after outlining what is meant by fields of practice in social work.

Fields of Practice

Fields of practice and practice methods are the two major descriptors of social work. Historically social work developed in the context of particular human issues such as health, income support and child protection. Social work has been in the forefront of developing appropriate policy and practice in some fields, as in child protection, but in most, it has needed to work with other disciplines and establish the contribution it can make, as in health.

For the purposes of this book, following Kamerman (2002), fields of social work practice are described as an amalgamation of program and service models; the population served; the legislative, organisational and administrative environment in which they operate; and the issues and problems they address. These four interacting components can be seen as the four planes of a solid triangle (Figure 1.1) where each influences and is influenced by the other aspects. Fields of practice in different countries also operate in an environment of history, a broader environment of the evolving shape of human services and social work's role within them, hopes for the future and strategies to achieve them. These strategies must include effective ways of evaluating practice against the stated aims of programs and individual pieces of work within that program. The whole defines the core components of practice in fields.

The current fields of practice reflect the overall development of human services, the way various issues are conceptualised and hence the form of practice that has developed in relation to these contexts. It is generally accepted that generic forms of social work practice are modified and developed in response to the demands and opportunities of specific fields of practice. What is learnt in specific settings may be applied more generally, just as generic ideas help to form specific forms of practice. It is difficult to talk about social work practice without referring to the context of that practice. This context is made up of what has gone before in terms of social work theory and skill development and the response of the state to those who are disadvantaged in contemporary society and the contemporary concerns about human services. This book identifies a range of critical issues in each of the fields and explores current responses and identifies some strategies for the future.

Figure 1. 1 The Defining Aspects of Social Work Practice in Fields

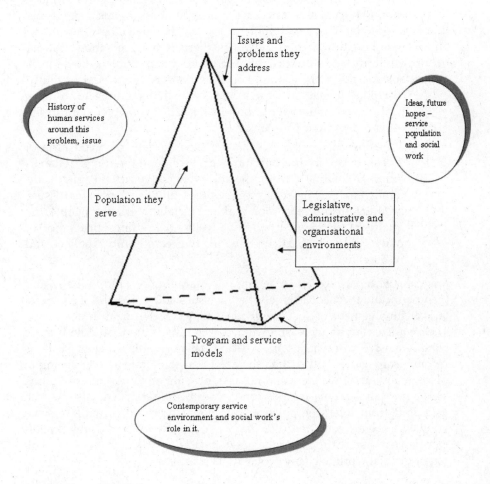

For example, in the field of ageing in Australia,

- *The population served* has been defined first in terms of age and then health status, income security and housing needs, and past service in the armed forces which entitled veterans to care as they aged. Older people's income levels have, at different times, determined access to some subsidised services. People (usually family members) who provide care are also included within the service network.
- *The legislative, administrative and organisational environment* is complicated with the States largely responsible for providing or funding services to people in the community with lower levels

of personal care needs, and the Commonwealth responsible for older people, screened by Aged Care Assessment teams, as eligible for services in residential facilities or packages of care in the community. Residential care, and increasingly community care, is highly regulated in terms of funding regimes, standards required and accreditation processes that must be followed to maintain funding. In all States there is a wide range of local authority, community or church-based organisations who address specific needs. In general social workers have worked in multi-disciplinary teams in their work with older adults to address health needs, and have traditionally had less involvement in the other issues older people face.

- *The issues and problems addressed* have largely revolved around access to care in the community and residential settings, rehabilitation following a major health event, advocacy in relation to family conflicts or access to resources, and to a less extent issues around substitute decision-making, the abuse of older people, the quality of life of older people in residential settings, promotion of older people's participation in the community, policy and research work.

Program and service models in ageing have largely been individually and therapeutically focused. This reflects the issues addressed and the general lack of involvement of social work in policy development in aged care. The awareness of an increasingly aged Australia is associated with more comprehensive approaches to meeting older people's needs such as income from sources other than the aged pension, housing and ageing in place, maintaining wellness and not just focusing on illness and disability. This approach is seen as empowering older people but it can also be seen as a shift from what the government should or could provide to what people can be expected to do or pay for themselves. These developments can be seen as creating more space for social workers as well as challenging social work to change some of its practices.

Issues in the Development of Welfare Services

It is generally noted that in many Western countries the post-Second World War social-democratic idea of the welfare state is being whittled away, under attack from both the political left and right (Hughes, 1998). As in other countries, the provision of community services in Australia has been described as a mixed economy of welfare with government, private and not-for-profit providers forming a significant industry in terms of expenditure and employees. Like other industries community services have undergone significant reform in recent years. These reforms are driven by a belief on the part of government that the delivery of programs and services can be accomplished more efficiently by the private rather than public sector (Raper, 2000), or at least that the market provides a model for efficiently providing integrated services as has allegedly happened in Britain, Canada and the United States.

The introduction of competition policies follows a trend across Western countries influenced by neo-liberal thinking that emphasises the ability of the market to meet demand by providing a competitive environment (Lyons, 2001). Such an approach includes the separation of the government's role as funder and purchaser of services, from the delivery of such services; increasingly contracting out services that were once delivered by government; the use of contracts for service accountability and encouraging fee for service contributions by service users (Rogan and Moore, 1999); a shift towards outcomes and outputs; and a new emphasis on community capacity building.

The community service sector has undergone a period of rapid transformation in the last decade in response to market reforms. These changes have impacted on trends in community service systems and on organisational structures and processes. Smaller organisations are particularly vulnerable (McDonald and Marston, 2002) because they tend to lack the energy and/or expertise to cope successfully with tendering, to meet service requirements when services are not fully funded (Meagher and Healy, 2003) or to remain viable if funds are reduced.

This environment requires that individual practitioners will be able to say what they are doing and why, make a case for its being 'best practice' in response to a particular issue at both macro and micro levels. Practitioners 'will require skills in benchmarking and quality assurance practices. They will need to understand the tendering, planning, auditing and evaluation processes. They need to be confident of the effectiveness of their interventions because in a competitive environment it is necessary to be able to demonstrate and articulate the outcomes and effectiveness of services' (O'Connor et al, 2003: 43).

Society as well as service structures have seen a number of significant changes that need to be accounted for in any attempts at best practice. These include changes in patterns of employment, the changing demographic structure of most societies, changing patterns of family life and changing underlying ideologies of social care. All of these will impact on the different fields of practice outlined in this book and need to be critically examined in the context of specific practice arenas to achieve best practice. For example a move towards greater family and community support and self-reliance may be seen as an attack on the ability or appropriateness of the welfare system to deliver change in social condi-tions or a willingness on the part of professionals to hand back to people control over their lives. In family and child welfare and corrections, notions of social and economic causes and responses are perhaps replaced by blaming individuals (O'Connor and Callahan, 1989). In child abuse cases resources have been concentrated in child protection on investi-gative tasks at a time when the levels of poverty and child poverty have increased, placing increased stress on families. To provide good practice in any environment we need to be aware of the impact of structural factors on the organisations we work for and the opportunities available or withheld from those we work with as well as a coherent and accountable approach to practice that can be explained to people called clients, consumers or communities.

Structure of the Book

Following this introduction, the book consists of 10 chapters, each with its own major theme or focus. Each chapter is a unique blend of theory, knowledge and empirical findings with a practice focus intended to be of direct use to the practitioner. The chapters are fully referenced, enabling further reading material to be found easily. In addition, a list of useful websites, containing a range of sources for accessing current research, policy initiatives and practice directions is found at the end of each chapter.

Chris Trotter argues in Chapter 2 that child protection in most industrialised countries places too much emphasis on risk assessment instead of 'treatment and a case management system which tends to be symptom focused rather than person focused'. He draws our attention to the importance of addressing the broader structural issues such as inequality and poverty which contribute to child abuse and maltreatment. Child protection workers should be equipped with a wide range of strategies, including role clarification, problem solving, risk assessment, case management, pro-social modelling, reinforcement and confrontation, and relationship skills.

In Chapters 3 and 4, Wing Hong Chui and Helen Cameron provide a thorough discussion on working with young and adult offenders respectively. More specifically, Wing Hong Chui provides a brief overview of key theories of delinquency, and then discusses various risk and protective factors for adolescent delinquency. He further reviews a number of formal responses such as early intervention and diversionary programs for juveniles in Australia. His chapter concludes by highlighting key principles of effective practice with young offenders in the community and custody. Helen Cameron opines that carefully designed and delivered programs for offenders that employ cognitive-behavioural theory in combination with crucial elements of effective programs such as accurate needs assessment and structured approaches to intervention would increase the chance of reducing offender recidivism. Both authors agree that working with offenders is difficult and demanding, and successful rehabilitation requires the application of treatments that are evaluated through research as most effective.

Chapter 5 examines a range of current issues in mental health practice, including policy development, case management, working with service users, working with families and the challenges imposed by evidence-based practice approaches to work. Robert Bland and Noel Renouf introduce several practice principles of working in mental health settings, namely encouraging positive expectations for the future, sustaining hope, supporting consumer decision-making and autonomy, and encouraging positive and supportive relationships with others.

Chapter 6 first outlines the policy and legislative context of the disability field and then examines theoretical underpinnings of our understandings of disability that may have impact on service delivery and practice. Major issues such as access and equity, dealing with stigma and social isolation, and communication issues and abuse that confront people with disability and their families are presented. Lesley Chenoweth also examines key approaches widely adopted in disability practice, specifically person-centred practice, family-centred practice and the strengths perspective.

Chapter 7 on Healthcare presents an overview of professional social work and human service practice in Australia, paying particular attention to the hospital and community health context. Definitions of health and illness are explored and their relevance for understanding how healthcare services are organised and delivered in Australia is examined. Two main frameworks of healthcare are reviewed, first, biomedicine, which includes the biopsychosocial approach, and which is most relevant to hospital and acute-care professional practice; and secondly, socioecology, which informs community-based health practice and emphasises wellness, health promotion and illness prevention within communities and populations. Key trends and developments in Australian healthcare policy are then described and discussed in terms of their potential impact on hospitals and community health services as organisational sites of professional healthcare practice. Sandy Taylor provides an overview of theoretical and professional knowledge relevant to professional healthcare practitioners in hospitals and community health with reference to the specific theoretical approaches of crisis theory and intervention, task or solution-based approaches, systems theories, strengths perspectives, anti-oppressive practice and models of ethical decision-making.

Deborah Setterlund, Jill Wilson and Cheryl Tilse point out in Chapter 8 that social workers, human service practitioners and older people encounter each other in a range of activities, such as assisting older people in hospital to access services, and facilitating older people to be involved in social action in a neighbourhood setting. They present a framework for practice designed to enable practitioners working with older people approach mutually agreed upon ethical outcomes. Critical theory which focuses on the role of power in influencing interactions between individuals and their social arrangements is introduced to guide our day-to-day practice.

Chapter 9 is concerned with social work in rural and remote communities. While rural practitioners and their urban counterparts share many methods and models, there are also many unique aspects which make the tasks required for living and working in a small community rewarding, varied, challenging and innovative and these features of practice are explored. Bob Lonne and Ros Darracott then examine the conceptual framework of domains, including society, structural, geographic, community, personal, professional, practice field and practice wisdom, that shape practice within these community contexts and outlines how practitioners' locations within these domains can assist them to attain best practice. Best practice approaches in rural child protection, healthcare, corrections and generalist practice are also examined, with particular emphasis on the particular characteristics, skills and demands required for these practice fields.

In partnership with an Aboriginal reference group, Joanna Zubrzycki and Bindi Bennett successfully articulate the essential skills and knowledge in working with Aboriginal Australians in social work and human services. Chapter 10 argues that developing the cultural courage to work with Aboriginal Australians requires both Aboriginal and non-Aboriginal workers to have a clear understanding of the historical and contemporary context of their work. Being culturally courageous means acknowledging the shared humanity and human rights of Aboriginal and non-Aboriginal Australians. While non-Aboriginal human service workers have to learn to work collaboratively and engage in practices that ensure cultural safety, Aboriginal workers must be able to work through the complex issues of identity and role. These aim at engaging the Aboriginal people in a process that is hopeful and empowering for them.

Working with migrants and refugees calls on the commitment to social justice, values and knowledge and is responsive to a range of factors such as race, gender, class and spirituality, as Jennifer Martin argues. Chapter 11 first explores the diverse backgrounds of migrants and refugees, followed by a discussion of changing legislative frameworks and issues and dilemmas related to resettlement and adjustment. A critical theoretical perspective that includes critical reflection, the naming of discriminatory practices, organisational considerations and the special needs of refugees and asylum seekers is introduced to highlight issues of power and domination and the political, social and economic dimensions related to resettlement and adjustment. Instead of seeing migrants and refugees as 'social problems', she believes that human service workers ought to challenge and move beyond this pathological view, and should be able to recognise the special needs of people who have migrated as refugees who may have experienced torture or trauma and the loss of loved ones.

This book introduces the reader to key fields of social work and human service practice. It encourages practitioners to be both active creators of knowledge and informed users of knowledge, to understand the historical background to situations, the contemporary service environment and the needs and hopes of those they engage with so that they can make the most appropriate response in a constantly changing society.

References

Biestek, FP (1961) *The Casework Relationship*, London: Allen & Unwin.

Drury-Hudson, J (1997) 'A model of professional knowledge for social work practice', *Australian Social Work*, 50(3), 35-44.

Ferguson, H (2003) 'Outline of a critical best practice perspective on social work and social care', *British Journal of Social Work*, 33(8), 1005-1024.

Gambrill, E (2003) 'Evidence-based practice: Sea change or the Emperor's new clothes?', *Journal of Social Work Education*, 38(1), 3-23.

Healy, K (2005) *Social Work Theories in Context: Creating Frameworks for Practice*, Basingstoke, Hampshire: Palgrave MacMillan.

Howe, D (2000) *On Being a Client: Understanding the Process of Counselling and Psychotherapy*, London: Sage.

Hughes, G (ed) (1998) *Imagining Welfare Futures*, London: Routledge.

Kamerman, S (2002) 'Fields of practice', in M Mattaini, C Lowery and C Meyer (eds) *Foundations of Social Work Practice: A Graduate Text* (pp 319-339), Washington, DC: National Association of Social Workers Press.

Lyons, M (2001) *Third Sector: The Contribution of Nonprofit and Cooperative Enterprises in Australia*, Sydney: Allen & Unwin.

Macdonald, G and Sheldon, B (1992) 'Contemporary studies of the effectiveness of social work', *British Journal of Social Work*, 22(5), 615-643.

McDonald, C and Marston, G (2002) 'Patterns of governance: The curious case of nonprofit organisations in Australia', *Social Policy and Administration*, 36(4), 376-391.

Meagher, G and Healy, K (2003) 'Caring, controlling, contracting and counting: Governments and nonprofits in community services', *Australian Journal of Public Administration*, 62(3), 40-51.

Milner, J and O'Byrne, P (1998) *Assessment in Social Work*, London: Macmillan.

Munro, E (2002) *Effective Child Protection*, London: Sage.

O'Connor, I (1989) *Our Homeless Children: Their Experiences*, Sydney: Human Rights and Equal Opportunity Commission.

O'Connor, I and Callahan, M (1989) 'Social crisis, social policy and sentencing in Queensland', *Australian and New Zealand Journal of Criminology*, 22(2), 109-123.

O'Connor, I, Wilson, J and Setterlund, D (2003) *Social Work and Welfare Practice* (4th ed), Sydney: Pearson Education.

O'Hagan, K (1996) 'Social work competence: An historical perspective', in K O'Hagan (ed) *Competence in Social Work Practice: A Practical Guide for Professionals* (pp 1-24), London: Jessica Kingsley.

Oldfield, S (1983) *The Counseling Relationship: A Study of the Client's Experience*, London: Routledge.

Polansky, N (1971) *Ego Psychology and Communication: Theory for the Interview*, Chicago: Aldine.

Raper, M (2000) *Examining the Futures of the Welfare State and the Need for Innovative Approaches to Service Delivery* (Formulating Strategies to Drive the Efficiency and effectiveness of Service Delivery in Government), Canberra: Australian Council of Social Service.

Rees, S and Wallace, A (1982) *Verdicts on Social Work*, London: Edward Arnold.

Rogan, L and Moore, C (1999) *Common Cause: Relationships and Reforms in Community Services*, Sydney: Australian Council of Social Service.

Schalock, R (1995) *Outcome-based Evaluation*, New York: Plenum Press.

Schon, D (1983) *The Reflective Practitioner*, New York: Basic Books.

Schon, D (1995) 'Reflective enquiry in social work practice', in P McCartt-Hess and E Mullen (eds) *Practitioner-research Partnerships: Building Knowledge from, in, and for Practice* (pp 31-55), Washington, DC: National Association of Social Workers Press.

Sheldon, B (2001) 'The validity of evidence-based practice in social work: A reply to Stephen Webb', *British Journal of Social Work*, 31(5), 801-811.

Sheldon, B and Chilvers, R (2000) *Evidence-based Social Care: A Study of Prospects and Problems*, Lyme Regis, Dorset: Russell House.

Thompson, N (2000) *Understanding Social Work: Preparing for Practice*, London: Macmillan.

Webb, S (2001) 'Some considerations on the validity of evidence-based practice in social work', *British Journal of Social Work*, 31(5), 57-79.

Chapter 2

Child Protection

Chris Trotter

Current Issues in Child Protection

The past few decades have seen a series of high profile child protection 'failures'. One of the most well-known examples is the case of Maria Colwell in the United Kingdom. In 1973 Maria, aged six, was placed in foster care because she was neglected. After about six months she was returned to her mother and stepfather under court supervision. About nine months later she was beaten to death by her stepfather. Between the time she was placed with her mother and stepfather and her death she was visited on 56 occasions by child protection workers and other professionals, and 30 complaints were made about her care and upbringing. Each of the professionals involved assumed that someone else was providing the primary service to the family (Howells, 1974).

The Daniel Valerio case in Australia was similar. Daniel was murdered by his de facto father in 1990. Daniel had been seen by more than 20 professionals, including doctors, social workers, medical specialists, police and community workers. Each of those who visited was suspicious that he was a victim of child abuse. None of them, however, took action to remove Daniel from the family or protect him from his father.

In these and in other high profile cases individual social workers have often been severely criticised by the courts and the press. When Kim Anne Poden, a 19-month-old child under the supervision of the Children's Aid Society in Canada, died of head injuries in 1976, the judge was highly critical of the way the case was handled by the Children's Aid Society. A subsequent judicial inquiry placed much of the blame at the feet of individual social workers.

These cases have led the courts, the press, the children's welfare organisations, the government departments and the politicians to question the systems which allowed these deaths to happen. They have also led to an increasing interest in and awareness of the dangers of child abuse.

No doubt as a result of this growing interest in child protection there has been an expansion in recent decades in many Western countries of government child protection and child welfare services. Alongside this expansion has been a dramatic increase in the numbers of child protection reports, in many cases as a direct result of the introduction of mandatory reporting systems which require professionals to report abuse to child protection authorities. In the decade between the mid-1980s and the mid-1990s most English speaking countries saw increases in reports of child abuse of more than 200 per cent. The United States today sees something like three million reports a year. So despite the increase in services the ability of the system to investigate and deal with these reports is often compromised (US Department of Health and Human Services, 2001). And the high profile child protection 'failures' have continued to occur.

The Climbie case in the United Kingdom is an example. In 2001 Victoria Climbie, in the words of Lord Laming, who conducted an inquiry into her murder, spent the cold winter months prior to her death 'bound hand and foot, in an unheated bathroom, lying in the cold bath in a plastic bag in her own urine and faeces and having to eat what food she could get by pressing her face onto the plate of whatever was put in the bath beside her' (Laming, 2003: 2). Yet Victoria had been known in the 10 months before her death to 'no fewer than 4 social service departments, 3 housing departments, two specialist child protection teams in the metropolitan police, she had been admitted to 2 different hospitals and referred to the National Society for Protection of Children'. The most striking feature of the case was the 'sheer number of occasions when the most minor and basic intervention on the part of the staff concerned could have made a material difference to the eventual outcome' (Laming, 2003: 2).

Risk Assessment

No doubt as a result of these high profile cases child protection services have become more and more concerned about risk assessment – about how to identify the families where there is a high risk of abuse or of repeated abuse. A lot has been written in recent years about risk assessment in child protection. One of the child abuse computer databases refers to more than 800 books and articles on the subject. There are many risk assessment profiles which require workers to work through a checklist of factors (see Holder and Salovitz, 2001 for examples of risk assessment criteria).

The risk assessment process provides a method of dealing with the increases in referrals. Scarce resources can be devoted to high risk cases. Low risk (and unsubstantiated cases) can be referred out to voluntary agencies for family support. There are, however, many critics of the current systems. It is argued that they are legalistic, they focus on surveillance rather than welfare and that they do not achieve the very purpose for which they have been set up – to protect children from harm. It is argued that much of the energy of child protection services is directed towards risk assessment rather than treatment and it is hardly surprising that families and children are not being helped. (Gough, 1993; Jack, 1997; Krane and Davies, 2000; Parton and O'Byrne, 2000).

There is certainly some evidence for this view. A study by Elaine Farmer (1999) examined case planning meetings in the United Kingdom in the early 1990s. She found that the meetings focused primarily on risk issues and whether children should be placed on the child protection register. Only about 15 per cent of the time was spent discussing treatment plans for the children and their families. A study by Gray, Higgs and Pringle (1997), also in the United Kingdom, suggested that clients feel they get little in the way of treatment from statutory child protection services. They suggest that clients feel that there are gaps in services and workers are often out of touch.

On the other hand a study I undertook in child protection in Victoria, Australia (Trotter, 2004) found that very high risk clients did receive help from their workers, whereas lower risk clients tended to be offered only short term investigatory approaches. This finding supports the view expressed by some commentators (for example, Thorpe, 1994) that many low risk child protection clients might be better dealt with through community-based family support services than through child protection services.

The critics of child protection services in the United Kingdom have pointed to the different nature of services in Western Europe. British, North American and Australian child protection services are characterised by many layers of command. A senior child protection worker reports to a team leader, who reports to a child protection manager, who reports to a regional manager and so on. Most important decisions, even decisions to continue working with a family, are taken by someone up the hierarchy.

Many child protection services in Europe, on the other hand, have different structures. They tend to have flatter management structures and give more responsibility to the front line workers. Decisions, even decisions to remove children, may be the ultimate responsibility of the child protection workers themselves. The focus of the child protection intervention is on helping the family with their problems, rather than determining whether abuse has occurred or the risk of future abuse. In only rare instances are children taken to court (Hetherington et al, 1997; Littlechild, 1998).

This approach is well illustrated in a child protection service I visited in Austria. The child protection workers would seek advice from expert panels rather than refer to other agencies or other expert workers. Those panels might include medical staff, drug and alcohol experts and other advisers and they would help the worker to work with the family. They would also help the worker to make decisions such as whether or not a family should be taken to court. The system provides for maximum continuity of contact between one worker and one client, something which does not occur in the more specialised case management or contracting models which operate in most English speaking countries.

The difference between the European and British systems is characterised by comments reputed to have been made by a child protection worker on an initial visit to a mother and father suspected of child abuse. The British child protection worker commented: 'We have had a report that you have been harming your children and I am here to investigate this'. The European child protection worker on the other hand commented: 'I have heard that you might be having some trouble with your children and I am here to see if I can help you with them or with any other problems you might have'.

It seems, however, that despite the increased focus on the investigatory function in English speaking countries and despite the arguments that child protection services are now too investigatory, some in the popular press are still not satisfied. As I mentioned earlier new child protection 'failures' continue to be publicised, usually with the suggestion that child protection workers failed to assess the situation adequately.

The controversy about the role of child protection is ongoing. High profile criticism of child protection failures has led to an increase in investigatory approaches. This has in turn led to criticism of the new focus on investigatory approaches and a push for more family support. Yet at the same time the push for more stringent investigatory approaches continues.

Case Management

Child protection services in some English speaking countries work on a case management or purchaser provider model, in other words, much of the helping or treatment work is done by voluntary agencies or specialist workers. Child protection workers are responsible for coordinating welfare or helping services rather than providing these services themselves. Individual clients within the child protection system, whether parents or children, could be seeing a family support worker, a school welfare worker, a psychologist, a drug counsellor, a domestic violence counsellor, or a court advice worker. A parent could also be involved with a financial counsellor, a parent support group or a domestic violence counselling group.

The extent to which this occurs varies within and between different countries. Christine Hallett (1995) for example found in a United Kingdom study that child protection workers did much of the direct work with children and families themselves. Hood (1997) on the other hand in a study of United Kingdom local authorities found that, while there was a lot of good work done in the view of the staff concerned, the practice of referring and contracting out led to concerns about miscommunication of information, duplication of roles, role confusion and de-skilling and disempowering of workers. The statutory workers often felt de-skilled as helpers. They often felt that they did not know families well enough to make decisions about them. Workers in the voluntary agencies, on the other hand, often felt disempowered in terms of decision-making.

A study undertaken in Illinois in the United States confirms the sense of disempowerment experienced by workers (McMahon, 1998). One of the workers is quoted: 'When I first came here it was more a personal kind of counselling. Now ... you just meet them and say that you need to go to a counsellor' (McMahon,1998: 38).

There has been much criticism of case management approaches on the basis that interventions should be person focused rather than symptom focused. Jones and Alcabes (1993) argue for example on the basis of the available research, that whether clients have mental health, drug use or criminal offending problems the key to effective practice relates to socialisation processes including role clarification and reaching agreement on problem definition and goals. This process takes time and may never occur if clients are exposed to repeated short term contacts with different specialist workers.

Cultural Issues

Cultural issues are often central to work with abused children and their families. Indigenous populations, along with a range of other minority groups are overrepresented in child protection services around the world. In fact there is a long history of indigenous populations and issues with child protection. One very good example of this is the debate which has raged in Australian newspapers in recent years about whether or not the Australian nation should apologise to the stolen generation – those children who, a generation ago, were forcibly removed from their families simply because they were Aboriginal. Similar debates have been seen in relation to North American indigenous populations.

David Gough and Margaret Lynch comment in a recent edition of *Child Abuse Review* devoted entirely to the issue of culture and child protection, that culture is 'the backdrop against which all circumstances and events affecting child protection occur' (2002: 341). They go on to discuss diversity within cultures and between cultures. Belief systems, child rearing practices and ways of communicating vary between cultures and between different groups within cultures.

Social Context of Child Abuse

Child abuse not only takes place in a cultural context but also in a social, economic and political context. Definitions of neglect or significant harm are socially constructed (see Jack 2004 for discussion about this issue). Parenting practices may vary depending on socioeconomic circumstances and the community in which people live. In the words of Margaret Bell (2004) in a recent edition of *Child Abuse Review* devoted to 'child protection at community level': 'Clearly effective child protection must look beyond the statutory and independent agencies set up to protect children from harm to the broader base of social structures wherein child abuse may begin, present and flourish' (p 364). She goes on to talk about the need to raise public awareness, to involve the broader community in promoting children's welfare and safety, and for social inclusion.

Intervention Methods

Child protection in English speaking countries today operates in a climate of media criticism, increasing and often unmanageable numbers of referrals, increasing focus on risk assessment rather than treatment and a case management system which tends to be symptom focused rather than person focused. Further it seems that little is being done to address the broader structural factors, which may contribute to child abuse. Is it possible for child protection workers to do effective work in this climate?

There is a body of evidence which suggests that individual child protection workers can do effective work within the current systems. The evidence suggests that the skills of the workers can make a substantial difference to the lives of the families with whom they are involved. These skills include: role clarification skills including a balanced approach to the investigatory/helping roles (Shulman, 1991; Rooney, 1992; Jones and Alcabes, 1993; Trotter, 2004, 2006); a willingness to work through problems with clients in a collaborative manner (Smokowski and Wodowski, 1996; Ethier et al, 2000; Gaudin et al, 2000; Trotter, 2004, 2006); a focus on the positive and pro-social things that clients say and do but simultaneously a willingness to challenge clients in relation to rationalisations or inappropriate behaviour (Trotter, 2004, 2006), and appropriate relationship skills (Shulman, 1991; Trotter, 2004, 2006). Case management skills, in particular preparing clients for and following through on referrals, may also be important.

In my book *Working with Involuntary Clients* (Trotter, 2006) I discussed the research about 'what works' and 'what doesn't' and presented some details about these effective practice skills. In *Helping Abused Children and their Families* (Trotter, 2004) I considered how these skills were applied in a child protection setting and described how the skills were used in practice. The study outlined in *Helping Abused Children and their Families* involved interviews with 50 workers and 280 clients. The book also includes a number of interview transcripts which provide examples of effective and not so effective practice. The reader is referred to the two books for more detail about the research and the application of the skills. Outlined below is a summary of the skills.

Role Clarification

Role clarification is about helping clients to understand the role of the worker and the role of the client in the child protection process. It involves frequent honest and open discussions about: the purpose of the intervention; the dual role of the worker as an investigator and helper; the clients' expectations of the worker; the nature of the worker's authority and how it can be used; what is negotiable and what isn't; and the limits of confidentiality.

In our child protection study we anticipated that when clients had an understanding of the dual role of the workers as both helper and investigator those clients would do better. This was clearly the case. When the clients saw their worker as both an investigator and helper they were much more likely to be satisfied with the outcome of the intervention, the workers were more likely to report that their families were progressing well, children were less likely to have been removed from their families and the cases were slightly more likely to have been closed.

This is perhaps not surprising. Lawrence Shulman (1991) came to a similar conclusion in his child protection study in Canada. He gave an example of the kind of comment the more effective workers in his study were likely to make: 'I am here because we received a call from someone who felt you might be neglecting your child. I have to investigate such calls to see if there is any truth in them. I also want to see if there is any way we might be helpful to you' (Shulman, 1991: 27). This theme was also very clear in an earlier study I did in corrections (Trotter, 1996). The more effective probation officers made it clear to their clients that they wanted to help as well as being clear about what must be done to comply with the probation order. Getting the balance right between social control and helping seems to be a very important skill in work with involuntary clients.

It was also apparent from our child protection study, however, that the clients often did not see their workers as embracing a dual role. They tended to perceive their workers either as helpers or as investigators. In only 10 per cent of cases did the clients describe their workers as both helpers and investigators (Trotter, 2004). So it is apparent that while helping the client to understand the dual role of the worker was helpful it occurred infrequently.

Our child protection study also provided support for the other role clarification skills. The outcomes were better when clients felt that their workers were clear about their authority and when their workers clarified and discussed issues such as the purpose of the intervention, the clients' expectations and confidentiality.

Problem Solving

Effective child protection workers make use of collaborative problem solving processes (sometimes referred to as working in partnership). They help clients to identify personal, social and environmental issues which are of concern to them. In doing this they are likely to canvass a wide range of issues: finances, housing, drug use, family background and relationships, friendships, work and schooling, health and mental health. They examine the client's situation in a broad context and they do it from the client's perspective. They help their clients identify issues of concern to them and of concern to the worker. They then help their clients develop goals and strategies to achieve these goals (Shulman, 1991; Jones and Alcabes, 1993; Smokowski and Wodarski, 1996; Gaudin et al, 2000; Ethier et al, 2000; Trotter, 2006).

The value of problem solving was strongly supported in our child protection study (Trotter, 2004). While the clients felt that their workers tended to minimise some of their problems (for example, finances stress financial relationships) the outcomes were clearly better when the clients and their workers identified specific problems and when these problems were defined by the clients, rather than the workers. The clients also did better if they set goals with the workers and if they set tasks to achieve the goals. The outcomes were also better when the workers carried out tasks as part of the problem solving process.

As I mentioned earlier, in most child protection services the child protection workers are expected to make assessments of the risk levels of the client or client family. They are asked to gather information from the client and other sources including relatives, doctors, schoolteachers and police, with a view to classifying the client family as high, medium or low risk. They consider factors such as the nature and severity of the abuse, children's individual physical, social and intellectual development, parental drug use or mental illness, parents' acknowledgment of the problem, attentiveness to children's needs, knowledge about child development, and so on. Effective child protection workers help the client to understand this process and how it interacts with the helping or problem solving process. In other words they link the role clarification process, the problem solving process and risk assessment.

Case Management

Reference was made earlier to criticisms of case management. Despite these criticisms child protection workers can help their clients by following some case management principles. Anne Fortune (1992) considers the role of case management in the context of inadequate resources and points to the advantages for clients of a coordinated approach. She points to a number of studies which suggest that casework outcomes are improved, for both voluntary and involuntary clients, when direct practice workers go beyond their 'comfortable' referral networks and when they have an understanding of bureaucratic procedures.

Gursansky, Harvey and Kennedy (2003) also point to key case management principles. They argue that case management should be designed around consumers needs, individualised, consumer driven and offer choice to consumers. It should involve contracts; services should be accountable and provide quality measurement, they should be timely, responsive and time limited. They should also involve evaluation and advocacy. There is some support in our study (Trotter, 2004) for these principles with more effective workers more inclined to be familiar with agencies to whom they refer, to be involved in initial meetings and to help the clients understand the purpose of referrals and their voluntary or involuntary nature.

Another aspect of working with other agencies in child protection involves case conferences. It has been argued that outcomes for clients are likely to be better if clients and families and other professionals are prepared for and involved in case conferences and if they are able to play a genuine role in decision-making (Holder and Corey, 1986; Sinclair, 1998; Farmer, 1999). This view was again supported in our study. Regardless of how the clients felt about the case conferences it was clear that the more they felt involved in the decisions the better the outcomes were. It seems that being clear about roles and working in a collaborative way leads to better outcomes whether in one to one work with clients and client families or in decision-making forums such as case conferences.

Pro-social Modelling, Reinforcement and Confrontation

A number of child protection studies have commented on the limitations of a partnership approach (Ammermann, 1998; Swenson and Hanson, 1998; Triseliotis et al, 1998; Trotter, 2006). Janet Stanley and Chris Goddard (2002) argue that child protection workers may effectively become hostages within family situations where they begin to accept the abuser's view. Rather than working in partnership with the abusing parent to deal with the problems of abuse, the child protection worker may inadvertently minimise the abuse and become an ally of the abusing parent.

Collaborative problem solving or partnership approaches need therefore to be balanced by a third group of skills involving a focus on clients' positive and pro-social actions and comments and the use of appropriate confrontation. Effective workers identify and reward the pro-social comments and actions of their clients. For example they praise comments by parents which acknowledge the harm that child abuse can cause. They would praise, for example, an attempt by a parent to use appropriate non-physical means of discipline or an attempt by a young person to reduce drug use. Effective workers also model the behaviours they are seeking from their clients. They also challenge the antisocial comments and actions of their clients. This approach is dealt with in some detail in *Working with Involuntary Clients* (Trotter, 2006) where some common criticisms of the pro-social approach are dealt with, in particular that it can be superficial, manipulative and judgmental. More detail about how child protection workers use the approach in practice is also provided in *Helping Abused*

Children and their Families (Trotter, 2004). Suffice to say at this stage that the evidence clearly suggests that the approach can be influential in helping clients to change their behaviour. For this reason it is an important skill in child protection work.

Certainly our study provided strong support for the use of pro-social modelling. According to the theory of pro-social modelling, if workers model appropriate behaviours their clients are likely to learn from those behaviours and they will in turn have better outcomes. Modelling pro-social behaviour involves, among other things, keeping appointments, being punctual and responding to phone calls. When the clients in our study believed that their workers had kept their appointments on time the outcomes were better. We found a similar trend when we asked the clients if their worker made phone calls when they were arranged, and returned the client's calls. Again we found strong associations with outcomes. The clients were almost twice as likely to be satisfied with the outcome, the workers were almost twice as likely to report that the client family was progressing well, 40 per cent fewer cases remained open and 30 per cent fewer children had been removed after 16 months. All of the associations are statistically significant, in other words unlikely to have occurred by chance.

It could be that the more reliable workers had lower case loads, or lower risk clients, and therefore had time to return phone calls and keep appointments. This could not, however, explain the differences. The case loads were reasonably evenly distributed among the workers and the risk levels were no different. Can it be that something as simple as keeping appointments and returning phone calls accounts for these substantial differences in client outcomes? Could it be that, what might be described as simple courtesies, are just as important, or even more important, than other direct practice skills such as working through problems? It certainly seems so from this study. This study is not, however, an isolated one. The importance of pro-social modelling is pointed to in a number of studies in corrections (see, for example, Andrews and Bonta, 2003). Two earlier studies of mine also provided similar outcomes, one with volunteer probation officers in juvenile justice (Trotter, 1990) and another with professional probation officers in adult corrections (Trotter, 1996). In both cases probation officers who scored high on a socialisation scale, a scale which measures the extent to which people are pro-social or pro-criminal in their attitudes, had clients with good outcomes. In both cases the clients were between 30 and 50 per cent less likely to reoffend if supervised by officers who scored high on the scale. One of the key characteristics of people who score high on the socialisation scale is their reliability.

Pro-social reinforcement, for example, praising clients and reducing frequency of contact in response to progress by the client, was also related to positive outcomes in our child protection study. The final aspect of pro-social modelling and reinforcement relates to confrontation or challenging clients' rationalisations or inappropriate behaviours. The use of confrontation in work with involuntary clients is controversial and there is little support in the research for direct or critical confrontation (for example, Shulman, 1991). This was supported in our study. The response which related most positively to the outcome measures was that of suggesting more positive ways of dealing with the situation. When the client indicated that their worker 'explored the reasons why they felt and acted in this way' or 'acknowledged that their negative feelings were justified' the worker and client outcomes were also positive. On the other hand when the clients reported that their worker did not respond or react, the outcomes were poor. The outcomes were also poor when the clients said that their workers pointed out the likely ill effects of the clients' views and behaviour, or criticised the client. It seems that the reservations expressed about the value of some types of confrontation may be well-founded. The concern expressed about ignoring rationalisations and antisocial comments also seems well-founded.

Relationship Skills

The fourth group of skills which the research suggests is related to positive outcomes includes relationship skills, in particular skills such as empathy, self-disclosure, humour and optimism (Shulman, 1991; Department of Health, 1995; Trotter, 2006). When child protection workers understand their clients' point of view, when they make appropriate use of self-disclosure, when they make appropriate use of humour and when they are optimistic about the potential of the client to change, they tend to have good relationships with their clients. In turn the good relationships may lead to improved outcomes, particularly if the worker also makes use of the other practice skills referred to above. Each of these skills was seen to be related to positive outcomes in our study.

Trotter (2004) outlines these effective practice skills in some detail and shows how they are actually used in practice. Only a brief summary has been presented here and readers who are interested in direct practice skills in child protection are referred to the book.

Summary

Child protection is currently facing a number of issues. There has been over the last three decades ongoing media scrutiny of deaths of children known to child protection services. In parallel with these high profile cases has been an increasing number of referrals and increasing resources to child protection services. In some cases, however, the resources have not been able to keep pace with increasing referrals and in other cases there have been problems with the organisation of the multiple services involved.

It seems clear that despite the resourcing and organisational problems faced by child protection services, child protection workers can do effective work with families if they follow certain practices. These practices include: being clear about their role, particularly their dual role of a helper and an investigator; working with clients and their families through a collaborative problem solving process which focuses on the issues which have brought the family to child protection services; making use of case management skills; pro-social modelling and reinforcing pro-social comments and actions of clients but at the same time challenging comments and behaviours which are supportive of abuse or neglect; and using appropriate relationship skills.

Review Questions

1. What are some of the key issues facing child protection services today?

2. What are the key principles of effective practice in child protection?

3. How can you deal with clients who have a different definition of their problems to that of the child protection worker?

4. What are the best ways to deal with client rationalisations for their abusive behaviour?

5. What is meant by pro-social modelling?

Useful Websites

National Child Protection Clearinghouse	http://www.aifs.gov.au/nch
Australian Institute of Health and Welfare	http://www.aihw.gov.au
Advocates for Survivors of Child Abuse (ASCA)	http://www.asca.org.au
British Association for the Study and Prevention of Child Abuse and Neglect (UK)	http://www.baspcan.org.uk
National Clearinghouse on Child Abuse and Neglect Information (US)	http://nccanch.acf.hhs.gov

References

Ammermann, RT (1998) 'Methodological issues in child maltreatment research', in JR Lutzker (ed) *Handbook of Child Abuse Research and Treatment* (pp 117-131), New York: Plenum Press.

Andrews, DA and Bonta, J (2003) *The Psychology of Criminal Conduct*, Cincinnati: Anderson Publishing.

Bell, M (2004) 'Child protection at the community level', *Child Abuse Review*, 13(6), 363-367.

Department of Health (1995) *Child Protection: Messages From Research*, London: HMSO.

Ethier, LS, Couture, G, Lacharite, C and Gagnier, J-P (2000) 'Impact of a multi-dimensional intervention program applied to families at risk for child neglect', *Child Abuse Review*, 9(1), 19-36.

Farmer, E (1999) 'Holes in the safety net: The strengths and weaknesses of child protection procedures', *Child and Family Social Work*, 4(4), 293-302.

Fortune, A (1992) 'Inadequate Resources', in WJ Reid (ed) *Task Strategies: An Empirical Approach to Clinical Social Work* (pp 250-279), New York: Columbia University Press.

Gaudin, JM, Wodarski, J, Atkinson, M and Avery, S (2000) *Outcomes of Social Network Interventions with Neglectful Families*, Washington DC: National Clearinghouse on Child Abuse and Neglect Information.

Gough, D (1993) *Child Abuse Interventions: A Review of the Research Literature*, Glasgow: Public Health Research Unit, University of Glasgow.

Gough, D and Lynch, M (2002) 'Culture and Child Protection', *Child Abuse Review*, 11(6), 341-344.

Gray, S, Higgs, M and Pringle, K (1997) 'User centred responses to child sexual abuse: The way forward', *Child and Family Social Work*, 2(1), 49-57.

Gursansky, D, Harvey, J and Kennedy, R (2003) *Case Management: Policy, Practice and Professional Business*, Sydney: Allen & Unwin.

Hallett, C (1995) *Interagency Co-ordination in Child Protection*, London: HMSO.

Hetherington, R, Cooper, A, Smith, P and Wilford, G (1997) *Protecting Children Messages from Europe*, Lyme Regis, Dorset: Russell House.

Holder, R and Salovitz, B (2001) *Child Safety and Child Neglect*, Duluth, GA: National Resource Centre on Child Maltreatment.

Holder, W and Corey, M (1986) *Child Protection Services Risk Management: A Decision Making Handbook*, Charlotte, NC: Action for Child Protection.

Hood, S (1997) 'The purchaser/provider separation in child and family social work: Implications for service delivery and for the role of the social worker', *Child and Family Social Work*, 2(1), 25-35.

Howells, JG (1974) *Remember Maria*, London: Butterworths.

Jack, G (1997) 'Discourses of child protection and child welfare', *British Journal of Social Work*, 27(5), 659-678.

Jack, G (2004) 'Child protection at the community level', *Child Abuse Review*, 13(6), 368-383.

Jones, J and Alcabes, A (1993) *Client Socialisation: The Achilles Heel of the Helping Professions*, Westport, CT: Auburn House.

Krane, J and Davies, L (2000) 'Mothering and child protection practice: Rethinking risk assessment', *Child and Family Social Work*, 5(1), 35-45.

Laming, L (2003) *The Victoria Climbie Inquiry Speech by Lord Laming*. Available at: <www.victoria-climbie-inquiry.org.uk>.

Littlechild, B (1998) 'Does family support ensure the protection of children?: Messages from child protection research', *Child Abuse Review*, 7(2), 116-128.

McMahon, A (1998) *Damned if You Do, Damned if You Don't Working in Child Welfare*, Aldershot: Ashgate.

Parton, N and O'Byrne, P (2000) *Constructive Social Work: Towards a New Practice*, New York: St Martin's Press.

Rooney, R (1992) *Strategies for Work with Involuntary Clients*, New York: Columbia University Press.

Shulman, L (1991) *Interactional Social Work Practice: Toward an Empirical Theory*, Itasca, ILL: FE Peacock.

Sinclair, R (1998) 'Involving children in planning their care', *Child and family Social Work*, 3(2), 137-142.

Smokowski, P and Wodarski, J (1996) 'Effectiveness of child welfare services', *Research on Social Work Practice*, 6(4), 504-523.

Stanley, J and Goddard, C (2002) *In the Firing Line*, Chichester, West Sussex: John Wiley & Sons.

Swenson, C and Hanson, R (1998) 'Sexual abuse of children', in JR Lutzker (ed) *Handbook of Child Abuse Research and Treatment* (pp 475-500), New York: Plenum Press.

Thorpe, D (1994) *Evaluating Child Protection*, Buckingham: Open University Press.

Triseliotis, J, Borland, M, Hill, M and Lambert, L (1998) 'Social work supervision of young people', *Child and Family Social* Work, 3(1), 27-35.

Trotter, C (1990) 'Probation can work: A research study using volunteers', *Australian Social Work*, 43(2), 13-18.

Trotter, C (1996) 'The impact of different supervision practices in community corrections', *Australian and New Zealand Journal of Criminology*, 29(1), 29-46.

Trotter, C (2004) *Helping Abused Children and their Families: Towards an Evidence-based Practice Model*, Sydney: Allen & Unwin.

Trotter, C (2006) *Working with Involuntary Clients: A Guide to Practice* (2nd ed), Sydney: Allen & Unwin.

United States Department of Health and Human Services (2001) *Child Maltreatment 2001 Summary of Key Findings*, Washington DC: National Clearinghouse on Child Abuse and Neglect Information.

Chapter 3

Young Offenders

Wing Hong Chui

Introduction

Juvenile delinquency and youth crime has long been recognised as one of the major social issues in most industrialised nations. The fear of youthful offending and what has been termed 'moral panics' tend to keep it a sensational subject matter, thereby attracting a great deal of public concern and political attention (Pearson, 1972; Cohen, 1980; Goode, 1994; Thompson, 1998). The study of juvenile crime is important because of its negative impact on young offenders and their families, the victims, and the community (Haines and Drakeford, 1998; Cunneen and White, 2002; Western, Lynch and Ogilvie, 2003; Bateman and Pitts, 2005). Youth justice professionals such as magistrates, judges, police, probation officers and correctional officers alike have attempted to identify and demonstrate cost effective measures to work with young offenders. A number of criminal justice researchers have looked for what the best method of dealing with at-risk children and juvenile offenders is in recent years (Alexander, 2000; Ellis and Sowers, 2001; Loeber and Farrington, 2001; Omaji, 2003; Burnett and Appleton, 2004; Hough and Roberts, 2004). While some are in favour of diverting the delinquents from the formal justice system (see, for example, Goldson, 2000; Morris and Maxwell, 2001), others hold the view that justice can be achieved in the court thereby imposing sanctions on young people's offending behaviour without infringing their legal rights. Despite various dispositions or sentencing options available for juvenile offenders, the question of how best to address criminality and reintegrate young offenders into the community has been a controversial one. There has been a renewed interest in identifying what works with offenders to reduce crime in the United Kingdom and North America (McGuire, 1995; Hollin, 2002; Andrews and

Bonta, 2003; Chui, 2003a; Burnett and Roberts, 2004) and Australia is no exception (Ogloff, 2002; Day, Howells and Rickwood, 2004). It is indeed our aim to create a better and safer society for us to live in, and to assist the disadvantaged people to lead a normal life.

This chapter turns to recent empirical research and literature on the effects of various intervention approaches on young people on court orders. More specifically, the aim of this chapter is to examine how research evidence informs practitioners what the best practice is, thus increasing probability of offender rehabilitation. The chapter is divided into four main sections. The first section provides an overview of theories of delinquency to understand the causes of the youthful offending. The second section is concerned with the risk and protective factors for adolescent delinquency, thereby highlighting the use of 'early intervention' and diversionary programs for juveniles. The third section first summarises key principles of effective practice with offenders in the community and custody, and then introduces various interventions by program type that have been found successful to reintegrate young offenders into the society. The concluding section discusses directions for future research and implications for professional practice.

Explanations of Adolescent Delinquency: A Brief Overview

What are the causes of juvenile crime? This question is not new, and much has been done to explain why some children offend and some do not offend. At the outset, it should be emphasised that no single theory or a single factor on its own can explain the complexity of juvenile crime, and researchers are still refining their theoretical explanations because of the ever changing political, legal, social and economic environment (Muncie, 2004; Byrne and Trew, 2005; Shoemaker, 2005). Three major traditional criminological perspectives on juvenile delinquency, namely biological, psychological and sociological explanations, are discussed briefly. (For more details, see Maguire, Morgan and Reiner, 2002; Shoemaker, 2005.)

Biological Explanations of Juvenile Crime

Are delinquents born to be criminals? The link between biology or physical traits and delinquent behaviour was first proposed by Cesare Lombroso, an Italian army physician in the 19th century (Bynum and Thompson, 2004). Lombroso's theory of atavism was derived from his research on adult prisoners, and asserts that certain people were 'born' criminals because of specific physical traits such as the shape of the skull (Gibson, 2002; Gelsthorpe, 2003). Earlier criminologists such as William Sheldon (1949) looked at how distinct physiques relate to particular types of juvenile delinquent behaviour. Sheldon (1949), an advocate of somatotype or body build school, contends that a person's body shape influences personality and then crime. In particular he classified three main somatotypes, namely endomorphs (that is, round shaped, relaxed, good humoured and sociable), mesomorphs (that is, muscular body, fit, violent and aggressive) and ectomorphs (that is, thin, skinny, shy and introvert). Sheldon's empirical studies found that among 200 juvenile delinquent boys aged from 15 to 24 years in a reformatory in Boston, delinquents were generally mesomorphs and were less likely to be ectomorphs (see also Ornstein, 1993; Muncie, 2004). However, Sheldon's explanation for juvenile crime is often criticised as over-simplistic largely because of numerous flaws such as biased sampling and lack of consistent measurement of the body type in his research. What is more, biological theories of crime completely ignore the role of various contextual and environmental factors which certainly have an impact on young people's decision to offend. Despite this, in recent years attempts have been made to explore the relationship between various biochemical factors such as diet, hormones and blood chemistry and juvenile delinquency (Siegel and Walsh, 2005; Shoemaker, 2005).

Psychological Explanations of Juvenile Crime

Are delinquents psychologically different? Earlier proponents of psychological explanations of crime such as psychiatrists and psychologists believe that delinquency is largely related to a wide range of personality, emotional and mental disorders. Following Freud's psychoanalytic approach, August Aichorn (1935) found that juvenile delinquents are impulsive, act on instincts and are absent of guilt feelings. In this respect, young criminals are viewed as id-dominated individuals largely due to maternal and love deprivation. Other researchers such as Glueck and Glueck (1950), Conger and Miller (1966) and Waldo and Dinitz (1967) found that male delinquents and non-delinquents can be identified by the standard personality tests like the Rorschach test and Minnesota Multiphasic Personality Inventory. Their studies confirm that young delinquents are more emotionally disturbed, egocentric and unhappier than the non-delinquent counterparts. Using Eysenck Personality Questionnaire, McEwan's study (1983) reveals that personality types such as extraversion, neuroticism and psychoticism are related to delinquent behaviour but personality types vary according to particular kinds of youthful offending. While psychological explanations of delinquency generally have more support than the biological perspective (see Chapter 4 of this volume), they are often criticised for their inability to examine the social and environmental causes of delinquency (Flowers, 2002).

Sociological Explanations of Juvenile Crime

How does the social structure and process affect the rate of delinquency? Sociological explanations are concerned with human social structures and their interactions, and emphasise the importance of understanding criminal behaviour in its social context. Examples of sociological explanations are social disorganisation theory (Shaw and McKay, 1969), anomie or strain theory (Merton, 1949), theories of delinquent subculture (Cohen, 1955), theory of differential opportunity (Cloward and Ohlin, 1960) and social control theory (Hirschi, 1969). Based on the arrest rates of juveniles throughout the city of Chicago in the early 20th century, Clifford Shaw and Henry McKay (1969) opined that delinquency was common in deteriorated neighbourhoods where industrial and commercial establishments were interspersed with residences. Subsequently, gang membership and subculture was a response to poor social conditions, and passed on from one generation to the next (cited in Drowns and Hess, 2000). Robert Merton's (1949) theory of anomie contended that youths either used 'illegitimate' or deviant means to achieve the goals or rejected 'legitimate' goals and substituted deviance. Combining social disorganisation and strain perspectives, Albert Cohen (1955) and Richard Cloward and Lloyd Ohlin (1960) attempted to investigate why some juveniles participate in delinquent gangs, and why gangs persist in urban neighbourhoods. In *Delinquent Boys*, Cohen (1955) found that juveniles had a strong desire to conform to lower class values such as short run hedonism, excitement, disrespecting authority and toughness, and these values are in conflict with those of larger society. Cloward and Ohlin's (1960) theory of differential opportunity further substantiated that while all young people share the same success goals, those in the lower class in general have limited means of achieving them, thereby generating increases in delinquency. Accordingly, these sociological perspectives shed insight on the importance of creating partnerships between the criminal justice agencies to attack social structure obstacles, especially for young people in lower class neighbourhoods.

Instead of asking why young people offend, Travis Hirschi (1969) 'seeks to explain the deviant and/or criminal by problematizing conformity' (Western, Lynch and Ogilvie, 2003: 3). His social control theory argues that positive social bonds which include attachments to significant others such as parents, teachers and peers, commitment to social conformity, involvement in conventional activities such as religion and school, and belief in values and social norms help control delinquency. In contrast, children engage in antisocial behaviours when these bonds are weakened, and recently Kaplan and Lin's (2005) study shows that '[i]f the person is alienated from the conventional world and does not anticipate rewards for conventional behaviour he or she will not decrease deviant behaviour even in the face of experiencing negative self-feelings in conjunction with a deviant identity' (p 301). Indeed attachments to parents and peers are considered to be the strongest predictors of the formation of offending predispositions during pre-adolescence and adolescent delinquency (Warr and Stafford, 1991; Western, Lynch and Ogilvie, 2003; Chapple, 2005; Farrington, 2005). Activity 3.1 may be a useful addition to understanding issues around youth offending behaviour.

Activity 3.1 Causes of Youth Crime

Brothers raped another two girls

The brothers' method was as simple as it was brutal. Find a vulnerable teenage girl, lure her back to the family home, ply her with alcohol and make sexual advances. If she refuses, rape her.

Three of four Pakistani-born brothers jailed last year for up to 22 years for gang raping two girls, aged 16 and 17, at knife point in 2002, have been convicted by a Sydney court in recent weeks of further sexual offences, also at the family home, in that year.

BAD BLOOD

MSK, MAK, MMK and MRK are the code names given to four brothers.

With reference to the case study, what are the theoretical explanations for the brothers to commit a crime? Are they genetically determined? Are they mentally insane?

Source: *The Australian*, 22/7/2005

Risk and Protective Factors in Juvenile Offending

Developmental Studies and Concepts

The abovementioned theories claim to generalise the causes of delinquency and predict who are likely to become delinquents. As with many social problems, the causal factors are multiple, and in particular, Hollin (1990), Farrington (1996, 2000) and Andrews and Bonta (2003) among others have noted the interaction of several individual, family, peer and environmental factors in the development of delinquency. According to Farrington (2000), '[t]he basic idea of [the risk factor prevention] paradigm is very simple: identify the key risk factors for offending and implement prevention methods designed to counteract them. There is often a related attempt to identify key protective factors against offending and to implement prevention methods designed to enhance them' (p 1).

Several studies have examined various factors or predictors associated with youth crime. For instance, common predictors of a young person committing an offence often include one or more of the following: inadequate parenting; childhood behaviour; problems at school; friends and leisure; housing; training and employment; and alcohol and drug abuse (Audit Commission, 1996: 58-60). Similar research findings are reported by the Home Office (1997), and that key factors related to youth criminality are: being male; being brought up by a criminal parent or parents; living in a family with multiple problems; experiencing poor parenting and lack of supervision; poor discipline in the family and at school; playing truant or being excluded from school; associating with delinquent friends; and having siblings who offend. In addition, Home Office (1997) reports that two most influences are persistent school truancy and affiliation with criminal peers, and the most important single factor in explaining youth crime is the quality of a young person's family, including parental care and supervision.

As shown in Table 3.1, the Office of the Surgeon General (2001) identifies the risk factors by age of onset of violence and corresponding protective factors among adolescent offenders (cited in Shader, 2003: 4). It is believed that a range of risk factors falling under five domains, namely individual, family, school, peer group and community may be offset by positive influences such as warm and supportive relationships with parents or other adults and commitment to school.

As shown in Table 3.2 (pp 34-35), the National Crime Prevention (1999) summarises the risk and protective factors suggested by seven influential longitudinal studies that have been linked to antisocial and criminal behaviour. These seven studies are: Bloomington Longitudinal Study, Cambridge Study in Delinquent Development, Concordia Longitudinal High Risk Project, Dunedin Multidisciplinary Study, Kauai Study, Mater-University of Queensland Study of Pregnancy and its Outcomes and Newcastle Thousand Family Study (National Crime Prevention, 1999: 135).

Increasingly in Australia and other industrialised countries, crime prevention programs are adopting a 'developmental pathways' approach which sees life as marked by a series of phases, points and transitions (Tremblay and Craig, 1995; Farrington, 2002). These phases and transition points are where developmental interventions aim to eliminate or modify risk factors and increase protective factors (National Crime Prevention, 1999). In this respect, there has been increasing recognition of the social and economic benefits of prevention and early intervention service delivery models (Farrington, 1996; Home Office, 1997; Lo, Wong and Maxwell, 2005).

Nipping Crime in the Bud

Undeniably there is no dispute that 'prevention is better than cure'. How can we prevent at-risk children and young people from becoming involved in the justice system? Various community safety initiatives have been suggested and research is underway to evaluate the effectiveness of these initiatives. An empirical study conducted by Stewart, Dennison and Waterson (2002) draws our attention to the fact that preventing different forms of child maltreatment is likely to produce a larger reduction in offending. Based on 41,700 children born in Queensland in 1983, their study discovered that 10 per cent of these children came into contact with the formerly Department of Families by the time they were 17 years old because of a child protection matter; and one of the predictors for youth

Table 3.1 Risk and Protective Factors for Violence at Age 15 to 18, by Domain

| Domain | Risk Factor | | Protective Factor* |
	Early Onset (age 6-11)	Late Onset (age 12-14)	
Individual	General offences Substance abuse Being male Aggression** Psychological condition: hyperactivity Problem (antisocial) behaviour Exposure to television violence Medical, physical problems Low IQ Antisocial attitudes, beliefs Dishonesty**	General offences Psychological condition: restlessness, difficulty concentrating**, risk taking Being male Physical violence Antisocial attitudes, beliefs Crime against persons Antisocial behaviour Low IQ Substance use	Intolerant attitude towards deviance High IQ Being female Positive social orientation Perceived sanctions for transgressions
Family	Low socioeconomic status/poverty Antisocial parents Poor parent-child relations (harsh, lax, or inconsistent discipline) Broken home (separation from parents) Other conditions Abusive parents Neglect	Poor parent-child relations (harsh, lax discipline; poor monitoring, supervision) Low parental involvement Antisocial parents Broken home Low socioeconomic status/poverty Abusive parents Other conditions: family conflict**	Warm, supportive relationships with parents or other adults Parents' positive evaluation of peers Parental monitoring
School	Poor attitude, performance	Poor attitude, performance Academic failure	Commitment to school Recognition for involvement in conventional activities
Peer group	Weak social ties Antisocial peers	Weak social ties Antisocial, delinquent peers	Friends who engage in conventional behaviour
Community		Neighbourhood crime, drugs Neighbourhood disorganisation	

*   Age of onset not known

**   Males only

Source: Office of the Surgeon General, 2001: Box 4.1 (cited in Shader, 2003: 4)

Table 3.2 Risk and Protective Factors Associated with Antisocial and Criminal Behaviour

RISK FACTORS

Child factors	Family factors	School context	Life events	Community and cultural factors
Prematurity	**Parental characteristics:**	School failure	Divorce and family break up	Socioeconomic disadvantage
Low birth weight	Teenage mothers	Normative beliefs about aggression	War or natural disaster	Population density and housing conditions
Disability	Single parents	Deviant peer group	Death of a family member	Urban area
Prenatal brain damage	Psychiatric disorder, especially depression	Bullying		Neighbourhood violence and crime
Birth injury	Substance abuse	Peer rejection		Cultural norms
Low intelligence	Criminality	Poor attachment to school		Concerning violence as acceptable response to frustration
Difficult temperament	Antisocial models	Inadequate behaviour management		Media portrayal of violence
Chronic illness	**Family environment:**			Lack of support services
Insecure attachment	Family violence and disharmony			Social or cultural discrimination
Poor problem solving	Marital discord			
Beliefs about aggression	Disorganised			
Attributions	Negative interaction/social isolation			
Poor social skills	Large family size			
Low self-esteem	Father absence			
Lack of empathy	Long term parental unemployment			
Alienation	**Parenting style:**			
Hyperactivity/ disruptive behaviour	Poor supervision and monitoring of child			
Impulsivity	Discipline style (harsh or inconsistent)			
	Rejection of child			
	Abuse			
	Lack of warmth and affection			
	Low involvement in child's activities			
	Neglect			

PROTECTIVE FACTORS

Child factors	Family factors	School context	Life events	Community and cultural factors
Social competence	Supportive caring parents	Positive school climate	Meeting significant person	Access to support services
Social skills	Family harmony	Pro-social peer group	Moving to new area	Community networking
Above average intelligence	More than two years between sibling	Responsibility and required helpfulness	Opportunities at critical turning points or major life transitions	Attachment to the community
Attachment to family	Responsibility for chores or required helpfulness	Sense of belonging / bonding		Participation in church or other community group
Empathy	Secure and stable family	Opportunities for some success at school and recognition of achievement		Community / cultural norms against violence
Problem solving	Supportive relationship with other adult	School norms re violence		A strong cultural identity and ethnic pride
Optimism	Small family size			
School achievement	Strong family norms and morality			
Easy temperament				
Internal locus of control				
Moral beliefs				
Values				
Self-related cognitions				
Good coping style				

Source: National Crime Prevention, 1999: Tables 3.3 and 3.4

offending is the experience of maltreatment and victimisation, including physical abuse and neglect. The link between child maltreatment and juvenile offending has also been discussed elsewhere (see Weatherburn and Lind, 1997; Hamilton, Falshaw and Browne, 2002; Howell et al, 2004; Malmgren and Meisel, 2004). However, this does not by any means suggest that all abused children are set to become criminals in the future. Yet the findings of Stewart et al (2002) are suggestive that a sound child protection system is essential in preventing children or young people from later offending.

Reviews of research literature by Utting (1996) have suggested that efforts to prevent children and young people from committing crime should focus on three main aspects, namely strengthening families, improving the school system and using sports and outdoor adventure activities. To address the family risk factors, home visitation provided by nurses and social workers should be made available to economically disadvantaged families with the intention of providing them with the necessary support, parent training, access to resources such as day care or play group and improving parenting skills (National Crime Prevention, 1999). In Queensland, a wide range of support services to families such as family support outreach services (where workers visit clients), family support centre-based services (where clients visit a service centre), high risk groups with specific needs including homelessness and substance abuse (where the service targets particular, high needs client groups), and specialist services (where the service is based around a specific issue such as sexual abuse) are delivered by the Department of Communities (2003). These early intervention programs intend to be provided at the earliest possible point in the conflict or crisis and before young people and their families become involved in the statutory child protection or juvenile justice systems (Chui, Kidd and Preston, 2005). To address the school-based risk factors, efforts should be made to improve the educational achievement of young people, especially in areas with long term problems of crime and criminality; prevent school exclusions and truancy; deal with school bullying; and increase the awareness of the consequence of crime and antisocial behaviour among the students in junior and high schools (Utting, 1996). In England and Wales, providing at-risk young people real opportunities for sport and leisure is seen as another option of preventing youth crime. Engaging young people or offenders into positive leisure opportunities not only enables them to use their time constructively but also facilitates them to learn 'discipline, cognitive skills, and social interaction demanded by many sporting and leisure activities as useful ingredients in wider ranging prevention initiatives' (Utting, 1996: 84). Learning from the British experience, programs should be implemented by committed and qualified youth workers with the skills to build trusting relationships with young people.

Diversionary Programs

Cautioning

In the light of the empirical findings and the United Nations Convention on the Rights of the Child, there has been a call to reduce the number of young people in the formal youth justice system and to increase the use of diversion as well as least restrictive alternatives in order to strengthen families (Lo et al, 2005). Dingwall and Harding (1998) consider diversion as 'a conscious decision not to use the formal process of prosecution and trial in cases where there is a fair expectation that it would otherwise have taken place' (p 2). Diversion can occur at various stages in the criminal justice process, ranging from the early phase of crime report to the juncture of sentencing, and on the initiative of different persons, be it the victim, the investigating authority, the prosecution or the court. It varies from informal and unofficial responses (such as victim waiver) to formal and legalistic ones (such as discharge by a court). Polk (2003: 2) specifies juvenile diversion as 'programs and practices which are employed for young people who have initial contact with the police, but are diverted from the traditional juvenile justice processes before children's court adjudication' which emerged in the Australian juvenile justice system as a consequence of work of the President's Crime Commission in the mid-1960s. Bartholomew (1992) articulates the rationales for introducing police cautioning in Western Australia: early contact with the criminal justice system can be counterproductive and may actually increase the likelihood of offending; offending by young people is often opportunistic and trivial; cautioning is a more efficient means of dealing with petty offenders; and cautioning would provide police with an opportunity to contact parents which would encourage parental involvement and responsibility. In other words, cautioning not only provides a child an opportunity to 'grow out of crime' but also is a method of diversion of juvenile offenders from prosecution. It is perceived as a more effective and appropriate way of dealing with young offenders by avoiding the undesirable effect of stigmatisation. In this respect, Coumarelos and Weatherburn (1995) opine that labelling theory underlies the diversion policy in Australia. But they reject the claim by labelling theorists that court proceeding is inherently criminogenic and thus increases recidivism as lacking empirical support. Polk's (2003) fieldwork study of juvenile diversion across the board in Australia reveals that the authorities did not pay due regard to diverting young offenders from pre-trial detention – many of those remanded in custody were subsequently not being sentenced to periods of detention. He considers that diversion is applicable to cases where the offender's conduct was trivial, experimental and one-off; these offenders are unlikely to be recidivists. The law enforcement agencies can 'clear' a case with fewer resources while the offender is not 'let off' (Dingwall and Harding, 1998: 13). Juvenile offenders may readily admit guilt for a quick disposal of their cases, but it does not relieve the government of the duty to ensure that the plea was voluntary, appropriate and proportional (Coumarelos and Weatherburn, 1995). However, this raises the concerns about the lower visibility of the diversion process, and the possibility of unstructured discretion and arbitrariness contrary to the legal protection and procedural safeguards as embedded in the criminal justice system (see Dingwall and Harding, 1998; O'Connor and Chui, 2002). Indeed, there are complicated issues of transparency, accountability, proportionality, consistency, fairness, effectiveness, costs, division of powers and implications for the justice system which are yet to be resolved. Polk (2003) recommends that measures should be taken to protect the legal and human rights of young offenders, for example, by assuring proper legal representations when appropriate, providing oversight and review of diversion processes and decisions, and ensuring that the diversion undertakings are proportional.

O'Connor (1992) believes that cautioning is a formal process in which a child admits his or her wrongdoing in front of a police officer and the parent or caregiver. The process can be highly stressful for a child and he or she is also made aware of what consequences would follow reoffending. Previous studies such as Leivesley (1984, cited in Lewis and O'Regan, 1992) and Potas, Vining and Wilson (1990) support the use of cautioning programs for young people for the following reasons. First, in general a formal court process is seen as an overreaction to some minor offending behaviour. Second, Potas et al (1990) argue that dealing with juvenile offenders in Queensland by cautioning is cheap, and the cost to the greater community in time, lost wages and productivity of witnesses, court and legal costs and the cost to other government departments would be much greater. Third, Lewis and O'Regan (1992) comment: 'Data on recidivist rates for juveniles coming to the notice of police is difficult to obtain, however indications are that between 70% and 85% of juvenile offenders never come to notice again ...' (p 247).

Restorative Justice

Following the passage of the *Children, Young Persons and Their Families Act 1989* in New Zealand, youth justice conferencing has been developed in all eight Australian States and Territories (Hayes and Daly, 2003). Conferencing emphasises the use of restorative justice principles. Marshall (1998) defines restorative justice as: '[a] process whereby all the parties with a stake in a particular offence come together to resolve collectively how to deal with the aftermath of the offence and its implications for the future' (p 32). Put simply, restorative justice programs bring the young offender, victim, their families, support persons and community representatives together to achieve a mutually agreeable resolution as a result of offending behaviour. In Queensland, both the police and the court can refer matters they consider appropriate to community conference, for young people aged from 10 to 16 inclusive when they commit the offence. Figure 3.1 illustrates the ways in which diversion to conferencing may occur at a number of different stages along the youth justice service continuum under the *Juvenile Justice Act 1992* (Qld).

Figure 3.1 Ways of Referrals Made to Community Conferences

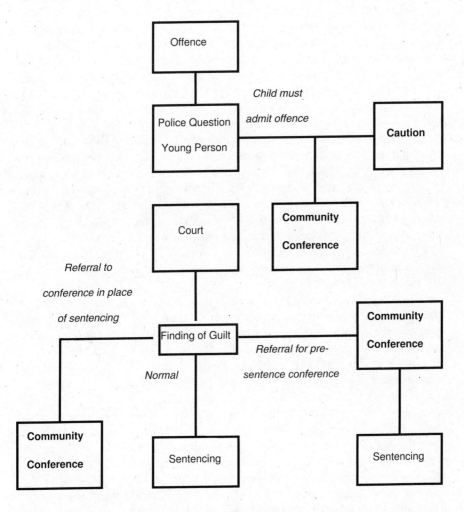

Source: Department of Communities, Youth Justice Operations Unit, Community Conferencing (2003, also cited in Chui, Kidd and Preston, 2005: 185)

The *Juvenile Justice Act 1992* (Qld) requires that before referring the young person to youth justice conferencing, four conditions should be met: the young person must admit the offence to the police; the victim (if there was a victim) must give consent; a caution is inappropriate, and the matter would have otherwise been sent to court if a referral to conference was not made; and the police officer considers that a referral is more appropriate than starting a proceeding.

Based on extensive literature review on conferencing, Hayes and Daly (2003) highlight two recurring themes. First, in most jurisdictions in Australia, evaluation studies have measured levels of satisfaction among victims and offenders in conferences as an indicator of effectiveness. It is not surprising that high levels of satisfaction with the process and outcomes were found among the participants in the actual conferences. Hayes et al (1998) also found that victims were more satisfied with the process than they would have expected to be through the courts, and recognised that their needs were attended to fully during the conferencing process. Hayes (2002) reports that variations in victim satisfaction rates across programs are influenced by the emphasis given to victim's rights and roles in the relevant legislative framework (pp 7-8). Second, research on conferencing evaluates the effectiveness of the conference according to the participant's sense of fairness and procedural justice (Hayes and Daly, 2003). The Re-Integrative Shaming Experiments (RISE) in Canberra compared conferences with courts in a randomised study (Strang et al, 1999). The RISE research found higher reported levels of procedural fairness and restorative justice (that is, repair of damage) than court. Also, victims reported that the process helped them understand why the offence occurred, and thus they were less fearful of the offender and were better able to move on and put the offence behind them (see also Hayes and Daly, 2003).

The New South Wales program published a study which indicated a 15 to 20 per cent reduction in reoffending when conference participants were compared to court cases (Luke and Lind, 2002). Furthermore certain studies conducted by Hayes and Daly (2001) in South Australia and by Maxwell and Morris (2001) in New Zealand have found a relationship between reoffending and whether the conference process generated feelings of remorse in the offender. Hayes (2002) found that 44 per cent of the young offenders conferenced did not reoffend even from three to five years post-conference in Queensland. Where young people did reoffend the median annual post-conference offending rates were nominal (one offence per year). These findings reveal that 'conference-specific factors, such as offenders' remorse and involvement in decision-making, are indicative of reduced reoffending' (Hayes and Daly, 2003: 756-757). Getting young offenders involved in the decision-making process in one way or another would enable them to face the consequences of their actions or assume active responsibility for their behaviours.

Effective Intervention with Young Offenders

While the early intervention and diversionary programs are tailor-made for those young offenders who commit petty offences, punishment in the form of community and custodial disposals is necessary to impose sanction on other young people who break the law to deter them from reoffending. Changing offending behaviour is not an easy task, especially for those who are involuntary clients and resistant to change. This section begins with an outline of the 'What Works' principles, and introduces promising approaches to work with young offenders.

Applying 'What Works' Principles

Drawing from various outcome literature, McGuire (1995, 2002), Andrews and Bonta (2003), and Day, Howells and Rickwood (2004) have identified a set of principles of effective intervention with offenders. These principles have also formed the basis for offender crime reduction strategy in England and Wales. They are:

- *risk classification* – matching between offender risk level based on criminal history and other variables and level of supervision or degree of service intervention;
- *criminogenic needs* – targeting the needs most related to offending, problems and features of offender's lives that contribute to, or are supportive of, or related directly to offending;
- *responsivity* – matching learning styles between supervising officers and offenders (more active, participatory methods of working are more desirable than the loose and didactic ones);
- *community base* – locating offender behaviour programs in the community yields more effective outcomes than those in institutions;
- *treatment modality* – applying a variety of models or approaches such as skills oriented, problem solving, social skills training, cognitive-behavioural theory to design and implement intervention programs (see McGuire and Priestley, 1995);
- *program integrity* – ensuring that the stated aims of programs are linked to the theories and methods being used, and that well trained and supported staff deliver the programs with adequate resources (Hollin, 1995; McGuire and Priestley, 1995); and
- *professional discretion* – valuing the practice wisdom and professional judgment of the program staff; and allowing practitioners to make decisions on the basis of other characteristics and situations not covered by the above principles (Day and Howells, 2002).

To summarise, the principles associated with effective interventions include effective risk management; targeting offending behaviour; addressing the specific factors linked with offenders' offending; ensuring relevance to offenders' learning styles; promoting community reintegration; and maintaining quality and integrity of program delivery (Underdown, 1998). These can of course be built on and refined still further. A recent meta-analysis conducted by the Department of Justice

(2005) in Canada rehearses some of these principles and gives 15 specific recommendations to program developers and deliverers regarding how to work with youth in conflict with the law:

1. conduct the treatment in a therapeutic environment using multiple forms of individual, group or family counselling (see also, Alexander, 2000);

2. screen youth for anger issues and provide an anger management program where suitable (see also, Howells et al, 2005);

3. directly involve educators within the treatment program and target school performance and attendance where necessary (see Sheldon, 1994);

4. target antisocial attitudes including respect for authority and for the institutions of the criminal justice system;

5. develop cognitive skills in order to improve problem solving, perspective taking and goal setting;

6. enhance social skills such as giving and receiving feedback, and the ability to work within groups;

7. encourage and teach positive communication within families;

8. provide parents with the appropriate skills to monitor and supervise youth;

9. increase employability of the youth by offering specific vocational training;

10. limit the program length to six months and provide a maximum of 20 hours of program exposure for low risk offenders and increase the treatment dosage for high risk offenders;

11. develop program manuals to ensure program compliance;

12. provide suitable interventions early in the lives of youth in conflict with the law;

13. encourage meaningful and substantial family involvement in the program;

14. involve the community such as the police, non-governmental organisations and community leaders in the treatment program where appropriate; and

15. address ambiguous and less promising treatment targets such as antisocial peers, relapse prevention, substance abuse and leisure when deemed appropriate on a case by case basis (Department of Justice, 2005: 1-2).

Effective Interventions for Young Offenders

In recent years, correctional agencies have been asked to scrutinise the models of service delivery and improve the effectiveness of rehabilitative or treatment programs for young offenders in order to reduce the rate of reoffending. It is indeed essential for youth justice practitioners to be informed about 'what works' and 'what doesn't work' with young offenders who often hold negative attitudes towards the criminal justice agencies (Chui and Nellis, 2003; Burnett and Roberts, 2004). Several researchers have attempted to review a large number of empirical studies to examine what types of programs are most likely to be successful, and identify the key strategies in designing successful programs. At the outset it should be emphasised that the models of intervention and programs introduced below are highly selective and are by no means exhaustive.

A Change Framework

One starting point to learn how to change an individual's behaviour, values and attitudes is to understand how people actually change (Fleet and Annison, 2003). DiClemente and Prochaska (1998) developed a model to assess a person's readiness to change and willingness to participate in treatment, and this is the so-called transtheoretical model of change. There are five stages of change, namely (1) pre-contemplative stage – 'your client is not considering changing'; (2) contemplative stage – 'your client is aware of the problem but is ambivalent to about changing'; (3) preparation stage – 'your client is preparing to take action soon'; (4) action stage – 'your client takes some action to make changes'; and (5) maintenance stage – 'your client changes behaviour successfully but needs to focus on sustaining these changes' (cited in Jarvis, Teubutt and Mattick, 1995: 24-25). The stages of change model can easily be used to assess the young offender's position in relation to offending, and give guidance as to what practitioners should do to motivate them to change. A change framework to work with violent male offenders has been developed by Dobash et al (2000) and it outlines the processes through which change can be achieved (see Table 3.3).

Table 3.3 A Change Framework

1. *Change is Possible* – Thinking what was previously unthinkable.
2. *Motivation to Change* – Desiring that which was previously unwanted.
3. *Why Change?* – Re-evaluating the costs and benefits of violence to self and others.
4. *What Changes?* – Transforming the self from 'object' to 'subject'.
5. *General Mechanisms of Change* – Shifting the regulation of behaviour from external constraints to internal controls.
6. *The Discourse of Change* – Replacing old ideas and words that support and justify violence with new ones that reject violence and acknowledge the harm done to others.
7. *The Medium of Change* – Talking and listening; thinking and learning; practising.
8. *Specific Elements of Change* – New skills and orientations.

Source: Dobash et al (2000: Table 1)

However, neither the model of change nor the change framework gives answers regarding how to promote changes with young offenders who are legally mandated to engage with service providers and those who experience social or non-legal pressures (Rooney, 1992).

Working with Involuntary Clients

Thibaut and Kelly (1959) believe that a therapeutic relationship is not voluntary if the client feels forced to remain in the relationship; feels that there are no other alternatives available; perceives the cost of leaving the relationship is higher than remaining; and feels disadvantaged in the relationship. However, an involuntary client is not always a resistant client, for example, a drug using criminal who has been court ordered to participate in a rehabilitation program may actually look forward to the program and actively want to change his or her behaviour (Longshore, Prendergast and Farbee, 2004). It is also important to note that resistance occurs on both sides of the transaction – that practitioners can be just as resistant within the therapeutic relationship as clients. Practitioner's resistance and client's resistance can be mutually reinforcing. Unless the resistance from the practitioner can be dealt with, the client's resistance may continue to exist, thus adversely affecting the quality of interventions (Hepworth and Larsen, 1993). For instance, labelling clients as 'incompetent' and 'lacking insight' enables the practitioners to avoid confronting deficiencies in their agencies or themselves.

To understand client's resistance, it is vital to acknowledge the loss of freedom or the lack of choices for the client (Ritchie, 1986; Rooney, 1988). The therapeutic relationship often takes place within the context of a power imbalance, whereby access to desirable alternatives is limited for the client. For example, a delinquent youth may have to choose between joining a community drug rehabilitation program and juvenile detention, while also harbouring resentment at the process of being coerced into treatment. As a consequence of these feelings, involuntary clients may react with resistance because the extent to which they choose to cooperate with the practitioner is one of the very few things which they still have control over (Rooney, 1992). Another reason why clients may be resistant towards therapeutic process is because it involves changing their current maladaptive behaviour. Changing old patterns of behaviour can be a painful process as it involves learning new ways of behaving that may cause tension and/or conflict (Cavanagh, 1990). Generally, people will not change their behaviour until there is a substitute behaviour that will be equally satisfying and does not raise their level of stress and anxiety.

Several strategies to work with involuntary clients have been suggested in existing literature. For example, Rooney (1992) advocates a 'socialisation' approach which involves practitioners and clients being clear about each other's roles, choices and goals, and being able to negotiate and bargain with each other until their goals are congruent. The process aims to decrease the power imbalance between practitioners and clients, thus promoting clients to become more voluntary. Major elements of 'socialisation' strategies include: making a distinction between acknow-ledged problems (that is, those problems that the client admits), and attributed problems (that is, those problems that others perceive the client having); clarifying client's rights and choices; and negotiating, bargaining and persuading between practitioner and client until both parties agree on the goals and the processes of obtaining the goals (Rooney, 1992).

Trotter (1999, 2004) developed a similar model of practice called a pro-social modelling (see Chapter 2 of this volume). In particular, Trotter (1999) believes that the following strategies are most effective: helping the client to understand the nature of the professional relationship; modelling and encouraging pro-social expressions and actions; rewarding or reinforcing pro-social attitudes and behaviours; employing a collaborative problem solving approach; and building a trusting relationship with the client. Sometimes the goals of involuntary clients can be inappropriate – however, research consistently points to the need to work with client's definitions of the problems and goals. The problem(s) should be clearly defined and understood by both parties – and the goals should be clear and achievable; and communication skills such as empathy and reflective listening should be displayed by practitioners.

Motivating Young Offenders to Change

In addition to learning how to deal with involuntary clients, McMurran (2002) judges that criminal justice practitioners should be equipped with the skills of assessing the offender's motivation to change. In order to assess people's readiness to change, Miller and Rollnick (2002) suggest four areas of concern, namely the person's judgment of a need to change; perception of actual changes; self-efficacy for change; and intention to change within a time frame. But how can young offenders be motivated to change their addictive and antisocial behaviour? A number of enhance-ment techniques have been suggested by Prochaska and Levesque (2002: 66-69) in relation to the transtheoretical model of change. For instance, *consciousness raising* can enable the offenders to be aware of their own defence mechanism such as denial and withdrawal and to understand the causes as well as consequences of maintaining destructive behaviour. This can be achieved by using mild confrontations, constructive feedback and reflection of feelings and contents. *Dramatic relief* intends to move people emotionally and arouse fear, guilt and hope by using psycho-drama, role-play and personal testimonies. *Self-liberation* attempts to convey the message that one can change so long as one is committed to change, thereby enhancing their motivation.

A number of commentators such as Trotter (1999) and Cordess (2002) opine that what is central to working with offenders effectively is to build and nurture a trusting and nurturing practitioner-offender alliance. Change often does not occur when alienated young offenders are not committed to change their personal and social circumstances. In this respect, their relationship with the practitioner is essential to sustaining their commitment to overcome obstacles and take risks in order to change their chaotic lifestyle. According to a probation study conducted by Chui (2003b), one element that is associated with probation success is the skill of communication. Young adult offenders who supported the view of a probation officer as one able to understand what they said and who had an ability to listen to their problems and concerns, were more likely to avoid reoffending. To achieve this takes patience, experience and good interpersonal skills. In addition, the young offenders would like to be treated as 'friends' rather than 'offenders'. Yet a friendly relationship does not mean collusion but requires honest and direct confrontation of unlawful and delinquent behaviours. A 'quality relationship' does not rule out a control element so long as offenders are treated fairly, openly and with respect. Indeed a youth justice practitioner may need to know when to be supportive and when to be more of a law enforcer and to use 'authority' appropriately. This is the real dilemma of being a youth justice practitioner – the underlying conflict between a rehabilitative aim and a social control aim (Hardiker, 1977; Garland, 1985).

Cognitive-behavioural Approaches

The value of cognitive-behavioural approaches have become widely recognised since late 1990s as an effective psychological intervention to address offending behaviour among young and adult offenders (McGuire, 2002; see Chapter 4 of this volume). Cognitive-behavioural theory is essentially cognitive theory with social learning or behavioural theory, and it is grounded in a notion that behaviour is modifiable by helping an individual to uncover dysfunctional and irrational cognition, thinking and beliefs (Kendall and Hollon, 1979). Hollin (1998: 127-130) examines a range of cognitive-behavioural programs for young offenders, and some examples are:

- *self-control and self-instructional training* intends to help children to gain self-control over their actions by developing self-statements;
- *anger management program,* which consists of three stages, namely cognitive preparation, skill acquisition and application training aims to reduce aggressive behaviour in the school and institutional settings;
- *role-taking* program is designed to help delinquents to see themselves from other people's perspective;
- *cognitive and social problem solving* aims to improve the young offender's ability to analyse the problems encountered, set realistic goals, and generate more solutions to problems;
- *moral reasoning development* should be fostered among those who fail to use reasoning to resolve moral dilemmas and lack victim empathy;

- *multimodal programs* combine a variety of techniques such as social skills training, behavioural modification, structured learning theory and moral education to improve young people's self-control and reduce their antisocial behaviour; and
- *parent management training* aims to improve the communication pattern and process between parents and their children (see Kazdin, 2005).

In reviews and meta-analyses of the outcome literature, cognitive-behavioural and multimodal programs have appeared to be more effective than punitive and unstructured counselling in reducing offending behaviour (Kurtz, 2002). Kurtz further elaborates that cognitive-behavioural programs work best when they involve training in problem solving or negotiation skills for delinquents. A review compiled by the Australian Institute of Criminology (2002) confirms that cognitive-behavioural training can help change how young people think and act, thereby showing positive impact on criminal activity, and it has proved to be successful in tacking truancy and discipline problems in schools.

A Rights-based Approach

Most at-risk young people and young criminals are the very marginalised young people. They are blamed for their irresponsibility and lack of competence. Indeed more should be done to examine the impact of structural inequalities on their individual lives, and perhaps structural changes are necessary to improve the social circumstances of the marginalised and excluded group (Drakeford and Vanstone, 1996; Smith, 1998). Crimmens and Whalen (1999) are in favour of using the rights-based approach which 'can enable practice with young people to be inclusive at a time when young people continue to be crudely categorised by policy makers and the media as either [un]deserving or deviant' (p 164). Crimmens and Whalen (1999) further highlight four core values underpinning the rights-based approach, namely treating all young people with respect and dignity which is in line with the principles contained in the United Nations Convention; listening to what young people have to say; communicating all information, especially on rights, in an accessible, young-person friendly way; and involving young people in the decision-making process (pp 170-171). Applying these values when working with young offenders would allow them to take more control in their lives and at the same time provide them with a chance to tell the practitioner what works best for them. Doherty (2004) notes that 'the emphasis on legal rights as the cornerstone of juvenile justice ... has been replaced by emphases on efficiency, expediency, crime prevention (in the sense of general surveillance rather than individual treatment) and public policy' (p 134). In this respect, how to safeguard the due process rights of a young person is a crucial issue worthy the practitioners' attention (O'Connor and Chui, 2002).

Summary

Based on varied research literature, major reasons for juvenile delin-quency and some intervention approaches to working with young offenders are discussed. Admittedly most of these empirical researches are carried out in the United States, Canada and England, and the Aust-ralian studies are sparse. Despite this, it is clear that causes of juvenile offending are many according to the risk factor paradigm, and young offenders often present multiple 'needs' and 'problems', which explains why tackling the causes of youth crime is a difficult task. Further research should look at the interrelationship between risk and protective factors, and explore why some young people exposed to various risk factors do not turn to crime.

There is evidence that the frequency and intensity of intervention should be in proportion to the seriousness of the current offence and the levels of risk of reoffending. The levels of risk of reoffending among young people vary according to their personal and social circumstances. Also, recent literature reveals that action should be taken earlier to prevent at-risk children and young people becoming involved in criminal and antisocial behaviour. In this chapter, it is argued that the early intervention programs and diversionary programs are geared towards the treatment of first time, minor and low risk offenders, especially in the pre-adjudication. However, there are concerns including differential policies and procedures on cautioning in different regions of England and Wales and prejudicial police decision-making against the ethnic minority communities (Gelsthorpe et al, 1995). A number of factors such as gender, ethnicity, class and parental attitudes are found to affect how a young offender is treated. Some research evidence shows that Aboriginal youth are less likely to benefit from police decisions to divert children from the court system in Australia (Gale, Bailey-Harris and Wundersitz, 1990; Cunneen and White, 2002). This experience requires us to look at the discretion exercised by the police and the family service officers in the diversionary process (Brants and Field, 1995).

This chapter also provides an overview of 'What Works' principles and what are effective interventions with the medium and high risk young offenders. Multi-modal offending programs that incorporate a range of intervention methods such as social skills training, pro-social modelling and cognitive-behavioural therapies have appeared to be more effective than unstructured and loosely organised programs in terms of reducing offending. However, it is far from clear whether these so-called promising approaches would work with Indigenous young offenders in Australia.

Review Questions

1. What do some young people break the law and others obey the law?

2. To what extent do you agree that young offenders should be diverted from the formal youth justice system? Give reasons to justify your answer.

3. In what ways do the 'What Works' principles help you guide your direct practice with at-risk youth and young offenders?

4. Critically evaluate whether cognitive-behavioural programs are the best intervention method to work with young offenders.

Useful Websites

Australian Clearinghouse for Youth Studies	www.acys.utas.edu.au
Australian Institute of Criminology	www.aic.gov.au
National Criminal Justice Reference Service (US)	www.ncjrs.org
Office of Juvenile Justice and Delinquency Prevention (US)	www.ojjdp.ncjrs.org
Youth Justice Board (UK)	www.youth-justice-board.gov.uk

References

Aichorn, A (1935) *Wayward Youth*, New York: Viking Press.

Alexander, R (2000) *Counseling, Treatment, and Intervention with Juvenile and Adult Offenders*, Belmont, CA: Wadsworth.

Andrews, DA and Bonta, J (2003) *The Psychology of Criminal Conduct* (3rd ed), Cincinnati: Anderson Publishing.

Audit Commission (1996) *Misspent Youth: Young People and Crime*, London: Audit Commission.

Australian Institute of Criminology (2002) *What Works in Reducing Young People's Involvement in Crime?*, Canberra: Australian Capital Territory Government.

Bartholomew, P (1992) 'Preventative and diversionary programs in Western Australia', in L Atkinson and S-A Gerull (eds) *National Conference on Juvenile Justice: Proceedings of a Conference Held 22-24 September 1992*, Canberra: Australian Institute of Criminology.

Bateman, T and Pitts, J (eds) (2005) *The RHP Companion to Youth Justice*, Lyme Regis, Dorset: Russell House.

Brants, C and Field, S (1995) 'Discretion and accountability in prosecution: A comparative perspective on keeping crime out of court', in P Fennell, C Harding, N Jorg and B Swart (eds) *Criminal Justice in Europe: A Comparative Study* (pp 127-148), Oxford: Clarendon Press.

Burnett, R and Appleton, C (2004) *Joined-up Youth Justice: Tackling Youth Crime in Partnership*, Lyme Regis, Dorset: Russell House.

Burnett, R and Roberts, C (eds) (2004) *What Works in Probation and Youth Justice: Developing Evidence-based Practice*, Cullompton, Devon: Willan.

Bynum, JE and Thompson, WE (2004) *Juvenile Delinquency; A Sociological Approach* (6th ed), Boston: Allyn and Bacon.

Byrne, CF and Trew, KF (2005) 'Crime orientations, social relations and involvement in crime: Patterns emerging from offenders' accounts', *Howard Journal of Criminal Justice*, 44(2), 185-205.

Cavanagh, ME (1990) *The Counseling Experience: A Theoretical and Practical Approach*, Prospect Heights, ILL: Waveland.

Chapple, CL (2005) 'Self-control, peer relations, and delinquency', *Justice Quarterly*, 22(1), 89-106.

Chui, WH (2003a) 'What works in reducing reoffending: Principles and programmes', in WH Chui and M Nellis (eds) *Moving Probation Forward: Evidence, Arguments and Practice* (pp 56-73), Harlow, Essex: Pearson Education.

Chui, WH (2003b) 'Experiences of probation supervision in Hong Kong: Listening to the young adult offenders', *Journal of Criminal Justice: An International Journal*, 31(6), 567-577.

Chui, WH and Nellis, M (eds) (2003) *Moving Probation Forward: Evidence, Arguments and Practice*, Harlow, Essex: Pearson Education.

Chui, WH, Kidd, J and Preston, C (2005) 'Treatment of child and juvenile offenders in Queensland, Australia: Alternatives to prosecution', in TW Lo, D Wong and G Maxwell (eds) *Alternatives to Prosecution: Rehabilitative and Restorative Models of Youth Justice* (pp 171-205), Singapore: Marshall Cavendish Academic.

Cloward, R and Ohlin, L (1960) *Delinquency and Opportunity*, New York: Free Press.

Cohen, A (1955) *Delinquent Boys: The Culture of the Gang*, New York: Free Press.

Cohen, S (1980) *Folk Devils and Moral Panics: The Creation of the Mods and Rockers*, Oxford: Blackwell.

Conger, JJ and Miller, WC (1966) *Personality, Social Class, and Delinquency*, New York: Wiley.

Cordess, C (2002) 'Building and nurturing a therapeutic alliance with offenders', in M McMurran (ed) *Motivating Offenders to Change: A Guide to Enhancing Engagement in Therapy* (pp 75-86), Chichester, West Sussex: John Wiley & Sons.

Coumarelos, C and Weatherburn, D (1995) 'Targeting intervention strategies to reduce juvenile recidivism', *Australian and New Zealand Journal of Criminology*, 28(1), 1-37.

Crimmens, D and Whalen, A (1999) 'Rights-based approaches to work with young people', *Ethical Issues in Youth Work* (pp 164-180), London: Routledge.

Cunneen, C and White, R (2002) *Juvenile Justice: Youth and Crime in Australia*, Melbourne: Oxford University Press.

Day, A and Howells, K (2002) 'Psychological treatments for rehabilitating offenders: Evidence-based practice comes of age', *Australian Psychologist*, 37(1), 39-47.

Day, A, Howells, K and Rickwood, D (2004) 'Current trends in the rehabilitation of juvenile offenders', *Trends and Issues in Crime and Criminal Justice*, No 284.

Department of Communities (2003), *Information Sheet 1: Prevention and Early Intervention Models of Service Delivery*, Brisbane: Department of Communities. Available at: <http://www.communities.qld.gov.au/department/future directions/publications/documents/pdf/info_sheet_01.pdf>.

Department of Justice (2005) *Treating Youth in Conflict with the Law: A New Meta-analysis*, Canada: Department of Justice. Available at: <http://canada. justice.gc.ca/en/ps/rs/rep/2003/rr03yj-3/rr03yj-3_00.html>.

DiClemente, C and Prochaska, O (1998) 'Toward a comprehensive, theoretical model of change: Stages of change and addictive behavior', in R Miller and N Heather (eds) *Treating Addictive Behaviors: Process of Change* (2nd ed) (pp 3-24), New York: Plenum Press.

Dingwall, G and Harding, C (1998) *Diversion in the Criminal Process*, London: Sweet & Maxwell.

Dobash, R, Cavanagh, K, Dobash, R and Lewis, R (2000) 'Domestic violence programmes: A framework for change', *Probation Journal*, 47(1), 18-29.

Doherty, M (2004) *Criminal Justice and Penology* (2nd ed), London: Old Bailey Press.

Drakeford, M and Vanstone, M (eds) (1996) *Beyond Offending Behaviour*, Aldershot: Gower.

Drowns, RW and Hess, KM (2000) *Juvenile Justice* (3rd ed), Belmont, CA: Wasworth.

Ellis, RA and Sowers, KM (2001) *Juvenile Justice Practice: A Cross-disciplinary Approach to Intervention*, Belmont, CA: Brooks/Cole.

Farrington, DP (1996) 'Individual, family and peer factors in the development of delinquency', in CR Hollin and K Howells (eds) *Clinical Approaches to Working with Young Offenders* (pp 21-56), Chichester, West Sussex: John Wiley & Sons.

Farrington, DP (2000) 'Explaining and preventing crime: The globalization of knowledge – The American Society of Criminology 1999 presidential address', *Criminology*, 38(1), 1-24.

Farrington, DP (2002) 'Developmental criminology and risk-focussed research prevention', in M Maguire, R Morgan and R Reiner (eds) *The Oxford Handbook of Criminology* (3rd ed) (pp 657-701), Oxford: Oxford University Press.

Farrington, DP (2005) 'Childhood origins of antisocial behavior', *Clinical Psychology and Psychotherapy*, 12(3), 177-190.

Fleet, F and Annison, J (2003) 'In support of effectiveness: Facilitating participation and sustaining change', in WH Chui and M Nellis (eds) *Moving Probation Forward: Evidence, Arguments and Practice* (pp 129-145), Harlow, Essex: Pearson Education.

Flowers, RB (2002) *Kids Who Commit Adult Crimes: Serious Criminality by Juvenile Offenders*, New York: The Haworth Press.

Gale, F, Bailey-Harris, R and Wundersitz, J (1990) *Aboriginal Youth and the Criminal Justice System*, Cambridge: Cambridge University Press.

Garland, D (1985) *Punishment and Welfare: A History of Penal Strategies*, Aldershot: Gower.

Gelsthorpe, L (2003) 'Theories of crime', in WH Chui and M Nellis (eds) *Moving Probation Forward: Evidence, Arguments and Practice* (pp 19-37), Harlow, Essex: Pearson Education.

Gelsthorpe, L, Nellis, M, Bruins, J and van Vliet, A (1995) 'Diversion in English and Dutch juvenile justice', in P Fennell, C Harding, N Jorg and B Swart (eds) *Criminal Justice in Europe: A Comparative Study* (pp 199-226), Oxford: Clarendon Press.

Gibson, M (2002) *Born to Crime: Cesare Lombroso and the Origins of Biological Criminology*, Westport, Conn: Praeger.

Glueck, S and Glueck, E (1950) *Unraveling Juvenile Delinquency*, Cambridge, MA: Harvard University Press.

Goldson, B (2000) 'Whither diversion? Interventionism and the new youth justice', in B Goldson (ed) *The New Youth Justice* (pp 35-57), Lyme Regis, Dorset: Russell House.

Goode, E (1994) *Moral Panics: The Social Construction of Deviance*, Oxford: Blackwell.

Haines, K and Drakeford, M (1998) *Young People and Youth Justice*, London: Macmillan.

Hamilton, CE, Falshaw, L and Browne, KD (2002) 'The link between recurrent maltreatment and offending behaviour', *International Journal of Offender Therapy and Comparative Criminology*, 46(1), 75-94.

Hardiker, P (1977) 'Social work ideologies in the probation service', *British Journal of Social Work*, 7(2), 131-154.

Hayes, H (2002) *Youth Justice Conferencing and Re-offending in Queensland* (Working Paper No 1), Brisbane: School of Criminology and Criminal Justice, Griffith University.

Hayes, H and Daly, K (2001) *Family Conferencing in South Australia and Reoffending: Preliminary Results from the SAJJ Project*, A paper presented at the Australian and New Zealand Society of Criminology 16th Annual Meeting, February 2001, Melbourne.

Hayes, H and Daly, K (2003) 'Youth justice conferencing and re-offending', *Justice Quarterly*, 20(4), 725-764.

Hayes, H, Prenzler, T and Wortley, R (1998) *Making Amends: Final Evaluation of the Queensland Community Conferencing Pilot*, Brisbane: Centre for Crime Policy and Public Safety, Griffith University. Available at: <http://www.gu/edu.au/school/ccj/amends.pdf>.

Hepworth, DH and Larsen, JA (1993) *Direct Social Work Practice: Theory and Skills* (4th ed), Pacific Grove, CA: Brooks/Cole.

Hirschi, T (1969) *Causes of Delinquency*, Berkeley, CA: University of California Press.

Hollin, CR (1990) *Cognitive-behavioral Interventions with Young Offenders*, New York: Pergamon.

Hollin, CR (1995) 'The meaning and implications of "programme integrity"', in J McGuire (ed) *What Works: Reducing Reoffending – Guidelines from Research and Practice* (pp 195-208), Chichester, West Sussex: John Wiley & Sons.

Hollin, CR (1998) 'Working with young offenders', in K Cigno and D Bourn (eds) *Cognitive-behavioural Social Work in Practice* (pp 127-142), Aldershot: Ashgate.

Hollin, CR (2002) 'An overview of offender rehabilitation: Something old, something borrowed, something new', *Australian Psychologist*, 37(3), 159-164.

Home Office (1997) *No More Excuses – A New Approach to Tackling Youth Crime in England and Wales*, London: Home Office. Available at: <http://www.homeoffice.gov.uk/documents/jou-no-more-excuses>.

Hough, M and Roberts, JV (2004) *Youth Crime and Youth Justice: Public Opinion in England and Wales*, Bristol: Policy Press.

Howell, JC, Kelly, MR, Palmer, J and Manqum, RL (2004) 'Integrating child welfare, juvenile justice, and other agencies in a continuum of services', *Child Welfare*, 83(2), 143-156.

Howells, K, Day, A, Williamson, P, Bubner, S, Jauncey, S, Parker, A and Heseltine, K (2005) 'Brief anger management programs with offenders: Outcomes and predictors of change', *Journal of Forensic Psychiatry & Psychology*, 16(2), 296-311.

Jarvis, TJ, Tebbutt, J and Mattick, RP (1995) *Treatment Approaches for Alcohol and Drug Dependence: An Introductory Guide*, Chichester, West Sussex: John Wiley & Sons.

Kaplan, HB and Lin, C-H (2005) 'Deviant identity, negative self-feelings, and decreases in deviant behaviour: The moderating influence of conventional social bonding', *Psychology, Crime & Law*, 11(3), 289-303.

Kazdin, AE (2005) *Parent Management Training: Treatment for Oppositional, Aggressive, and Antisocial Behavior in Children and Adolescents*, Oxford: Oxford University Press.

Kendall, PC and Hollon, SD (eds) (1979) *Cognitive-behavioral Interventions: Theory, Research, and Procedures*, New York: Academic Press.

Kurtz, A (2002) 'What works for delinquency? The effectiveness of interventions for teenage offending behaviour', *Journal of Forensic Psychiatry*, 13(3), 671-692.

Leivesley, S (1984) *Juvenile Aid Bureau: An Evaluation of Police Work with Juveniles 1970-1983*. (Unpublished)

Lewis, A and O'Regan, C (1992) 'Police cautioning – Effective diversion or experience?', in L Atkinson and S-A Gerull (eds) *National Conference on Juvenile Justice: Proceedings of a Conference Held 22-24 September 1992*, Canberra: Australian Institute of Criminology.

Lo, TW, Wong, D and Maxwell, G (eds) (2005) *Alternatives to Prosecution: Rehabilitative and Restorative Models of Youth Justice*, Singapore: Marshall Cavendish Academic.

Loeber, R and Farrington, DP (eds) (2001) *Child Delinquents: Development, Intervention, and Service Needs*, Thousand Oaks, CA: Sage.

Longshore, D, Prendergast, ML and Farabee, D (2004) 'Coerced treatment for drug-using criminal offenders', in P Bean and T Nemitz (eds) *Drug Treatment: What Works?* (pp 110-122), London: Routledge.

Luke, G and Lind, B (2002) *Reducing Juvenile Crime: Conferencing versus Court* (Contemporary Issues in Crime and Justice No 69), Sydney: New South Wales Bureau of Crime Statistics and Research.

Maguire, M, Morgan, R and Reiner, R (eds) (2002) *The Oxford Handbook of Criminology* (3rd ed), Oxford: Oxford University Press.

Malmgren, KW and Meisel, SM (2004) 'Examining the link between child maltreatment and delinquency for youth with emotional and behavioural disorders', *Child Welfare*, 83(2), 175-188.

Marshall, T (1998) *Restorative Justice: An Overview*, St Paul: Centre for Restorative Justice and Mediation.

Maxwell, G and Morris, A (2001) 'Family group conferencing and reoffending', in A Morris and G Maxwell (eds) *Restoring Justice for Juveniles: Conferences, Mediation and Circles* (pp 243-266), Oxford: Hart Publishing.

McEwan, AW (1983) 'Eysenck's theory of criminality and the personality types and offences of young delinquents', *Personality and Individual Difference*, 4(2), 201-204.

McGuire, J (ed) (1995) *What Works: Reducing Reoffending – Guidelines from Research and Practice*, Chichester, West Sussex: John Wiley & Sons.

McGuire, J (2002) 'Integrating findings from research reviews', in J McGuire (ed) *Offender Rehabilitation and Treatment: Effective Programmes and Policies to Reduce Re-offending* (pp 3-38), Chichester, West Sussex: John Wiley & Sons.

McGuire, J and Priestley, P (1995) 'Reviewing "what works": Past, present and future', in J McGuire (ed) *What Works: Reducing Reoffending – Guidelines from Research and Practice* (pp 3-34), Chichester, West Sussex: John Wiley & Sons.

McMurran, M (ed) (2002) *Motivating Offenders to Change: A Guide to Enhancing Engagement in Therapy*, Chichester, West Sussex: John Wiley & Sons.

Merton, RK (1949) *Social Theory and Social Structure*, New York: Free Press.

Miller, WR and Rollnick, S (2002) *Motivational Interviewing: Preparing People for Change* (2nd ed), New York: Guilford.

Morris, A and Maxwell, G (eds) (2001) *Restorative Justice for Juveniles: Conferencing, Mediation and Circles*, Oxford: Hart.

Muncie, J (2004) *Youth and Crime: A Critical Introduction* (2nd ed), London: Sage.

National Crime Prevention (1999) *Pathways to Prevention: Developmental and Early Intervention Approaches to Crime in Australia*, Barton, ACT: National Crime Prevention.

O'Connor, I (1992) 'Issues in juvenile justice in Queensland: New laws, old visions', in L Atkinson and S-A Gerull (eds) *National Conference on Juvenile Justice: Proceedings of a Conference Held 22-24 September 1992*, Canberra: Australian Institute of Criminology.

O'Connor, I and Chui, WH (2002) 'Rights and justice', in P Swain (ed) *In the Shadow of the Law: The Legal Context of Social Work Practice* (2nd ed) (pp 184-197), Sydney: Federation Press.

Office of the Surgeon General (2001) *Youth Violence: A Report of the Surgeon General*, Washington, DC: US Department of Health and Human Services, Office of the Surgeon General. Available at: <http://www.surgeongeneral.gov/library/youthviolence/toc.html>.

Ogloff, JRP (2002) 'Offender rehabilitation: From "nothing works" to what next?', *Australian Psychologist*, 37(3), 245-252.

Omaji, PO (2003) *Responding to Youth Crime: Towards Radical Criminal Justice Partnerships*, Sydney: Hawkins Press.

Ornstein, R (1993) *The Roots of the Self: Unraveling the Mystery of Who We Are*, New York: Harper Collins.

Pearson, G (1972) *Hooligan: A History of Respectable Fears*, London: MacGibbon and Kee.

Polk, K (2003) *Juvenile Diversion in Australia: A National Review*, A paper presented at the Juvenile Justice: From Lessons of the Past to a Road Map for the Future conference, 1-2 December 2003, Sydney.

Potas, I, Vining, A and Wilson, P (1990) *Young People and Crime: Costs and Prevention*, Canberra: Australian Institute of Criminology.

Prochaska, JO and Levesque, DA (2002) 'Enhancing motivation of offenders at each stage of change and phase of therapy', in M McMurran (ed) *Motivating Offenders to Change: A Guide to Enhancing Engagement in Therapy* (pp 57-73), Chichester, West Sussex: John Wiley & Sons.

Ritchie, MH (1986) 'Counseling the involuntary clients', *Journal of Counseling and Development*, 64(8), 516-518.

Rooney, RH (1988) 'Socialization strategies for involuntary clients', *Social Casework: The Journal of Contemporary Social Work*, 69(3), 131-140.

Rooney, RH (1992) *Strategies for Work with Involuntary Clients*, New York: Columbia University Press.

Shader, M (2003) *Risk Factors for Delinquency: An Overview*, Washington, DC: Office of Justice Programs, US Department of Justice. Available at: <http://www.ncjrs.gov/pdffiles1/ojjdp/frd030127.pdf>.

Shaw, CR and McKay, HD (1969) *Juvenile Delinquency and Urban Areas*, Chicago: University of Chicago Press.

Sheldon, B (1994) 'Social work effectiveness research: Implications for probation and juvenile justice services', *Howard Journal of Criminal Justice*, 33(3), 218-235.

Sheldon, W (1949) *Varieties of Delinquent Youth*, New York: Harper & Row.

Shoemaker, DJ (2005) *Theories of Delinquency: An Examinations of the Explanations of Delinquent Behavior* (5th ed), New York: Oxford University Press.

Siegel, LJ and Welsh, BC (2005) *Juvenile Delinquency: The Core* (2nd ed), Belmont, CA: Thomson/Wadsworth.

Smith, D (1998) 'Social work with offenders: The practice of exclusion and the potential for inclusion', in M Barry and C Hallett (eds) *Social Exclusion and Social Work: Issues of Theory, Policy and Practice* (pp 107-117), Lyme Regis, Dorset: Russell House.

Stewart, A, Dennison, S and Waterson, E (2002) 'Pathways from child maltreatment to juvenile offending', *Trends and Issues in Crime and Criminal Justice*, No 241, Canberra: Australian Institute of Criminology.

Strang, H, Barnes, G, Braithwaite, J and Sherman, L (1999) *Experiments in Restorative Policing: A Progress Report on the Canberra Reintegrative Shaming Experiments (RISE)*, Canberra: Australian Federal Police and Australian National University. Available at: <http://www.aic.gov.au/rjustice/rise/progress/1999.html>.

Thibaut, JW and Kelley, HH (1959) *The Social Psychology of Groups*, New York: Wiley.

Thompson, K (1998) *Moral Panics*, London: Routledge.

Tremblay, RE and Craig, WM (1995) 'Developmental crime prevention', in M Tonry and DP Farrington (eds) *Strategic Approaches to Crime Prevention: Building a Safer Society* (pp 151-236), Chicago: The University of Chicago Press.

Trotter, C (1999) *Working with Involuntary Clients: A Guide to Practice*, Sydney: Allen & Unwin.

Trotter, C (2004) *Helping Abused Children and their Families: Towards an Evidence-based Practice Model*, Sydney: Allen & Unwin.

Underdown, A (1998) *Strategies for Effective Offender Rehabilitation: Report of the HMIP What Works Project*, London: Home Office.

Utting, D (1996) *Reducing Criminality among Young People: A Sample of Relevant Programmes in the United Kingdom* (Home Office Research Study No 161), London: Home Office.

Waldo, G and Dinitz, S (1967) 'Personality attributes for the criminal: An analysis of research studies, 1950-1965', *Journal of Research in Crime and Delinquency*, 4(2), 185-202.

Warr, EM and Stafford, M (1991) 'The influence of delinquent peers: What they think or what they do?', *Criminology*, 29(4), 851-866.

Weatherburn, D and Lind, B (1997) *Social and Economic Stress, Child Neglect and Juvenile Delinquency*, Sydney: New South Wales Bureau of Crime Statistics and Research.

Western, JS, Lynch, M and Ogilvie, E (eds) (2003) *Understanding Youth Crime: An Australian Study*, Aldershot: Ashgate.

Legislation Cited

Children, Young Persons and Their Families Act 1989 (NZ)
Juvenile Justice Act 1992 (Qld)

Chapter 4

Adult Offenders

Helen Cameron

Introduction

Adult offenders may be those who have been sentenced to a term of imprisonment, to a period of community-based surveillance through the parole system or are under some kind of community service order. In general, most adult offenders are juvenile clients all grown up but whereas there is often hope that juvenile offenders can be turned away from crime by well-targeted programs or will grow out of what is termed 'delinquency' in referring to offences by young people, with adult offenders there is frequently much less faith in positive outcomes. Nonetheless, professional work with these individuals is important to the civil management of society as it often focuses on the rehabilitation of socially disadvantaged people who have been through the mill of the justice system. In more recent times, a shift has occurred; from incarcerate punishment to understanding the perspective of criminal offenders and the application of increasingly popular cognitive-behavioural therapies and interventions with offenders (Howells and Day, 1999, 2003; see also Chapter 3 of this volume). If deviance is indeed socially, historically and culturally situated, then this means that not only will offenders vary according to context, so will their treatment. It is clear that all aspects of crime and punishment are likely to be crucial in the constitution of deviance in a number of ways, varying in history and between cultures (Eardley, 1995).

The motivation to work with adult offenders comes in many forms. Social workers, human service workers, psychologists and others may find themselves drawn to working with adult offenders for a number of reasons. Pragmatically it may be where the available jobs are, but others may have professional interest in the welfare of offenders and in the nature of crime and those who commit it. Whatever the basis of motivation, to gain employment in this field it is essential to understand the foundations of adult offending and the most effective processes for assisting the rehabilitation of these clients. These are the purposes of this chapter. This chapter is too broadly brushed to offer a full understanding of criminology or of crime, the social significance of which Garland and Sparks (2000: 3) describe as 'so pervasive, so complex, and so contentious' that it is beyond most scientific understanding. Despite this, crime and its partner punishment, sit centrally within the social imagination of our time. Criminology, crime, punishment and rehabilitation are the focus for a suite of academic programs and for a continuous series of television programs, movies and books. As well, the management of offenders through processes of punishment or rehabilitation is economically important in most modern societies in that it provides employment for many people within a variety of organisations and services. Crime is big business in a range of ways.

Understanding Deviance and Crime

Part of any understanding about crime and offending is the issue of social deviance but all sorts of social deviance, not just criminal behaviour, contain something of a paradox. While it may seem, at some points in time within a society or culture, that certain acts are judged as self-evidently *deviant* in nature, these judgments are never fixed in time or culture. On the contrary, the ways in which people appraise others and their behaviour are subject to a wide range of forces and influences. This means that notions of deviance vary over time and place, never staying inert. In other words, deviance is not only a shifting social phenomenon across social settings and in time, it is also a social phenomenon distinct to any given social setting. The variability of 'deviance' flows from the capacity of humans to continuously (but not self-consciously) construct and shape their social worlds. The modernist view of deviance as correctable (not necessarily an accepted view in other times or places) is intrinsic to the very nature of current offender management or to principles of rehabilitation. As Giddens (1991) notes, 'the idea that human beings can be subject to corrections was necessarily bound up with the notion that social life itself is open to radical change' (p 158).

It is with attention to these kinds of ideas and processes that we can begin to contextualise the world of offenders. Yet, in order to do this, we need understand also that the world of 'justice' is not unproblematic, prefigured, nor consistent in form. Justice, like other domains of the social and political world, is 'constructed'. For example, within a courtroom, accused persons commonly explain their motives, intentions, goals or behaviour from within their personal constructs of events. Consider Cressey's landmark interactionist work on embezzlement as summarised in Hester and Englin (1995: pp 349-350):

> The first major symbolic interactionist study in this genre was Cressey's (1953) work, *Other People's Money*. After interviewing numerous persons convicted of embezzling from their places of employment, Cressey

theorized that in addition to being in positions of financial trust and experiencing 'non-shareable financial problems' embezzlers employed 'vocabularies of adjustment', which permitted them to engage in embezzling behaviour. Such permission not only preceded these illegal acts but it was also necessary, argued Cressey. This was because the offenders conceived of themselves as essentially non-criminal. Vocabularies of adjustment or rationalizations such as the characterization of the act as only 'borrowing' enabled the embezzler to take the money and at the same time preserve a sense of him or herself as non-criminal, at least for the initial acts of embezzlement.

Cressey's interactionist approach has similarities with approaches that examine the internal 'talk" of offenders, when they justify, rationalise and reframe their offences, all processes related to criminogenic need. Understanding the personal constructs of offenders is related to the socially, culturally and historically located views of crime and justice in general. Thinking back over the course of the last few decades in Australia it is possible to trace changes in social behaviour, attitudes or inclinations that have been widely socially accepted or rejected at different times. Such examples include behaviour such as cigarette smoking and other drug use; gender roles and sexuality; women, childcare and the paid workforce; the adoption of the mobile phone; shopping hours and related traditions or driving habits. As well as variation within a particular society over time, deviance also varies within and between societies. Notions of deviance vary between various Western locales and the contrast between Western legal responses to crime and non-Western responses more sharply reveals the cultural cast of deviance. Cross-cultural comparisons concerning 'deviance' provide us with opportunities to appreciate how crime is socially, culturally and historically constituted. However, the paradoxical nature of deviance is such that most people experience and perceive deviance and 'deviants' as at the one time both 'natural' and aberrant.

Already it can be seen that deviance is not an easy concept to categorise. This attribute is reflected in the literature to a large extent. While 'deviance' is studied within a number of disciplines, there is considerable variation both within and across disciplines regarding the most appropriate form of analysing, explaining and confronting deviance in contemporary society. For example, the sociology of deviance does not approach deviance uniformly or unproblematically (Anleu, 2006). On the contrary, the sociology of deviance comprises an array of divergent views, explanations and premises about the social forces that help shape human behaviour and transgressions of social order. Within the sociology of deviance, we may encounter schools of thought that privilege variables such as conflict, power, gender, particular social groups, ideology, functionality, the family, representations of certain subordinated groups in the media, economic structures or religious orthodoxy.

Three characteristics are often associated with the study of deviance, especially in viewing the notion of deviance with a critical eye: many parts of our everyday lives appear to be neatly and uncomplicatedly categorised into clear, perhaps stable classes of knowledge. Deviance, however, is not such a clear-cut phenomenon and the first point is that its study cannot proceed via commonsense or assumed understandings of the concept (Downes and Rock, 2003). The second issue concerns the ambiguity around rule breaking and other disruptions or threats to established social order. In other words, a particular behaviour or instance of behaviour may be judged as borderline between what is certainly deviant and what is certainly acceptable. Social judgments of deviance depend on 'context, biography and purpose' (Downes and Rock, 2003: 4). The third issue concerns the differing views and interpretations about its proper investigation, the theoretical base that underpins it and the forces that shape it in social settings. Deviance remains a contested, debated phenomenon both across and within disciplines such as sociology, psychology and social work.

However, the difficulties that are inherent in examining deviance as part of the study of crime do offer a particular kind of insight into the phenomenon. Deviant acts, such as criminal offences, cannot be viewed as occurring in a social vacuum. On the contrary, perceptions about deviant behaviour are always located within a sociohistorical context and thus there are no 'universal' truths within the sociology of deviance. In turn, the social context is configured and shaped by a range of forces, influences, processes and phenomena. For example, Erving Goffman's (1963) seminal work on the phenomenon of social stigma, its potency and its (difficult) management, highlights the quintessentially social forces that surround and help constitute stigma as a part of deviance and as a process of 'spoiled identity'. Gerstel's (1994) perspective alerts us to an essential aspect of working with offenders – that is, it is all too easy to assume certain contours of another's experiences, probably erroneously so. This idea is underlined when it is accentuated that many 'clients' in correctional and justice settings are likely to be more marginalised and excluded from social opportunities than many others in society. The correctional system includes high populations of those with socially disadvantaged backgrounds, with mental illness and with low levels of educational achievement.

Deviance as a Social Stereotype

Marginalised groups in particular tend to be reported in stereotypical ways that reproduce the super-ordination of dominant groups (Hall, 1997). Crime, perceived as a threat to an imagined social order, is no exception. Stereotypes often underpin the ways in which marginalised groups are dealt with in the media, including speaking for them rather than recognising their capacity to speak for themselves. Hall (1997: 258) suggests that stereotyping 'facilitates the 'binding' or bonding together of all of us who are 'normal' into one 'imagined community' and it sends into symbolic exile all of Them – 'the Others' – who are in some way different – 'beyond the pale'. This links with Bauman (2001: 114-122) who notes society's uses of poverty, where the sight of the poor 'other' provides solace or warning, inspiring self-control and conformity in the non-poor who may see themselves only a pay packet away from destitution.

The self is situated within a range of social contexts and processes, from the family, to wider kin networks, friends, work and leisure associates and other influential groups. In this chapter the reader's attention is directed to the influences of life chances (or lack of) on the development of criminal behaviour. This underlines the fact that it is the individual that is the focus for the vast bulk of attention and responsibility for actions in our society. Note, as an aside, that in many other societies, it may not be the individual or the person that is the main 'unit of attention' for major responsibility regarding adherence to social, ritual or customary norms or strictures; it may well be the lineage, clan, moiety or some other social group. However, in Western societies, as noted by McGuire (1995), it is the individual that is the prime unit of attention in relation to bearing responsibility for criminal actions and for rehabilitation, especially through the efforts and expert knowledge of the helping professions.

The Flip Side to Deviance – Understanding Conformity

It is important to consider the fact that individuals live in environments that are dense with influence – whether they offend against the laws of society or carefully tow the line. Influence may be in the form of a boss encouraging productivity, a policeman directing a person's car in traffic, or a lecturer encouraging a student to write a paper. Each day, everyone is subjected to an uncountable number of influence attempts. A particular feature of this influence concerns the phenomena of conformity and deviance and how groups operate as both *encouragers* and *containers* of individual behaviour. Understanding how correctional treatment approaches operate to influence the behaviour of individuals is central to both the theoretical concepts surrounding the occurrence of much criminal behaviour and to the principles supporting effective work with offenders. Brown (2000: 124-166) discusses the power of the majority and the pervasive forces that cause individual conformity to group rules and norms, often through subtle processes. Social psychological studies of conformity behaviours have a long history, from the work of Sherif (1937) and Asch (1955) as cited in Myers (1993: 222-228), Milgram's 1965 study (in Lippa 1994) and Anleu's book (2006). These and the current interest in the importance of control theory in human motivation as in Beck (2000) and particularly in Andrews and Bonta (2003) in reference to criminal conduct, all attest to the widespread and longstanding application of conformity theory to understanding aspects of human behaviour.

It is worth emphasising here that conformity has particular social value. Imagine if everyone needed daily coercion to conform to social rules; for instance, the lecturer needed to shout at students to convince them to write that paper, bosses had to punch employees to make them work harder, or policemen shot out motorists' car tyres for doing 65 kilometres in a 60 kilometre zone. Persuasion, cooperation and conformity all oil the workings of society. Successful persuasion (for example, through education and advertising), produces the level of conformity that makes most physical coercion unnecessary, interpersonally, socially and internationally. Working with offenders may often be about assisting them to find the motivation and self-control to stay within the rules of society; in other words, to conform without feeling resentful about being coerced and teetering on the edge of recidivism. With some adult offenders with a long history of deviance from social norms, this is a challenging, although not impossible task.

Some situations move beyond requests for action and entail direct orders from one person to another. Surprisingly, a demand often results in obedience for many people, even if the authority figure involved lacks the power to enforce an order. For example, the psychologist Stanley Milgram, (as cited in Lippa, 1994) conducted a famous experiment in which he asked the participants to administer what they believed were electric shocks to a person who was making apparent errors in a learning experiment. The results of Milgram's study revealed that 65 per cent of the subjects complied with the experimenter's request to provide a shock at a level that they believed was both extremely painful and dangerous to the other (Lippa, 1994: 570-577). It is interesting to note that in 1974, after repeating this experiment many times, Milgram concluded: 'I am certain that there is a complex personality basis to obedience and disobedience. But I know we have not found it' (cited in Myers, 1993: 248). While it is accepted that personality features may persist across situations (Lippa, 1994), it seems to be the situation rather than stable personality type that holds the key to understanding conformity (Myers, 1993). Developmental influence issues are relevant here too, as Brown (2000: 139-140) notes that higher levels of conformity peak between 11 and 13 and then decline slightly after that, however, he stresses that that 'peer group influence is by no means confined to adolescence'. This point is demonstrated by adult offenders becoming caught in webs of social group influence that hold them back from full rehabilitation – often accounting for conditions of parole being broken in reference to the ruling about *not* associating with other known criminals.

The size of a group impacts on the conformity pressures within it. Lippa (1994) in referring to Asch and similar work by Brown (2000) suggests that three or four is the optimum size for pressures towards conformity in a group. People become suspicious of mob rule in larger groups, and so may resist conformist pressures. Group membership or belonging brings powerful pressures to conform to norms and rules.

Group attractiveness and cohesiveness (the degree to which we are strongly attracted to a group and desire to maintain membership in it) increases the occurrence of conformity. For example, Brown (2000: 133-137) cites a range of research studies which show that people conform to group norms when they like and admire the other group members, when the group goals are positive and when the group is successful. Most people do not back losing groups and when they have a choice about which groups to join are more likely to support a successful one.

But some people do not conform and forces within society attempt to deal with these in a variety of ways. Brown (2000: 141-143) describes studies that attest to the cross-cultural validity of findings about how deviates (or minorities) are not appreciated and that groups try a range of ways to manage them. However, as Brown notes, deviates can exert some influence on group decisions. He describes the attractiveness and power of nonconformity in some group situations.

Overall though, conformity is seductive and most people conform to social expectations. Brown (2000) suggests that people are likely to conform when they depend on the group for information they need about the society in which they live; can achieve a personal goal as a result of cooperating with the group to achieve its goals; receive approval from others through belonging to a group; and gain social identity through the acceptance of others in groups. Lippa (1994) points out that a person's status in a group will impact on how willing they are to deviate from group norms and that both 'high-status people ... and low-status people (minority out-groups) often conform less' (p 552). This seems to be about how much a person has to lose. So, the more accepted one is in social groups, the higher the need for such acceptance and this may determine degrees of deviance from group norms and standards.

Connectedness to others is a powerful force towards conformity. In new parlance this is termed 'social capital' (Winter, 2000). Graycar and Nelson (1999) link low social capital directly to offending behaviour on a number of levels. They suggest that society is really only a 'vast network of mutual agreements' (p 1), and that higher crime is partly the result of looser connections between individuals and their groups in society. If an individual has nothing to lose by way of acceptance in a group, then he or she is much less likely to care about the group's norms or its spoken or unspoken rules. As noted previously, the individual or the person may not be attributed full responsibility in some societies even though this tends to be the case in most Western ones (Bankart, 1997; Gudykunst and Kim, 1997).

It is apparent that all individuals are products of society and their daily behaviour and general presentation bear testament to the power of various social forces that usually elicit conformity from most people at a number of levels and in a range of locations. At this point, Activity 4.1 may be a useful addition to understanding issues around conformity.

Activity 4.1 Pressures Towards Conformity and Urges Towards Deviance

Consider the number of direct attempts that other people make to control your thoughts and behaviour on a single day. This may include people directly requesting you to do things, manipulating you to do things, forcing you to do things, pressuring you to buy things, imposing rules about where and when to stop and go and suggesting how you should think or feel about things. Even if you avoided the newspaper and commercial radio programs, you would still find a large number of incursions on your free will each day.

Begin by drawing up two columns with the first headed 'conformity' and the second 'deviance'. Then under each list the forces in your life that keep you conforming to social expectations and the urges that open the way to more deviant responses. Then work with another person to discuss what you have noted and to share ideas.

So far in this chapter the discussion of deviance has been located within a sociological framework even though traditionally the individual has been at the core of research-based explanations of deviance in Western settings. Recently, the incidence of criminal behaviour has found explanation in two additional perspectives, through biological and psychological explanations. Perspectives that foreground the (autonomous) individual, such as psychological and biological ones, tend to foreground the issue of prediction in one form or another to make sense of and explain deviance and crime. In fact, Andrews and Bonta (2003) assert that sociology highjacked the debate about criminal behaviour from early in the last century, to the detriment of the science of criminal prediction and of effective rehabilitation processes. Only recently, in the 1990s, has the new *Psychology of Criminal Conduct*, with its focus on prediction and influence, gained precedence over sociological perspectives that blamed society for deviant and criminal behaviour (Andrews and Bonta, 2003).

Biological Explanations of Deviance and Crime

Biological perspectives look to the determinative, or at least the highly influential quality of some physical ingredient in the makeup of people to explain the occurrence and specific instances of deviance. Like all explanations of deviance, these perspectives (and their popularity) have altered over time (Holman and Quinn, 1992). This is not a new idea – as some examples of biological explanations of deviance are suggested in the early research by Lombroso (1835-1909) who saw links between behavioural variations and physical signs of difference (Melossi, 2000). In his later work, Lombroso's theories about phrenology led to attempts to understand 'types' of offending through particular 'bumps' on the surface of the cranium. Sheldon's (1942) study explained criminal disposition through somatotypes – so that according to one's physical shape (any one of only three alternatives – endomorph, ectomorph or mesomorph), one's personality could be explained and understood (see also Chapter 3 of this volume).

Hormonal structures have received some attention in recent times, although there seems to be limited support for simplistic links between levels of circulating hormones such as testosterone and violent behaviour (Miczek et al, 1994: 227) except where there is misuse of administered steroids, especially in individuals with pre-existing pathologies of the endocrine system. Some do see a closer match between male hormone patterns and aggression and violence. Moir and Moir (1998: 5) suggest some 'hard-wired' features that they track back to concepts of old and new brain, where males are described as 'primed for ambush' at a consistent level, all because of their hormones. While the link between testosterone and criminal violence, as indicated in behavioural research, is acknowledged by Dabbs, Strong and Milun (1997: 557), they also question the comprehensiveness of such research or its applicability for society and say the link is tenuous. They do not deny the importance of testosterone in a person's personal style, but reject it is inevitably linked to violence. Rather they prefer to link it with energy, good performance and alertness. They rightly point out that testosterone is present in the hormonal profiles of both males and females and also varies in levels between individuals within gender groups. So at this point it seems advisable to put aside the idea that genderised hormonal profiles provide any real explanation for violent crime or any other kind. This includes family studies that seek to explain deviance or criminality by inheritability – the transmission of predispositions to crime through genetic material.

However, a range of other physiological features of a person can set up predispositions to crime, especially that involving aggression. Scherwitz and Rugulies (1992) cite a meta-study (which is a study of a wide range of research on a particular topic) that examines a constellation of physical health features such as levels of smoking cigarettes, use of marijuana and alcohol, total calorie intake and waist/hip ratio. Findings indicate that combination of some of these variables appear to predict higher levels of hostility, with links to aggressive and violent crime.

Miczek et al (1994) review a range of drugs other than alcohol and their impact on violent behaviour and crime. Amphetamines have some impact on increased aggression, for instance, but only in high and chronic dosages where low impulse control may occur, and opiates or narcotics seem to be linked to crime only when linked to maintaining supplies and interacting with drug dealers. Cannabis in fact increases submissive and flight behaviours, leading to low rates of both crime and victimisation (Miczek et al, 1994). Other drugs such as cocaine and Phencyclidine (PCP or Angel Dust) are less predictable in their influences as they are often part of poly-drug patterns of use, and may involve the user with violent social liaisons in gaining and maintaining supplies (Miczek et al, 1994). It may be reassuring to some to note that caffeine does not appear to positively correlate with crime or violence (Scherwitz and Rugulies, 1992).

In contrast the place of alcohol as a factor in violent crime is indicated from research spanning 30 years as cited in Miczek et al (1994) and Scherwitz and Rugulies (1992). But the relationship is complex. Miczek et al (1994: 384) show that high chronic doses do seem to be linked to violent behaviour including rape and that there are also consistent linkages between high use and being a victim of violent crime, which also holds for cocaine. But alcohol alone does not seem to increase violence. In laboratory experiments for instance high doses reduce aggression. So while it is accurate to say that alcohol is certainly associated with crime, 'there is controversy about whether 'the association is causative' (MacDonald and Brown, 1996: 20). Alcohol's disinhibiting effects are implicated in less personal control, but why this may lead to crime in some people (and loquaciousness, laughter and loud singing in others) clearly depends on a range of other factors. Grabosky (1999) sets alcohol use among a range of other factors, including social capital, race, gender and culture, as a risk factor for violent crime. This web of influences holds the key to understanding the role of alcohol in crime, but is hard to unravel. By way of caution here, biological explanations privilege so-called *scientific* physically based explanations, especially if they offer attractively simple, quick and possibly irreversible explanations of a deviant disposition towards crime. Biological factors and drug effects including alcohol, provide no complete explanation for crime and all must be viewed in conjunction with a complex set of psychological and social determinants that also appear to be associated with patterns of offending.

Psychological Explanations of Deviance and Crime

Psychological explanations of deviance vary considerably, but generally, like biological ones, depend on pathology at the site of the individual in one way or another. Psychological explanations look to the develop-mental experiences of the person in identifying aberrations in behaviour (Hollin, 1989). Some examples of psychological explanations of deviance are those which perceive human activity as fuelled by a sense of the irrational or subconscious and the sway of latent factors. Andrews and Bonta (2003: 104) find value in the Freudian explanation of 'control factors' for instance, suggesting 'the motivation for rape, murder, suicide and theft, is within all of us'. So, crime can be understood as a result of psychic imbalance or as a form of neurosis where lack of control opens up as opportunities to offend and also to receive punishment. Criminal offending is also viewed as deriving from suppressed inner turmoil, related to the 'frustration-aggression hypothesis' (Andrews and Bonta, 2003: 104). Since human drives are always in conflict, satisfactions are about both pleasure and guilt and so with tension constant, especially if inner control is weak, offending is but one possible cathartic result.

Behavioural theory brought to centre stage the importance of social learning so that crime is explained not just by inner drives and conflicts, but rather as the result of either *actively learning how to behave*, or of *failing to learn how to behave*. Similarly, the values and motivations that accompany crime are learned over time, through interaction with significant others, especially close family and friends. According to this kind of perspective, offending occurs when the values and motivations that support offending outweigh the values and motivations that inhibit offending. Because of the learned nature of offending in such perspectives, the potential for *learning to change* offers considerable hope.

Central to psychological explanations of criminal deviance are studies about the importance of impulse control and impulsiveness in offending, in contrast to self-control and self-efficacy. There is a link to studies, already cited in this chapter, around physiology, gender and drugs. McGuire (2004) suggests it has been demonstrated that 'poor social-control is an important predictor of crime across a broad spectrum of offence types' (p 39). None of this means that people with high levels of self-control and self-efficacy do not commit crime – although maybe those with higher levels are better organised and less likely to be apprehended? Seriously though, people with good levels of self-control, self-efficacy and an internal locus of control, are more likely to be able to take greater direction over their lives and achieve personal goals through delaying gratification rather than giving into their impulses.

Self-control, esteem and skill are all products of a person's socialisation, rebuilt on a daily basis through current experiences with other people and one's own self-talk. Bandura (1996: 15) suggests that it is futile to focus just on 'mastery motivation' or belief in oneself (such as using processes of internal self-persuasion – for example, 'I think I can, I think I can'). Rather, he points out that personal competence takes time and effort to produce. He believes that the only effective way to make changes is to set challenging but realistic goals about desired things and to succeed in reaching these goals. Others, like Marmot and Wilkinson (1999) suggest that self-control and related factors of self-esteem can be encouraged through educational and health policy changes that will give better support to socially disadvantaged families.

Social Disadvantage, Crime and Deviance

As well as seeing the relevance of biology and psychology in understanding conformity and deviance, in terms of criminal behaviour it is important to note that many offenders start life with few life chances in society. Socioeconomic factors are all statistically implicated, through a range of studies in rates of violent crime for instance (Schwartz and Milovanovic, 1996). MacDonald and Brown (1996: 22) cite Farrington and the US National Committee on Violence to demonstrate the coincidence between social disadvantage and reported violent crime across the major

Western world. It is noted here that much intra-familial violence is under-reported and that both child abuse and domestic violence occurs across all socioeconomic strata. Nonetheless, income inequality is an indicator for crime, as is personal unemployment, family unemployment and disadvantaged neighbourhoods. Andrews and Bonta (2003: 211) implicate the 'breakdown of parental monitoring and exposure to delinquent peers' in 'early onset chronic offending'. According to Sampson and Lauritsen (1994), features of family structure, such as single parent households, are also statistically significant as backgrounds for a range of crimes, though they too stress quality of parenting rather than family structure per se. It is apparent then that when social disadvantage is combined with lack of parental monitoring, interaction with antisocial associates and low self-control, the individual's ability to respond to life's challenges is impacted negatively, increasing the incidence of deviance and crime. Activity 4.2 will expand our understanding about self-control in particular.

Activity 4.2 Examining Self-attributions about Locus of Control

For this exercise it is best to work in pairs and conduct a short interview with your partner. The objective of the exercise is to examine some of the attributions you make for positive and negative events that have occurred in your life.

Working with your partner, you should each make two lists. The first is a list of all the things in your life which you consider to be positives, advantages, good things or items about which you feel happy, excited, stimulated or comfortable. The second list is the opposite: all the negatives, disadvantages, bad things about which you feel resentful, guilty, bad or uncomfortable.

Next look at the two lists, marking each item according to whether you believe it was due to your own actions/your efforts or errors (1) or due to the actions of others/external forces outside your control (2).

When you have finished, examine the pattern of your allocations and see whether any general themes emerge about positive/negative and internal/external attribution. Are there any items which could in principle be re-allocated as a result of actions you could take?

An essential aspect of professional work with offenders will be in assisting them to either build or regain their positive self-control and find positive paths that do not include further offending. Most clients of correctional systems are trying to cope with the effects of changes they perceive to have been imposed on them as a result of circumstances that they believe are beyond their control, due to perceptions about self-control discussed so far here. Consequently, some will be resentful, disillusioned and struggling to believe in either themselves or society. A 'what works' approach (McGuire 1996) sees offenders as agents in their own lives and focuses on employing processes to engage them in reconstructing their cognitive and behavioural responses to the world. This focuses on their thinking, processing of feelings and actual behavioural outcomes, that is, doing things that are effective (and within the law) to attain their goals.

Mukherjee (1999: 6) notes that '[i]f an individual is found to be lacking in education and proficiency in English language, his/her chances of engaging in legitimate, gainful employment will be diminished' and given links between unemployment and crime it is not surprising that there might be some overrepresentation of ethnic groups in crime statistics. 'Ethnicity and crime' is not an easily summarised topic of social research. Apart from the fact that it has not been systematically and thoroughly researched in Australia, popularly assumed links between ethnicity and crime require excavation and clarity of social inquiry.

In summary, although aspects of both biology and individual psychology go some way towards explaining criminal deviance, workers in the criminal justice system need to include a broader appreciation of the complex network of factors that produce and sustain criminal behaviour. Current researchers in criminology 'are retaining causal status for *antisocial attitudes*, the *personality complex*, the *bonding set* (family in particular) and *antisocial associates*' [italics added] (Andrews and Bonta, 2003: 131).

The Value of Predicting Crime

Clearly, in reference to the previous material in this chapter on biological, psychological and social determinants of crime, it seems possible to predict who is most likely to offend. In fact, Andrews and Bonta (2003: 260) assert that 'criminal behaviour can be predicted' and 'there is no need to dispute this statement'. Prediction is a necessary and useful function, as at the core of therapeutic intervention with offenders is prevention of further offending, through identifying and treating criminogenic needs. A criminogenic needs assessment involves systematically appraising various factors and circumstances in an offender's life, highlighting those factors that are linked to risk of offending (or reoffending) and identifying interventions that will address those factors and thus reduce the likelihood. This is a pivotal aspect of the psychology of criminal conduct and of criminogenic needs assessment. In economic terms alone, addressing the criminogenic needs of an offender has the potential to save the community justice costs in the future.

It is asserted that 'official records provide underestimations of the overall level of criminal activity in the community' (Andrews and Bonta, 2003: 45) and this means the completeness of any picture of offenders' characteristics thus has to be questioned. Nonetheless, there are certain factors that tend to be common predictors in the lives of those offenders who are apprehended. By their very nature, some of these factors are tied to the development of the individual within his or her social context and his or her 'bonding set' (Andrews and Bonta, 2003: 131).

Personality theories provide explanations of crime that make predictions possible by highlighting the relationship between personality patterns and offending. There is some current consensus about five broad personality traits – neuroticism, extraversion, openness, agreeableness and conscientiousness (Soldyz and Vaillant, 1999). For example, high neuroticism is associated with emotionality and impulsiveness. Personality theory attributes the presence or absence of these traits as fairly durable features of the personality and Soldyz and Vaillant (1999: 226) found them 'robust and stable over a 40-year period'. If this is so, it has implications for modes of treatment. Langston and Sykes (1997) link the Big Five to belief structures and consequent behaviour, with obvious connections to the concept of internal dialogue and its impact on outcomes. Andrews and Bonta (2003: 86) extend this field in their summary of the research about the personality patterns which are related to criminogenic need, defined then as *risk factors*. Andrews and Bonta (2003) suggest there are the 'Big Four' or the 'Big Eight'. The eight factors are: 'antisocial attitudes; antisocial associates; a history of antisocial behaviour; antisocial personality pattern; problematic circumstances at home (family/marital); problematic circumstances at school or work; problematic leisure circumstances; and substance abuse' (Andrews and Bonta, 2003: 86). The 'Big Four' are the first four of these related to antisocial attributes. Andrews and Bonta (2003) note that the antisocial personality pattern of adult offenders is characterised by 'high energy, impulsiveness, low self-control, and sensation seeking' (p 187), clearly linking to neuroticism.

Those offenders whose criminal 'career' is quite short tend to have their offending concentrated in ages from 17 to approximately 22. Yet despite these broad age patterns, offences tend to exhibit definite peaks, as indicated in Table 4.1 (Howells and Day, 1999).

Table 4.1   Peak Age Groups for Some Offence Categories

Offence category	Peak Age group
Shoplifting/vandalism	11
Burglary/theft of vehicle	14-15
Sex/drugs	17-19

Howells and Day (1999) define a different eight factors as antisocial in nature, some associated with childhood development and others with antisocial behaviour and criminal offending in adulthood. These include trouble at school; childhood lying and aggression; bullying; heavy drinking; heavy drug use; gambling; anti-authority attitudes; and school truancy. It is important to bear in mind that one of these factors alone cannot determine or even heavily influence offending behaviour in adulthood. However, when a number (or most) of these factors are present over a considerable time period, they can predict persistently troublesome behaviour. When established over time, these factors may indicate the establishment of what Andrews and Bonta (2003: 242) refer to as 'ties to crime' these being 'a history of criminal behaviour', 'self-management deficit, procriminal sentiments; and antisocial associates'. There are consistent patterns in this material demonstrating that crime thus emerges and becomes established as a repertoire of behaviour within a broader context of antisocial behaviour. As an example, poor anger management – a self-management deficit and a criminogenic factor – may also be linked to another one of alcohol and drug abuse to lead to violent behaviour. Note, however, that in this example these factors do not necessarily predict of all crimes of violence, such as armed robbery.

Risk factors that form part of the predictive frame of criminality mean that offending cannot be simply explained as a free choice by any individual at any time. Crime is more often one aspect of a broader established pattern of antisocial behaviour set within socialised skill deficits in responding to life's stresses and opportunities. When these patterns are consistent over time, it is possible to predict propensity to offend with some accuracy (but never deterministically). Effective intervention provides countervailing influences to these destructive environmental influences and to the psychological and criminogenic patterns of the individual. At this point Activities 4.3 and 4.4 encourage some exploration of issues around control and consequences in terms of behaviours and feelings.

Activity 4.3 Recording Dysfunctional Thoughts or Feelings

Complete this as a privately reflective and recording activity.

(a) Consider the last occasion in which you engaged in a behaviour or experienced a feeling where you would like to have been in better control. Focus on this event, and try to bring it clearly to mind. Draw up three columns and label each A = Antecedents; B = Behaviour; C = Consequences. Write down details of your behaviour in the middle column. Complete the other two columns by recording information about the circumstances (personal and involving others) immediately *prior* to the event in the *Antecedents* column; and immediately *following* it in the *Consequences* column.

(b) Add to this by recording the *automatic thoughts* that were in your mind at the time of the event. Write them down and also record your level of belief in each of these as justifiable ways of seeing things.

This sequence of analysis and recording can be followed for several instances of problem behaviours or feelings.

Activity 4.4 Self-monitoring of Mood and Emotion

Reflect on changes in your moods and try to discover the main things which affect them. This exercise will probably be easier if done in pairs in which one individual helps the other and then swaps to give the other a turn.

Over the course of a week, sometimes even within a single day, our moods fluctuate and often the reason for these changes is not obvious to us. You can work at understanding these reasons through the following activities:

(a) Compile a list of the factors you are aware of which you know influence your moods. Explore the situation and attempt to elicit the causal factors in each case.

(b) Examine some critical recent event, in which you were in a rather extreme mood (from your own point of view). Recreate in memory the sequence of events and discuss the points at which your mood seemed most out of control or more open to influence or change.

What Works?

This chapter now moves on to consider the nature of intervention strategies that 'work' in helping offenders change criminogenic patterns and deviant behavioural repertoires. The 'What Works' initiative is also referred to as 'evidence-based practice', or 'evidence-based focus' in intervention with offenders, where effectiveness is measured in terms of rates of recidivism. In some locations, the work of entire organisations or arms of government is being driven by evidence-based practice. (For examples of the breadth and depth of this tendency in England and Wales, consult websites of the British Home Office listed at the end of this chapter.)

When correctional and other justice agencies organise their work and their strategic plans around evaluated intervention, the justice system can be seen to be investing heavily in the idea of evidence-based practice. One implication of evidence-based practice is that organisational goals, strategies and the allocation of resources reflect the desire to measure success in terms of reductions in recidivism rather than rates of arrest and/or incarceration. Considering various options around engaging offenders in processes that are rehabilitative and remedial involves weighing the advantages of one-to-one intervention and group-based intervention. Yet, in order to do this, a shared foundation of assessment, intervention method and client engagement will be necessary. At the core of such alliances is the clear identification of criminogenic factors and needs or risks, of the possibility of predicting who will offend/reoffend and of employing intervention processes that work.

The 'What Works' debate is part of a body of literature that explores precisely what interventions, under what conditions, result in reduced recidivism rates for offenders and the degree of such a reduction in crime. In this chapter, we are especially interested in drawing on those elements of the 'What Works' literature that indicate strategies for conducting effective rehabilitation programs with adult offenders. The 'What Works' material is presented here with two priorities in mind: to summarise the research and to highlight those dimensions of the research that signal how therapeutic intervention with offenders can be successful.

The 'What Works' literature did not arise in a vacuum. On the contrary, inquiring and debating various issues concerning 'what works' with offenders developed real energy from the discourse occurring in response to a publication in 1974 by Robert Martinson, a researcher in the US, whose paper was taken as concluding that 'nothing works' in terms of correctional rehabilitation. Martinson was commissioned to review the research concerning the 'rehabilitative' effects of imprisonment in New York State. It was somewhat paradoxical that while Martinson's paper pointed to a number of features and issues associated with the effectiveness of correctional intervention and programs, the reactions to Martinson's paper, in the 1970s and 1980s, although selective and political, have been rather more influential than the paper itself, especially in the US. As discussed by several authors, for example Lösel (1995); Gendreau and Goggin (2000) and McGuire (2000a, 2000b), the heading 'nothing works' was intended only as a question and was not apparently presented as an assertion nor intended as a conclusion. Martinson sought to highlight the limitations of various interventions at the time including psychotherapy, but his paper was taken as a kind of definitive finding that 'nothing works' with offenders. This interpretation quickly gained wide acceptance by many correctional administrators, since it suited political interests, including the de-legitimisation of 'treatment' for offenders and was able to be presented as not only supporting, but requiring a 'just desserts' or punitive approach to sentencing and offender management.

Although Martinson's paper was to become something of a landmark in criminology and penology, it was in fact the responses to it combining perspectives from psychology and psychotherapy that led to the formulation of cognitive-behavioural therapy (CBT) in criminal rehabilitation. The foundations for this approach were constructed in the mid-1970s, with the appearance of a number of books and articles which combined ideas from the behavioural and the cognitive traditions within psychological research and practice, suggesting a range of practices that could work to treat offending. Goldfried and Merbaum (1974), Mahoney (1974) and Meichenbaum (1977) are well-recognised early proponents of this approach.

Origins of Cognitive-behavioural Therapy

McGuire (2000a) suggests a range of behavioural and/or cognitive techniques as the most effective in helping clients to change or to improve their responses to situations. Current CBT derives from a history too complex to do it justice in this chapter. McGuire (2000b) describes how the early theorists such as Mahoney (1974) and Meichenbaum (1977) adopted key principles including the role of the environment in learning. These included the idea of 'breaking complex behaviour into simple, more comprehensible units; the possibility of behaviour change in gradual, clearly defined steps; and the universal importance of monitoring and evaluation from outset to completion of the process, including follow-up to examine maintenance of change' (McGuire, 2000b: 20). As well, the ideas circulated between these early authors included what McGuire (2000b: 20) suggests were 'converse principles including the use of self-reports'. These processes acknowledge the central importance of inner language or what I call *self-talk*, thus recognising the 'central place of cognitive processes in self-regulation and self-perception' (McGuire, 2000b: 20). The combination of this range of approaches that married cognitive and behavioural approaches, formerly not well connected, produced what McGuire (2000b: 20) terms, 'powerful new approaches to understanding the complex dynamic relationships between thoughts, feelings and behaviour'. It seems odd that it took theorists and practitioners so long to understand that criminal behaviour in a particular individual is a product of cognition and behaviour, all surrounded by affect or feelings, yet until this linkage occurred, approaches that were effective in mediating criminal behaviour remained elusive. This understanding was slow in developing. According to Meichenbaum (1995), CBT had three principal stages in its evolution and as McGuire (2000b: 28) suggests 'they reflect wider developments in psychology itself' providing 'different metaphors for understanding the change processes in individuals'. These three stages are as follows:

1. *Conditioning* – Learning theory is a basic premise of cognitive-behavioural approaches, with change conceptualised in terms of alterations in learning processes in the nervous system, involving thoughts, feelings and behaviours. As McGuire says (2004: 53), 'the conceptual framework of cognitive learning theory continues to evolve' and provides the 'underpinning theoretical model' for most interventions that comprise the CBT repertoire.

2. *Information Processing* – The focus on cognitive events as prime factors influencing individuals and their difficulties took a strong hold in work with mental health problems but more generally the key notions of cognitive therapies were spelt out by Ellis and Harper (1974) and their Activity-Behaviour-Consequences (ABC) analysis and in Beck (1989) and others. This was followed by research according to McGuire (2000b: 28) 'on how cognitive patterns support dysfunctional feelings and behaviour and on the nature and causes of these patterns themselves'. As, at least to some extent, consequences derive from the individual's management of their feeling reactions to events, this intersecting with the important principle of self-control as noted also in its application to working with offenders in Andrews and Bonta (2003).

3. *Self Attribution and Constructive Narrative* – As it became clearer that behaviour was closely related to thoughts and beliefs, or to cognitive events, ways to intervene to effect positive change in working with clients became better understood. How individuals constructed these cognitive patterns, which are termed 'stories' by Ivey and Ivey (2003), was seen as the way individuals create their own lives. McGuire (2000b: 29) describes this view of 'individuals as architects of their own individual existences' as a shift in the development of CBT, not yet fully resolved.

Current Cognitive-behavioural Approaches

An important point to recognise in discussing CBT is that there is no single cognitive-behavioural method or theory and that a variety of techniques and methods qualify for inclusion. McGuire (2000b) describes CBT as a family or collection of methods rather than a single technique. It is suggested by McGuire (2000b: 21) that self-instructional training (SIT) is the 'core method of cognitive-behavioural therapy' and when viewed as such, SIT may be seen as 'the essence (sometimes even as the sum total) of the approach'. McGuire (2000b) sees that several cognitive and/or behavioural methods with slightly different origins and modes of application 'bear strong resemblances to SIT and overlap with it in several ways' (p 21). A relationship can be noted between this and Cressey's interactionist approach. McGuire (2000b: 21) believes that attempting a sharp definition of what qualifies as CBT is 'a fairly vacuous and ultimately futile exercise'. He also suggests that 'cognitive-behavioural approaches focus too heavily on internal, psychological events at the expense of external, environmental ones' (p 27) and this is a timely suggestion here about clients' existences within complex sets of influences which need to be considered in all stages of the rehabilitation process. Change-based approaches with clients will benefit much more from a flexible approach in which a range of methods can be adopted to take into account the psychological and emotional needs of the client, situated within their usual environment. The following two activities provide a focus on the use of some of the techniques discussed so far.

Activity 4.5 Examples of Personal Change

This exercise should be conducted in pairs where you interview each other in turn. Each person discusses one personal change or type of change you have made in your life. The objective is to examine *personal* change and to attempt to identify the mechanisms which were involved in its occurrence. In particular, note whether it is possible to identify whether the first indication of this personal change was a cognitive, emotional or behavioural event.

Activity 4.6 Self-Instructional Training

This activity is designed to illustrate the nature of cognitive/self-instructional training methods.

Participants work in pairs and focus on some problems identified in the previous activities. Pairs work together to formulate sets of self-instructions or coping self-statements which can be used to replace the dysfunctional patterns.

In order to understand how this 'What Works' wisdom for working with offenders has been determined, the chapter now provides an overview of the current research base of CBT and the systematic review of its application in corrections, referred to as meta-analyses.

Meta-analysis and Correctional Intervention

The bulk of research on correctional effectiveness in the decades since Martinson's paper was published has involved what is termed meta-analyses. Meta-analyses or meta-evaluations strive to 'provide a highly systematic, representative and objective integration of research findings by using statistical methods' (Lösel, 1995: 80). In other words, a meta-analysis is:

> A technique that enables a reviewer to objectively and statistically analyse the findings of each study as data points ... the procedure of meta-analysis involves collection of relevant studies, using the summary statistics from each study as units of analysis, and then analysing the aggregated data in a quantitative manner using statistical tests. (Hollin, 1998: 132)

Indeed, researchers are more focused now on *which programs reduce recidivism* in *which kinds of ways*, under *what kinds of conditions*, rather than continuing to question whether programs can reduce recidivism at all. As Gendreau and Ross (1999) note:

> [T]he debate on correctional effectiveness should no longer focus on whether treatment programs are effective. That should now be viewed as an overly simplistic question. A more meaningful question which should now be addressed is which programs work. Equally important, questions should be asked about why some programs work and some do not. (p 356)

One of the primary advantages of meta-analyses is that a wide range of studies have been completed, highlighting certain factors concerning the programs that 'work', as well as programs that do not 'work'. Programs that are based purely on non-directional counselling and undirected client self-help programs do not systematically reduce recidivism (Gendreau and Ross, 1999). Gendreau and Ross define five features of effective programs:

1. *Authority* – where rules or formal legal sanctions are clearly spelled out;
2. *Anti-criminal modelling and reinforcement* – where the development of pro-social and anti-criminal attitudes, cognitions and behaviours are engendered and reinforced by appropriate modelling of pro-social behaviour;
3. *Problem solving* – where the client is assisted in coping with personal or social difficulties, particularly in the instances where they relate to fostering attitudes which have led him or her to experience pro-social behaviour;
4. *Use of community resources*; and
5. *Quality of interpersonal relationship* – where effective relationships are seen as consisting of empathy, open communication and trust (p 358).

Critical Dimensions of Effective Intervention with Offenders

Andrews and Bonta (2003: 437) say 'there is now a human science of criminal conduct' featuring 'how to make use of what works'. Several key aspects of offender intervention feature techniques and programs based around CBT. One of the most critical aspects of effective programs for offenders is matching the services and intervention to the carefully assessed needs and risks of the person concerned (Bonta, 1996; Andrews and Bonta, 2003). The 'What Works' literature not only highlights the importance of careful assessment of risk and need, it also emphasises the centrality of distinguishing criminogenic needs from more generalised 'needs' for the person concerned. It has become apparent that the complexities of offenders' criminogenic needs are tied closely to their offending behaviours and are thus vital aspects of all programs based on intervention with offenders.

It is generally agreed then that risk, need and responsivity are all crucial dimensions of effective intervention. The risk principle refers to the requirement to match intensity and duration of intervention to the degree of risk of further offending by the client. Active work with clients in programs designed to reduce recidivism needs to take place on the basis of soundly assessed risk. Assessing the degree of risk posed involves differentiating between fixed or static variables in the client's background and dynamic variables, which are open to change. While risk assessment will focus on both types of variable, it is dynamic variables that constitute the focus for change in offenders' lives. At the same time, the need principle suggests that criminogenic needs, rather than undifferentiated needs, should be the major focus of intervention, treatment or program inclusion. Yet identifying risk and need will only be usefully translated into practice if the responsivity principle is applied. The responsivity principle requires that the service being offered is matched to the offender's learning style. This all resonates with the principles of motivation as a basis for effective treatment as discussed by Miller and Rollnick (2002). As well McGuire (2000a) stresses the importance of active and experiential learning rather than processes dominated by didacticism and 'telling'.

This style of engaging with and influencing offenders can only be translated into practice through programs containing all these elements mixed coherently. For example, substance abuse programs usually 'entail a combination of medical and psychosocial approaches' (McGuire, 2004: 162) and engage the client in setting goals, monitoring their own behaviour and changing aspects of lifestyle. Such active client involvement follows from thorough needs assessment, accompanied by skills training. Similarly, programs aimed at addressing violent and aggressive behaviour will be founded on the point that aggressive and violent behavioural repertoires are learned but, as Howells and Day (2003) note, these must include the central importance of readiness for change for offenders, as discussed also by Miller and Rollnick (2002). Thorough assessments are required to clarify how behavioural regimes arise in the first place, as well as identifying the social and interpersonal factors that maintain offending behaviours. The client will then be recruited as an active agent in working on cognitive-behavioural domains.

While research still contains a good degree of contention and debate, certain aspects of research on intervention have emerged as beyond conjecture, with four key principles of effective work with offenders emerging (McGuire, 1995, 2000a, 2000b).

First, particular interventions with offenders (such as probation, imprisonment, periodic detention, home detention, community service and fines) do not have the same effects, in terms of likelihood of recidivism. Interventions that focus on changing offenders' ways of thinking – or their cognition – and their behaviour and self-control, are significantly more effective than non-directive therapy or punishment. In other words, interventions that actively change cognitive and behavioural patterns significantly reduce recidivism and thus make a contribution to the prevention of crime in the community.

Secondly, programs for offenders can indeed 'work' but only if they are delivered in certain ways. As many researchers emphasise, the provision of a cognitive-behavioural intervention will not automatically, of itself, result in reduced recidivism. Similarly, approaches that 'sheep-dip' all offenders through programs in the hope that something will work are ineffective. However, programs that are designed and delivered in such a way as to match offenders' learning styles and their criminogenic needs can be highly effective. As McGuire notes (1995: 22), 'evidence concerning the responsivity principle highlights the vital need for staff to relate to clients in a manner that combines sensitivity and constructiveness'. Andrews and Bonta (2003: 314) describe effective workers as those who 'are successful with their clients' and who are able to '(a) establish high quality relationships with them, (b) demonstrate anti-criminal expressions [modelling], (c) approve of client's anti-criminal expressions [reinforcement], and (d) disapprove of the client's procriminal expressions [punishment], while at the same time demonstrating alternatives'. They also say that correctional workers will be ineffective if they 'are explicitly non-supportive of the system, enamored with the positive aspects of criminal activity, or accepting of the rationalizations for law violations' (Andrews and Bonta, 2003: 316).

Thirdly, cognitive-behavioural techniques that actively teach certain skills within a therapeutic context are likely to be most effective. In other words, these techniques teach 'how' to perform the desired behaviour as well as explaining the importance of not thinking or behaving in certain ways. Old ways of thinking and behaving are removed from habituation through the use of processes that construct new understandings about thought (cognition) and then by behaving in more positive ways. Such processes obviously also need to include the client as an active agent.

Fourthly, cognitive-behavioural intervention is most likely to be effective with offenders if (and only if) certain conditions apply. These conditions include identifying precisely which needs and other factors actively contribute to offending, using active engagement with offenders rather than passive 'education' contexts, matching the type of intervention to the assessed risk of further offending. In addition, it must be ensured that programs are conducted exactly as per 'design specifications' so that goals and methods or modules of the program are not modified over time, this being referred to as program integrity (Gendreau and Ross, 1999). Program integrity also includes the requirement for the programs to be delivered by adequately trained and qualified staff (Hollin, 1996). Raynor and Vanstone (1998) provide a further example of how program integrity is implemented in a group-based program for adult offenders. It is quite apparent then that one of the most critical aspects of all effective programs for offenders is matching the services and intervention to the carefully assessed needs and risks of the person concerned.

Summary

In summary, it seems the best chances of reducing offender recidivism, come from programs for offenders that employ CBT in combination with crucial features such as careful assessment of needs, structured rather than unstructured approaches to intervention and program integrity (McGuire, 2000a, 2000b). As well, the effectiveness of correctional workers is a key variable, as noted by McGuire (1995) and Andrews and Bonta (2003).

While many topics remain hotly debated about the applicability of CBT to all groups of adult or juvenile offenders (Andrews and Bonta, 2003; Cameron, 2004), there is substantial agreement and conclusive research demonstrating the efficacy of carefully designed and delivered programs for offenders. It is proven through a range of research and literature that all offender programs, both custodial and community-based depend for their efficacy on a range of variables, one of which is the customisation of programs to address the needs of offenders. Successful rehabilitation then depends on the application of the right kind of treatment, one matched to the criminogenic needs of the person, and applied effectively as demonstrated through the meta-analyses noted in Andrews and Bonta (2003) and the 'What Works' literature (McGuire, 1995, 2000a, 2000b, 2004) as featured in this chapter. These guidelines are often overlooked in selecting treatment approaches for offenders and deserve a much stronger emphasis. It cannot be denied that working with adult offenders is challenging, given that many have backgrounds of previous offences and may be classified as 'hardened criminals'. This field of work requires commitment to this enterprise and the application of interventions that are evaluated through research as most effective. Ongoing reviews of efficacy are essential, however, as even with the current background of intensive research into effective practices with offenders the question will go on being asked: What works?

Review Questions

1. How does an understanding of deviance and conformity inform beliefs about criminal conduct and offender rehabilitation programs?

2. Consider the balance between 'antisocial attitudes, the personality complex, the bonding set (family in particular) and antisocial associates' in influencing criminal behaviour as suggested by Andrews and Bonta (2003: 131).

3. Review the features of effective offender programs according to Gendreau and Ross (1999) and discuss what these require in terms of changes in correctional procedures in society and the resources needed to make these changes.

4. Consider how well-equipped are most workers for being effective in the correctional system, according to Andrews and Bonta's (2003) list of requirements.

Useful Websites

Australian Institute of Criminology	http://www.aic.gov.au
Home Office (UK)	http://www.homeoffice.gov.uk/
Home Office reports on what work in corrections (UK)	http://www.homeoffice.gov.uk/rds/
Crime Reduction (UK)	http://www.crimereduction.gov.uk/cpindex.htm
David Willshire's forensic psychology and psychiatry links	http://members.optusnet.com.au/dwillsh/

References

Andrews, DA and Bonta, J (2003) *The Psychology of Criminal Conduct* (3rd ed), Cincinnati: Anderson Publishing.

Anleu, SLR (2006) *Deviance, Conformity & Control* (4th ed), Sydney: Pearson Education.

Asch, SE (1955) 'Opinions and social pressure', *Scientific American*, 193(5), 31-35.

Bandura, A (1996) *Self-efficacy: The Exercise of Control*, New York: WH Freeman.

Bankart, P (1997) *Talking Cures: A History of Western and Eastern Psychotherapies*, Pacific Grove, CA: Brooks/Cole.

Bauman, Z (2001) *The Individualized Society*, Cambridge: Polity.

Beck, AT (1989) *Cognitive Therapy and the Emotional Disorders*, London: Penguin.

Beck, R (2000) *Motivation: The Theories and Principles* (4th ed), Upper Saddle River, NJ: Prentice Hall.

Bonta, J (1996) 'Risk-needs assessment and treatment', in A Harland (ed) *Choosing Correctional Options That Work* (pp 18-32), Thousand Oaks, CA: Sage.

Brown, R (2000) *Group Processes: Dynamics Within and Between Groups* (2nd ed), Malden, MA: Blackwell.

Cameron, H (2004) 'Cognitive-behavioural group work: Its application to specific offender groups', *Howard Journal of Criminal Justice*, 43(1), 47-64.

Cressey, DR (1953) *Other People's Money*, Glencoe, ILL: Free Press.

Dabbs, J, Strong, R and Milun, R (1997) 'Exploring the mind of testosterone: A beeper study', *Journal of Research in Personality*, 31(4), 577-587.

Downes, D and Rock, P (2003) *Understanding Deviance: A Guide to the Sociology of Crime and Rule Breaking* (4th ed), Oxford: Oxford University Press.

Eardley, T (1995) 'Violence and sexuality', in S Caffrey and G Mundy (eds) *The Sociology of Crime and Deviance: Selected Issues* (pp 135-150), Dartford: Greenwich University Press.

Ellis, A and Harper, R (1974) *A Guide to Rational Living*, Hollywood, CA: Wilshire Book Co.

Garland, D and Sparks, R (eds) (2000) *Criminology and Social Theory*, Oxford: Oxford University Press.

Gendreau, P and Goggin, C (2000) 'Correctional treatment: Accomplishments and realities', in P Van Voorhis, M Braswell and D Lester (eds) *Correctional Counseling and Rehabilitation* (4th ed) (pp 289-297), Cincinnati: Anderson.

Gendreau, P and Ross, RR (1999) 'Correctional treatment: Some recommendations for effective intervention', in KC Haas and GP Alpert (eds) *The Dilemmas of Corrections: Contemporary Readings* (pp 355-368), Prospect Heights, ILL: Waveland.

Gerstel, N (1994) 'Divorce and stigma', in PA Alder and P Alder (eds) *Constructions of Deviance: Social Power, Context and Interaction* (pp 237-248), Belmont, CA: Wadsworth.

Giddens, A (1991) *Modernity and Self-Identity: Self and Society in the Late Modern Age*, Cambridge: Polity.

Goffman, E (1963) *Stigma: Notes on the Management of Spoiled Identity*, Englewood Cliffs, NJ: Prentice Hall.

Goldfried, MR and Merbaum, M (eds) (1974) *Behavior Change Through Self-control*, New York: Holt, Rinehart and Winston.

Grabosky, P (1999), 'Managing violence and health: Strategies, solutions, research and methodological issues', Paper presented at the *WHO Global Symposium on Violence, and Health* in Kobe, Japan. Available at: <http://www.aic.gov.au/conferences/other/grabosky_peter/1999-10-kobe.html>.

Graycar, A and Nelson, D (1999) 'Crime and social capital', Paper presented at the *Australian Crime Prevention Council 19th Biennial International Conference on Preventing Crime, Melbourne.* Available at: <http://www.aic.gov.au/conferences/other/graycar_adam/1999-10-acpc99.html>.

Gudykunst, WB and Kim, YY (1997) *Communicating with Strangers: An Approach to Intercultural Communication* (3rd ed), New York: McGraw-Hill.

Hall, S (1997) 'The spectacle of the "other"', in S Hall (ed) *Representation: Cultural Representations and Signifying Practices* (pp 223-279), London: Sage, in association with the Open University.

Hester, S and Englin, P (1995) 'Justice and symbolic interaction', in S Caffrey and G Munday (eds) *The Sociology of Crime and Deviance: Selected Issues* (pp 349-362), Dartford: Greenwich University Press.

Hollin, C (1998) 'Working with young offenders', in K Cigno and D Bourn (eds) *Cognitive-behavioural Social Work in Practice* (pp 127-142), Aldershot: Ashgate.

Hollin, CR (1989) *Psychology and Crime: An Introduction to Criminal Psychology*, London: Routledge.

Hollin, CR (ed) (1996) *Working with Offenders: Psychological Practice in Offender Rehabilitation*, Chichester, West Sussex: John Wiley & Sons.

Holman, JE and Quinn, JF (1992) *Criminology: Applying Theory*, St Paul: West Publishing.

Howells, K and Day, A (1999) 'The rehabilitation of offenders: International perspectives applied to Australian correctional systems', *Trends and Issues in Crime and Criminal Justice*, No 112, Canberra: Australian Institute of Criminology.

Howells, K and Day, A (2003) 'Readiness for anger management: Clinical and theoretical issues', *Clinical Psychology Review*, 23(2), 319-337.

Ivey, AE and Ivey, MB (2003) *Intentional Interviewing and Counselling: Facilitating Client Development in a Multicultural Society* (5th ed), Pacific Grove, CA: Thomson.

Langston, C and Sykes, WE (1997) 'Beliefs and the big five: Cognitive bases of broad individual differences in personality', *Journal of Research in Personality*, 31(2), 141-165.

Lippa, RW (1994) *Introduction to Social Psychology* (2nd ed), Pacific Grove, CA: Brooks/Cole.

Lösel, F (1995) 'Increasing consensus in the evaluation of offender rehabilitation? Lessons from recent research', *Psychology, Crime and Law*, 2(1), 19-39.

MacDonald, D and Brown, M (1996) 'Indicators of aggressive behaviour', *Research and Public Policy Series* (No 8), Canberra: Australian Institute of Criminology. Available at: <http://www.aic.gov.au/publications/rpp/08/index.html>.

Mahoney, MJ (1974) *Cognition and Behavior Modification*, Cambridge: Ballinger.

Marmot, M and Wilkinson, R (eds) (1999) *Social Determinants of Health*, Oxford: Oxford University Press.

Martinson, R (1974) 'What works? – Questions and answers about prison reform', *The Public Interest*, 35(Spring), 22-54.

McGuire, J (1996) 'Community-based interventions', in CR Hollin (ed) *Working with Offenders: Psychological Practice in Offender Rehabilitation* (pp 63-93), Chichester, West Sussex: John Wiley & Sons.

McGuire, J (2000a) 'Defining correctional programs', *What Works in Corrections*, 12(2). Available at: <http://www.csc-scc.gc.ca/text/pblct/forum/e122/e122b_e.shtml>.

McGuire, J (2000b) *Cognitive-behavioural Approaches: An Introduction to Theory and Research*, London: Home Office.

McGuire, J (2004) *Understanding Psychology and Crime: Perspectives on Theory and Action*, Buckingham: Open University Press.

McGuire, J (ed) (1995) *What Works: Reducing Reoffending – Guidelines from Research and Practice*, Chichester, West Sussex: John Wiley & Sons.

Meichenbaum, D (1977) *Cognitive-behavior Modification: An Integrative Approach*, New York: Plenum.

Meichenbaum, D (1995) 'Cognitive-behavioral therapy in historical perspective', in B Bongar and LE Beutler (eds) *Comprehensive Textbook of Psychotherapy: Theory and Practice* (pp 140-158), New York: Oxford University Press.

Melossi, D (2000) 'Changing representation of the criminal', in D Garland and R Sparks (eds) *Criminology and Social Theory* (pp 149-181), Oxford: Oxford University Press.

Miczek, K, Haney, M, Tidey, J, Vivian, J and Weerts, E (1994) 'Neurochemistry and pharmacotherapeutic management of aggression and violence', in A Reiss, K Miczek and J Roth (eds) *Understanding and Preventing Violence* (pp 425-514), Washington DC: National Academy Press.

Miller, WR and Rollnick, S (2002) *Motivational Interviewing: Preparing People for Change* (2nd ed), New York: Guilford.

Moir, A and Moir, B (1998) 'Sense and sensitivity: A review of why men don't iron: The real science of gender', *The Weekend Australian*, October 17-18.

Mukherjee, S (1999) 'Ethnicity and crime', *Trends and Issues in Crime and Criminal Justice*, No 117, Canberra: Australian Institute of Criminology.

Myers, DG (1993) *Social Psychology* (4th ed), New York: McGraw-Hill.

Raynor, P and Vanstone, M (1998) 'Adult probationers and the STOP programme', in K Cigno and D Bourn (eds) *Cognitive-behavioural Social Work in Practice* (pp 143-162), Aldershot: Ashgate.

Sampson, RJ and Lauritsen, J (1994) 'Violent victimization and offending: Individual, situational, and community-level risk factors', in AJ Reiss and JA Roth (eds) *Understanding and Preventing Violence* (pp 1-115), Washington DC: National Academy of Science.

Scherwitz, L and Rugulies, R (1992) 'Life-style and hostility' in H Friedman (ed) *Hostility, Coping & Health* (pp 77-98), Washington DC: American Psychological Association.

Schwartz, M and Milovanic, D (1996) *Race, Gender and Class in Criminology: The Intersection*, New York: Garland Publishing.

Sheldon, WH (1942) *The Varieties of Temperament: A Psychology of Constitutional Differences*, New York: Harper & Row.

Sherif, M (1937) 'An experimental approach to the study of attitudes', *Sociometry*, 1(1/2), 90-98.

Soldz, S and Vaillant, GE (1999) 'The big five personality traits and the life course: A 45 year long study', *Journal of Research in Personality*, 33(2), 208-232.

Winter, I (ed) (2000) *Social Capital and Public Policy in Australia*, Melbourne: Australian Institute of Family Studies.

Chapter 5

Mental Health

Robert Bland and Noel Renouf

Introduction

Mental health has traditionally been a major area of social work practice. The focus on the social context and consequences of mental illness, key concepts informing practice, has established social work leadership in the broader social aspects of mental health interventions. The current context for practice remains challenging, yet social aspects of illness continue to be of vital importance to comprehensive care of people with mental illness. This chapter explores the conceptual basis for social work practice in mental health, and then examines a range of current issues and areas of practice – policy development, case management, working with service users, working with families and the opportunities offered by evidence-based practice approaches to work.

Social Work in the Mental Health Field in Australia

Within the Australian human services sector social workers are employed in a range of mental health services. Within the public health system, employment includes hospital and community mental health services in traditional clinical positions, working in intake and assessment services, case management, primary care and rehabilitation services. In recent years there has been an expansion of the psychiatric disability support area largely provided through the non-government sector. Social workers are employed in child and adolescent services, in adult services and in aged care services. Social workers have also moved into management and leadership positions throughout the sector.

As a direct consequence of the deinstitutionalisation movement, and the trend for people with mental illness to live in the community, social workers in all human service areas will encounter people with mental illness among their client group. Social workers in such diverse areas as child protection, family welfare, housing, income security, domestic violence and community development need to have an understanding of mental illness and its impact on the lives of individuals and their families.

Within Australian social work, recent studies have defined the domain of social work in mental health as the social context and social consequences of mental illness. The purpose of practice is to restore individual, family, and community wellbeing, to promote the development of each individual's power and control over their lives and to promote principles of social justice. Social work practice occurs at the interface between the individual and the environment: social work activity begins with the individual, and extends to the contexts of family, social networks, community and the broader society (Australian Association of Social Workers (AASW), 1999).

Key concepts then include social context, social consequences and social justice. At the level of 'social context', social work is concerned with the way each individual's social environment shapes their experience of mental illness. Its concerns include issues of individual personality, vulnerability and resilience, family functioning, strengths and stressors, support networks, culture, community, class, ethnicity and gender. Beyond the intrapsychic aspects of ego functioning, self-esteem and meaning making, and interpersonal aspects of family functioning and personal relationships, its concerns include broader social issues of economic wellbeing, employment and housing. At the level of 'social consequences', social work is concerned with the impact of mental illness on the individual, the family and personal relationships, and the broader community, including the impact on sense of self, on life chances, on family wellbeing, and on economic security, employment and housing. Social work is concerned with the interface between mental illness and broader health and welfare issues such as child protection and domestic violence. At the level of 'social justice', social work is concerned with issues of stigma and discrimination, of political freedoms and civil rights, of promoting access to necessary treatment and support services, and of promoting consumer and family carer rights to participation and choice in mental health services. It is concerned with making all human services more accessible and responsive to the specific needs and wishes of people with mental illness, and their family carers. It recognises that people with mental illness are also likely to be poor, unemployed, marginalised and stigmatised (Rapp, 1998).

Mental health practice in recent years has been strongly influenced by the emergence of the consumer movement and related influential principles such as strengths perspectives, empowerment and recovery (Dewees, 2002). The *strengths perspective* (Saleeby, 1996; Rapp, 1998) challenges the pathologising discourse of mental illness to encourage practitioners to focus on the client's capacities, strengths and resilience. While not denying the torment of the symptoms of severe mental illness, the emphasis is on the client's hopes and dreams, and finding ways to achieve these. It considers the client the expert in his or her own life and culture. It emphasises community integration, normalisation and citizenship. In assuming the shared humanity of the worker and client, it challenges the 'clinical distance' that accompanies traditional clinical work.

The concept of *empowerment* in mental health is generally applied at the individual level emphasising the development of a greater sense of personal control over one's life, yet there is much in the consumer and family carer movements in recent decades to suggest a more structural concept of empowerment. Consumers have recognised their shared sense of oppression in a treatment system which is experienced as dehumanising, and in a community that is hostile, stigmatising and denying of human rights. Collective action through the activities of the consumer movement has helped to develop a more positive and potent sense of self, a more critical analysis of the mental health services and society, and strategies for collective political action. The work of advocacy groups such as the Mental Illness Fellowships of Australia and National Alliance for the Mentally Ill in the United States are examples of highly successful political activity to achieve empowerment.

Recovery principles, building on the concepts of strengths perspective and empowerment, have emerged in recent years as a major influence in service development and practice. Recovery challenges the negative and pathologising discourse of chronicity. Using empirical long term outcome studies of mental illness, Harding, Zubin and Strauss (1992) showed that many people with severe illness made good recoveries over time. Rather than accept and adjust to chronic disability, consumers and workers should expect recovery and improvement over time. Studies of first person accounts of recovery from illness by Hatfield and Lefley (1993) and Rapp (1998) were used to identify key principles of recovery. These included a recognition that the illness is a partial and not a complete identity, personal control over choices, hope, purpose, support from others and personal achievement. Recovery principles emphasise personal responsibility and growth through relationships. For workers, key practice principles include encouraging positive expectations for the future, sustaining hope, supporting consumer decision-making and autonomy, and encouraging positive and supportive relationships with others.

Evidence-based Practice

Within the field of mental health, concepts of evidence-based practice (EBP) have emerged as dominant influences in the way all disciplines provide clinical services (Tanenbaum, 2003). Originating in the Evidence-Based Medicine (EBM) movement (Evidence-Based Medicine Working Group (EBMWG), 1992), EBP involves the conscientious, explicit and judicious application of best research evidence to a range of clinical domains: diagnostic tests and interventions of therapeutic, rehabilitative and preventative nature (Gilgun, 2005). EBP focuses on locating and evaluating research evidence according to research methods in which randomised clinical trials are seen to constitute the strongest evidence for efficacy. Qualitative studies, case studies, anecdotal and 'expert consensus' evidence is less highly valued. There is an emphasis on quantitative indicators of outcome, and an insistence that interventions that have consistently failed to be proven effective should be replaced by evidence-based interventions. EBP demands an active engagement with the research literature as the foundation for practice. It is clearly most applicable in those clinical settings where interventions can be explicitly defined around tightly controlled variables, and where outcomes are clearly defined. Some researchers have argued that EBP also includes a recognition of the need to accommodate the expectations, concerns and values of the client and the need for practitioners to be aware of their own values (Singer and Todkill, 2000).

Within the social work literature there is an emerging disagreement about the value and applicability of EBP to social work practice. Champions of EBP such as Sheldon (2001) and Thyer (2001) emphasise the opportunities for social workers to embrace EBP to provide a solid research base for the many interventions applied by social workers, allowing the profession to emphasise the science, as well as the values or ideology, of interventions. The evaluation of psychosocial interventions is seen as a particularly important site for social work research. Critics of EBP, such as Webb (2001), challenge the scientific positivism fundamental to EBP, arguing that the construction of knowledge here is a political process that privileges science and managerialism over alternative knowledge and theory. It threatens to entrap social workers within a mechanistic form of technical rationality. At one level this is an epistemological debate though there are clear practice issues for social workers employed in mental health settings (Murphy and McDonald, 2004).

To some extent, this ambivalent attitude to EBP approaches is due to the problem that the voices advocating for the evidence for biomedical interventions are so much stronger than those speaking to psychosocial issues (Bland, 2004). As a result, the whole discourse of 'evidence' may be heard and experienced by social workers as yet another marginalising practice within the contested mental health workplace (Holloway, 2001; Filc, 2004), associated with other professions whose training and traditions are more closely aligned with scientific discourse.

Other problems may lie with the nature of the work itself. Many of the activities of social work, in areas such as case management, family work, advocacy, community work and resource development, do not easily fit the conceptual framework of EBP. It is not always easy to demonstrate the effectiveness of broadly based interventions (Webb, 2001). For example, high levels of depression may be evident in a community with a high rate of unemployment and a collapse of social capital. Social workers in a community health setting might recognise the need for a broadly based approach to community development, supporting the community members to work towards solving some of their problems through collective action. Such an intervention flows clearly from social work's values and traditions. It is more difficult, however, to define or demonstrate the effectiveness of such an approach. A cognitive-behavioural approach to intervention with identified depressed individuals, though not necessarily appropriate in this context, is by contrast definable and demonstrably effective.

These challenges notwithstanding, there is now a very strong body of existing evidence for effective psychosocial interventions in the mental health area (Sands, 2001), and a lot of potential for developing evidence in under-researched areas such as the interplay of mental health issues with income, housing and employment (Huxley and Thornicroft, 2003). There is also an increasing recognition of the need to place evidence alongside values, such as the 'two-feet' principle that decisions should be based on facts and values (Woodbridge and Fulford, 2004), which provides mental health social workers with a potential framework for a measured and critical engagement with the evidence base. There is, perhaps, the opportunity for mental health social workers to promote and explore broader forms of 'evidence' (Mykhalovskiy and Weir, 2004) that pay attention to the social processes of care, and consider the voices of consumers, families and the community.

Ferguson (2003) suggests a four part approach to engaging with the knowledge base for practice which provides some direction for resolution of some of these tensions. He argues that social workers need to search out the 'best practice' knowledge in each sphere of work, that they apply critical theory to this knowledge as an 'interpretive framework', that they identify the evidence base for any interventions in order to establish 'what works', and that they identify 'practice-based evidence' which relates to experiential knowledge and the social actions and processes that go to make up the very nature of social work in practice (Ferguson, 2003: 1006).

Policy Context for Practice

Before 1990, mental health was considered a responsibility of the States, and each State managed its own services under State policy and mental health legislation. In the last 15 years the Commonwealth and State governments have worked together to develop a common mental health strategy and policy. Despite attempts to secure common legislation this has not yet been achieved. Mental health services are still administered by State governments but the Commonwealth remains active in a range of policy development areas.

The National Mental Health Strategy developed over the past 15 years has been articulated in four major documents (Ash et al, 2001): the *National Mental Health Policy* (Australian Health Ministers, 1992a), the *National Mental Health Plan* (Australian Health Ministers, 1992b), the

Mental Health Statement of Rights and Responsibilities (Australian Health Ministers, 1991) and the Medicare Agreements that provided the funding arrangements to support the reform process. Key principles of the Strategy included an emphasis on positive consumer outcomes, priority for those with the most severe mental health problems, protection of the human rights of consumers, consumer participation in decision-making, multidisciplinary service delivery and workforce education and training. There was an emphasis on mainstreaming of mental health services and the effective linking of mental health services with the broad range of other health and welfare services used by mental health consumers. Subsequent plans (*Second National Mental Health Plan 1998-2003*, and the *National Mental Health Plan 2003-2008*) have extended the original scope of the strategy to include an emphasis on prevention and promotion, partnerships among service providers and consumers, and on population health principles. The policies which have shaped the reform process in Australia are reflected in developments elsewhere, including Britain (Department of Health, 1999, 2002) and New Zealand (Mental Health Commission, 1998, 2003).

As a result, there has been outstanding service reform in the clinical services, and considerable development of non-government services oriented towards rehabilitation and recovery. Although implementation of the National Plans has been uneven (Commonwealth Department of Health and Ageing, 2002; Groom and Hickie, 2003), their principles have been translated into many State-based and local service reform initiatives. To cite a recent example of particular relevance to social workers in mental health, the Victorian 'Action Plan for Carer Involvement in Victorian Public Mental Health Services' (Mental Health Branch, 2004) aims to achieve widespread improvement in the involvement of family carers, based explicitly on the principles of the Mental Health Statement of Rights and Responsibilities (Australian Health Ministers, 1991), the three Mental Health Plans and the National Standards for Mental Health Services (Australian Health Ministers Advisory Council, 1997).

One radical feature of the strategy has been a recognition of the importance of consumer participation in all aspects of mental health activity, from planning services with individual consumers, through agency management and evaluation, and in the education and training of mental health professionals. There is also a growing acknowledgment of the need to extend such participation to the families of consumers (Bland, 2002).

Case Management

Systems of case management are fundamental to the organisation of many contemporary mental health service systems, and many social workers perform much of their work within this role, although case management practices vary considerably according to context. The term case management is a difficult one because it may be taken to imply that clients are 'cases' rather than individuals or families, and that the worker's task is a form of 'management' – a term with does not capture, and even contradicts, the centrality of relationship, partnership and therapeutic alliance. Nevertheless, case management has developed as a fundamental practice through much of the contemporary human service system (Furlong, 1997). Some of its roots lie in social casework (National Association of Social Workers, 1992), and certainly the values, knowledge and skills of social workers are suited to the construction and implementation of an approach to case management that is client driven and focused on the interaction of the individual with the environment.

Bachrach's (1993) conceptualisation of models of case management perhaps captures the range most clearly and simply, from 'brokerage' at one end of the continuum, through models that are based on 'relationship' and 'continuity of care', to 'clinical case management' including specialist interventions and rehabilitation, and 'intensive case management' at the other end of the continuum.

There is an extensive literature on the efficacy and effectiveness of case management systems of various kinds. Despite the well-publicised Cochrane Review finding that 'case management is an intervention of questionable value, to the extent that it is doubtful whether it should be offered by community psychiatric services' (Marshall et al, 1998), and a number of studies producing equivocal results (Bedell, Cohen and Sullivan, 2000), there remains a strong commitment to the practice underpinned by an extensive research literature (Ziguras and Stuart, 2000). There is better empirical evidence for the efficacy of more intensive 'full service' models of case management such as Assertive Community Treatment (ACT) (Marshall and Lockwood, 1998; Bedell et al, 2000; Phillips et al, 2001), which have strong social work origins (Mowbray and Holter, 2002). Rosen and Teesson (2001) concluded that 'there is strong evidence for the efficacy and effectiveness and cost-effectiveness of case management in psychiatry, the closer it conforms to active and assertive community treatment models' (p 731). Nevertheless, the picture is a complex one, and it can be difficult to discern from the empirical studies precisely what case management components can be predicted to have a specific effect on different outcome measures, such as improvement in symptoms, reduced hospitalisation, improved 'cooperation' with treatment services, social and occupational functioning, quality of life, client and/or family satisfaction, cost-effectiveness and so on (Hemming and Yellowlees, 1997; Björkman and Hansson, 2000; Schaedle and Epstein, 2000).

What is clear is that it is not enough to reconfigure a service system to ensure that case management services are available, but it is necessary to focus on the process of case management to ensure that it is provided skilfully (Gournay and Thornicroft, 2002). The particular approach or style of the case manager (Hromco, Lyons and Nikkel, 1997) is critical to its effectiveness.

Kanter's (1989) influential 'clinical' model remains one of the clearest and best descriptions of the main elements of effective case management, integrating clinical acumen, personal involvement and environmental interventions. The model identifies the following principles: continuity of care, use of the case management relationship, titrating support and structure, flexibility and facilitating the client's resourcefulness. Kanter describes specific case management interventions related to engagement, assessment and planning, as well as interventions focused on three domains: the environment (linkage with community resources, consultation with families and other caregivers, maintaining and expanding social networks, collaborating with treatment services, and advocacy); the client (intermittent individual psychotherapy, developing living skills, psychoeducation); and both the client and the environment (crisis intervention and monitoring).

This is consistent with the strengths model of case management (Rapp, 1998), in which the emphasis is on client self-determination and strengths rather than pathology, and the case manager works optimistically and assertively, viewing the community, for example, as an 'oasis of resources'. Strengths-based social work provides a strong conceptual basis for transforming practice away from 'pathologising' discourses (Morley, 2003) towards a focus on 'resilience, rebound, possibility, and transformation' (Saleebey, 1996: 297).

The quality of partnership, engagement and relationship between the client and the worker – the amount of 'client-orientation' (Schaedle and Epstein, 2000) – is an important aspect of effective mental health care in general (McCabe and Priebe, 2004) and case management in particular (Howgego et al, 2003; Meaden et al, 2004). There are elements of skill involved here, but also human qualities and values. For example, Intagliata (1982) identified 'the quality of the personal commitment that case managers develop toward their clients' (p 673) as perhaps the most influential aspect of the case management process. One of the important early descriptions of case management in mental health emphasised the human relationship factor in the following terms:

> Simply stated, the human element cannot be taken out of the human service system. When connecting with clients, the case manager establishes a close bond with the client. The case manager treats the client as a "person" rather than a client, attending to the client's need to be physically, emotionally, intellectually, and spiritually close to another person. (Anthony et al, 2000: 101)

Perhaps one of the reasons for the near ubiquity of case management systems in community mental health services is their suitability – at least potentially – for simultaneously providing support and services, while also managing risk (Rose, 1998). There is a potential contradiction here, and a real challenge for mental health social workers and other case managers. For example, when case management was introduced as a cornerstone of the Victorian framework for service delivery (Psychiatric Services Branch, 1994; Department of Human Services, 1998), there were two clear messages. The first was that all clients were to have access to a high quality clinical case management that emphasised the strengths of consumers, the importance of the helping relationship, and the collabo-rative achievement of goals developed in comprehensive individual service plans. The second message was that case management would be established as the mechanism for ensuring accountability for the risks of mental health problems in the community. In the ensuing decade, there has been an increasing emphasis on the assessment and management of risk, while the quality of mental health services continues to fall well short of community expectations. In this context, it is not surprising that there is sometimes a tendency towards a debased, defensive form of case management practice that has more to do with meeting the demands of service management and the worker's anxiety than the needs and wishes of the client.

Furlong's (1997) argument that it is essential that both the 'care' and the 'control' functions of case management be acknowledged and articulated is pertinent here. It may be that best practice lies in the capacity to hold both dimensions in an appropriate balance, on the basis of a negotiated partnership with the client and family carers. But this is a sophisticated undertaking, requiring great skill as well as a well-managed and well-resourced service system. The construction and maintenance of a best practice approach to case management needs to take account of effective ways to manage risk.

Case management models require comprehensive and individualised service planning over a range of domains including: emotional and mental wellbeing; dealing with stress; personal response to illness; personal safety and the safety of others; friendships or social relation-ships; work; leisure and education; daily living skills; family's response to relative's illness; income; physical health; housing; and rights and advocacy (Department of Human Services, 1998). Yet, in the face of a service system that is not always responsive to individual client needs and serious inadequacies in opportunities and resources for housing, employment, recreation and so on, case managers need to work with their clients in creative ways in order to be effective. Trevillion (1999) has dubbed case managers 'the alchemists of welfare', 'constantly seeking to transform inadequate resources and inappropriate services into the philosopher's stone of a genuinely needs led service' (p 104). Flexibility of approach is another important factor (Simpson, Miller and Bowers, 2003). While much empirical support for case management derives from the efficacy of intensive case management models, most clients are unlikely to require such interventions in perpetuity, and recovery will be enhanced by providing the right amount and mix of interventions for the right duration (Sherman and Ryan, 1998).

Partnership between professionals and service providers has been seen as a cornerstone of the best case management, but there is clear potential to develop consumer run programs and services (Test, 1998), as well as consumer participation in existing case management programs through the active employment of consumers as case managers or by supporting consumers to work in partnership (or as aides) with other professionals (Sherman and Porter, 1991; Dixon, Krauss and Lehman, 1994; Solomon, 1994; Solomon and Draine, 1995; Bedell et al, 2000).

Good case management practice has always required that, on the basis of an effective collaborative partnership with the client, the social worker will collaborate with a range of other service providers and community members, as required by the specific needs and circumstances of each client. Mental health case management is not a 'one stop shop'. The need for social network interventions is increasing in the current environment, because the complex needs of many clients require joint work across the boundaries of multiple service systems (income security, child protection and family welfare, justice, health and so on) and sometimes engagement with important systems in the client's life (employment, education, extended family systems and so on). Mental health service systems are frequently criticised for being unresponsive and poorly integrated with the community and other health and welfare services. Social workers need to adopt an informed, planned and skilled approach to working at the interface between the mental health service system and the community, to ensure that mental health care is provided in an integrated way, to advocate alongside their clients for their needs to be adequately met, and to build new service networks to address the many glaring service gaps, such as inadequacies in affordable and accessible housing and vocational opportunities.

Working with Families of People with Mental Illness

Social workers have traditionally worked with families in mental health settings (Bland, 1987) and there is now an increasing recognition of the importance of this area of activity, based largely on the strength of evidence for the effectiveness of family work, and the efforts of family carers and their representatives in working for reform of a mental health service system that has tended to focus too narrowly on the treatment of the individual.

The effectiveness of certain defined family interventions for people with mental illness (especially schizophrenia, which is the group where most studies have been conducted) is one of the very strong themes of contemporary mental health service research (Dixon and Lehman, 1995; Dixon et al, 2001; McFarlane et al, 2003). On this basis, the Royal Australian and New Zealand College of Psychiatrists (2005) recommend that family interventions should be integrated at all stages and with all aspects of care, should include psychoeducation, communication and problem solving modules, and that referrals should be made to consumer and carer networks.

Implicit in these recommendations is the recognition of the value of family carers as a resource, and a developing appreciation of the impact of mental illness on families. The empirical evidence suggests that the recommended interventions have a significant effect in reducing relapse (Mari and Strenier, 1994; Mueser and Bond, 2000; Bustillo et al, 2001; Pitschel-Walz et al, 2001), and decreasing the difficulties and burden experienced by families (Cuijpers, 1999), especially when they are provided in a sustained manner over time (Dixon and Lehman, 1995).

While further research is required to identify the most effective ingredients of family work, there is considerable consensus about many of the core features of good practice. Sometimes these are subsumed under the rubric 'family psychoeducation', which may be a misleading term. Certainly, it is essential to provide information (education) to relevant family members about mental illness, its causes, precipitants and manifestations, what is known about prognosis, and the rationale for various treatments. But much more than this is required: families will often want and need support and encouragement in a no-fault atmosphere from the start; they will often want to hear and discuss recommendations for coping with the disorder; often they will benefit from assistance in improving the clarity of family communication in the wake of painful and traumatic events and dislocation of family life, and help with problem solving to deal with everyday hassles as well as major stressful life events; and of course they will benefit from active assistance at times of crisis, or when there are incipient signs of recurrence of mental health problems (Goldstein and Miklowitz, 1995).

An authoritative statement from the World Fellowship for Schizophrenia and Associated Disorders (1999) identifies 15 principles, which begin with the fundamental requirement of ensuring 'that everyone is working towards the same goals in a collaborative, supportive relationship. Working together ensures that the goals for treatment and care are understood and agreed by the treatment team which includes the family. This will overcome the isolation that is experienced by both professionals and families'. While this might seem so fundamental as to be obvious, such a principle actually suggests a radical reworking of strongly entrenched traditions of mental health work, which have tended to split the needs and perspectives of individuals and their families, when the latter have been considered at all. The construction of a 'team' that includes professionals, the client and the family is a complex and sophisticated undertaking. For example, particular skill is required sometimes in negotiating issues of confidentiality (Furlong and Leggatt, 1996), and in negotiating situations in which family relationships have been badly damaged, perhaps even by family violence and abuse.

Mental health service policies now routinely recognise family carers as important partners in the service system (Department of Health, 1999;

Mental Health Branch, 2004), but the values, knowledge and skills required to translate this into practice have not always been developed. Most important is the recognition of the unique knowledge and expertise that family members bring to bear on the situation, and a respect for the efforts that families have been making to address the difficulties they are experiencing. This requires an assumption of 'least pathology': family members undoubtedly will be experiencing problems when a family member has a mental illness, but this does not mean that families *are* the problem. It might be useful to conceptualise much of the work that needs to be done with families more as 'consultation' (Wynne, McDaniel and Weber, 1987; Wynne, 1994) than as therapy, treatment or even 'psycho-education'. The consultation model aims at a meaningful collaboration or equal partnership, which means that the 'consultant must approach the family as an entity that has its own needs, rights and responsibilities, which include, but go beyond, the impact of the patient's illness' (Wynne, 1994: 131).

On this basis, there are a number of practice issues that require skills and knowledge of social workers. The complex and often poorly under-stood emotions of loss, guilt, anger and shame that may be experienced by families with a mentally ill member call for a sensitive and skilful response (Bland, 1998; Davis and Schultz, 1998; Jones, 2004; Godress et al, 2005). It is often in the family setting that cultural differences come to the fore, adding additional complexities and opportunities. Here as elsewhere it is important to acknowledge 'the value of aspects of family and commu-nity structures and function, as opposed to problematising them and claiming superiority through offering new ways of being' (Burman, Gowrisunkur and Walker, 2003: 72). Where there is a particular context of oppression, as with Indigenous people (Westerman, 2004) and refugees (Walker, 2005), the challenges can be immense for a social worker, and here it may be especially important to operate from a broad psychosocial practice framework that incorporates community social work and group work.

The needs of children of people with a mental illness require special attention, because the impact on children's lives (for example, interaction with their parents and living arrangements) can be profound. Individual workers need to work to promote family wellbeing and reduce risk, to support families and their children, to specifically address grief and loss issues, ensure there is good access to information, education and decision-making, and to ensure the care and protection of children (Australian Infant, Child, Adolescent and Family Mental Health Association, 2004). Social workers thus need to pay particular attention to navigating the interrelationship between the child protection and mental health service systems in a way that protects and respects the needs and interests of children and their parents (Cousins, 2004) and, beyond this, to support adults in their parenting as much as possible, to contribute to optimal family functioning (Sayce, 1999) and to mediate any negative impacts

(Smith, 2004) and to ensure that children's own needs receive specific and sensitive attention (Cowling, 1999).

Partnership Principles in Working with Consumers and Family Carers

Since the development of the National Mental Health Strategy through the last 15 years there has been an emphasis on the inclusion of consumers and family carers in all aspects of service planning, implementation, and evaluation. As argued earlier in this chapter, engaging in collaborative endeavour, working in partnership, with both consumers and family carers is seen as fundamental to the practice of all of the mental health disciplines. The term 'partnership' implies that consumers and family carers work together with service providers towards common goals. It includes the concept of 'participation' (Bland, 2002) but extends this to suggest mutuality of endeavour and a sense of shared or more equal power.

There are many sites of the application of partnership and participation principles in mental health services. In all States there are services that employ people with mental health problems as 'consumer consultants' in the expectation that they will work as part of the multi-disciplinary team to provide a range of services for consumers. Advocacy for individuals is typically seen as an appropriate role for consumer consultants. Less commonly, family carers are also employed in services to support and advocate for the families of people receiving treatment and support from a service. Both consumers and family carers are also employed in management advisory roles in services provided by government and non-government organisations.

There is increasing evidence of the successful involvement of consumers and family carers in the education and training of the mental health workforce (Deakin Human Services, 1999). In Victoria, for example, NorthWestern Mental Health has employed a consumer educator as a member of their in-service education team. Both La Trobe University and the University of Tasmania have engaged consumer and family carers as partners in the development and teaching of mental health units in undergraduate and postgraduate teaching. At a broader policy level, consumers and family carers have been active members of Ministerial advisory bodies (Community Advisory Groups) and the Mental Health Council of Australia.

Beyond these formal sites for participation, a key area of activity remains the work between individual mental health practitioners and their clients. This remains, perhaps, the most challenging and poorly understood site for partnership. The questions here relate to the extent to which social workers and others can engage individual consumers, and their family carers, in activities that are experienced as respectful and empowering. If services are unable to provide their consumers and their families with such services, then the formal application of partnership principles in service management will be ineffective.

In reviewing the literature on consumer participation in mental health services, Bland (2002) argues that the arguments in favour of consumer participation can be reduced to two claims:

- Participation is a right of consumers. In any competitive market-place consumers of services can choose among competing options. Where no choice is possible, consumers have a right to be consulted about the nature of services provided.
- Participation ensures better services. When service providers consult consumers about the services provided then services are more responsive to consumer need. Participation then leads to better services.

He argues that there is, as yet, little empirical evidence to support the second proposition and that most services apply participation strategies to honour the principle of participation by right.

Developments in the area of education and training have provided a well-articulated rationale for the importance of partnership principles in mental health. The Deakin Human Services project 'Learning Together' (1999) engaged members of the mental health disciplines, including social work, with consumers and family carers in developing an agenda for the education and training of the mental health workforce. The project identified two principles of mental health that were considered fundamental to services. The first of these required that mental health professionals should value the lived experience of mental heath, of consumers and families, as a starting point for helping. The second required professionals to recognise the importance of the healing relationship as the basis for helping. These radical principles acknowledged that consumers and family carers were experts in the experience of both illness and treatments, and that a knowledge of, and respect for, that experience was essential to provide services. The principles suggest the importance of the human encounter, that helping comes through relationships, rather than the technology of helping. Once we accept the centrality of those principles, then working in partnership with consumers and family carers in all aspects of mental health care and education is essential to good practice.

While many services throughout Australia have attempted to apply participation or partnership principles with consumers and family carers, and a few exemplary models of service have been developed (Wadsworth, 2001), many problems remain. Working in partnership will mean giving consumers and family carers greater power to influence decision-making. The mental health workplace remains a site for intense inter-professional contestation (Bland and Renouf, 2001) and social workers usually do not feel particularly powerful themselves. Confronted with feelings of their own relative powerlessness, giving away power to consumers and families may not appeal. Secondly, it cannot be assumed that the interests and wishes of consumers and family carers are homogenous. On any one issue we can expect there to be many different consumer and family carer perspectives. It is probably better to speak of 'consumer and family perspectives' expecting a range of positions rather than a single position. How can we then accommodate many competing voices?

Consumer consultants struggle with trying to represent a wide diversity of consumers, with different types of mental illness and with varying degrees of disability. When employed by mental health services consumer consultants risk the danger of co-option by the system that employs them. How can they represent and advocate for individual consumers while they are employed by the service? The experience of mental illness, and the very qualities of sensitivity and compassion that consumers bring to their work, may make consumers more vulnerable to the stresses of working in the mental health system. Finally, many services are reluctant to provide sufficient resources to support effective consumer participation. All too frequently services might employ a single consumer or family carer consultant, ensuring the position is both highly isolated, but also carrying high expectations.

Despite these difficulties there are a number of best practice arrangements to ensure that social workers work more effectively in partnership with consumers and family carers.

- *Developing a respectful relationship* – Partnership starts with respecting the lived experience of mental illness, respecting that the consumer or family carer has special understandings about illness that complement the formal knowledge and skills of the worker. Developing partnership arrangements take time and commitment. Epstein (2004) calls the process of respectful sharing a 'deep dialogue'. In this process, consumers and workers can find shared understandings, and priorities for action.

- *Allocating resources* – For partnerships to work there must be adequate resources to support activity. For example, consumers invited to give lectures to students about mental illness have to be paid at standard rates. It may be necessary to invite a small group of consumers, rather than a single consumer, to contribute to a committee.

- *Timely consultation* – Real partnership may require consumer involvement at key points in a process. 'Consult early and often' is a good principle. There is little real respect for consumer input when researchers want to add the name of a high profile consumer to a research proposal at the last minute with a view to enhancing the appeal of the proposal to potential funding bodies.

- *Dealing with conflict* – Partnership includes the potential for conflict. Be prepared to work through potential conflicts in a respectful manner. Encouraging an independent and empowered consumer or family carer voice will invite the opportunity for productive disagreements.

Summary

Best practice in mental health social work should be based in a clear understanding of the social work domain, with an emphasis on the social context and consequences of mental illness, and social justice. The contemporary policy context offers a solid basis for community-based psychosocial interventions in collaboration with consumers and their families as the key stakeholders. There is a growing body of knowledge and evidence about effective work within case management models, and working with family carers, and in developing true and effective partnerships with consumers and family carers. Good social work practice in the mental health area requires a critical engagement with the developing knowledge and evidence base, interpreting and integrating this knowledge with the fundamental principles of social work practice.

Review Questions

1. What are the key principles of social work case management in mental health?
2. Why is it important for social workers to work with the families of people with serious mental illness?
3. What are the specific activities of working in partnership with consumers and family carers?
4. What are the values and areas of knowledge and skills that are unique to social work in the mental health area?

Useful Websites

Website of Sane Australia (extensive links to world wide mental health resources)	http://www.sane.org/
Beyondblue website (an excellent resource for depression)	http://www.beyondblue.org.au/
Sainsbury Centre for Mental Health (UK)	http://www.scmh.org.uk/
Social Perspectives Network for Modern Mental Health (UK)	http://www.spn.org.uk/

References

Anthony, WA, Cohen, M, Farkas, M and Cohen, BF (2000) 'Case management – More than a response to a dysfunctional system', *Community Mental Health Journal*, 36(1), 97-106.

Ash, D, Benson, A, Fielding, J, Fossey, E, McKendrick, J, Rosen, A, Singh, B and Weir, W (2001) 'Mental health services in Australia', in G Meadows and B Singh (eds) *Mental Health in Australia* (pp 51-66), Melbourne: Oxford University Press.

Australian Association of Social Workers (AASW) (1999) *Practice Standards for Social Work and Mental Health*, Canberra: Australian Association of Social Workers.

Australian Health Ministers (1991) *Mental Health Statement of Rights and Responsibilities*, Canberra: Australian Government Publishing.

Australian Health Ministers (1992a) *National Mental Health Policy*, Canberra: Australian Government Publishing.

Australian Health Ministers (1992b) *National Mental Health Plan*, Canberra: Australian Government Publishing.

Australian Health Ministers Advisory Council (1997) *National Service Standards for Mental Health Services*, Canberra: Commonwealth Department of Health and Family Services.

Australian Infant, Child, Adolescent and Family Mental Health Association (2004) *Principles and Actions for Services and People Working with Children of Parents with a Mental Illness*, Canberra: Commonwealth Department of Health and Ageing.

Bachrach, LL (1993) 'Continuity of care and approaches to case management for long-term mentally ill patients', *Hospital and Community Psychiatry*, 44(5), 465-468.

Bedell, JR, Cohen, NL and Sullivan, A (2000) 'Case management: The current best practices and the next generation of innovation', *Community Mental Health Journal*, 36(2), 179-194.

Björkman, T and Hansson, L (2000) 'What do case managers do? An investigation of case manager interventions and their relationship to client outcome', *Social Psychiatry and Psychiatric Epidemiology*, 35(1), 43-50.

Bland, R (1987) 'Social work with the family of the schizophrenic patient', *Australian Social* Work, 40(2), 25-30.

Bland, R (1998) 'Understanding grief and guilt as common themes in family response to mental illness', *Australian Social Work*, 51(4), 27-34.

Bland, R (2002) 'Policy reform in Australia and family roles: Learning from experience', in HP Lefley and DL Johnson (eds) *Family Interventions in Mental Illness: International Perspectives* (pp 195-208), Westport, Conn: Praeger.

Bland, R (2004) 'Social work practice in mental health', in M Alston and J McKinnon (eds) *Social Work: Fields of Practice* (pp 109-121), Melbourne: Oxford University Press.

Bland, R and Renouf, N (2001) 'Social work & the mental health team', *Australasian Psychiatry*, 19(3), 238-241.

Burman, E, Gowrisunkur, J and Walker, K (2003) 'Sanjhe Rang / Shared colours, shared lives: A multicultural approach to mental health practice', *Journal of Social Work Practice*, 17(1), 63-76.

Bustillo, JR, Lauriello, J, Horan, W and Keith, SJ (2001) 'The psychosocial treatment of schizophrenia: An update', *American Journal of Psychiatry*, 158(2), 163-175.

Commonwealth Department of Health and Ageing (2002) *National Mental Health Report 2002: Seventh Report. Changes in Australia's Mental Health Under the First*

Two Years of the Second National Mental Health Plan 1998-2000, Canberra: Commonwealth of Australia.

Cousins, C (2004) 'When is it serious enough? The problems of children of parents with a mental health problem, tough decisions, and avoiding a "martyred" child', *Australian e-Journal for the Advancement of Mental Health (AeJAMH)* 3(2). Available at: <http://www.auseinet.com/journal/vol3iss2/index.php>.

Cowling, V (1999) 'Providing services to children and families where the parent has a mental health problem: The Australian experience', in A Weir and A Douglas (eds) *Child Protection and Adult Mental Health: Conflict of Interest?* (pp 163-172), Oxford: Butterworth Heinemann.

Cuijpers, P (1999) 'The effects of family interventions on relatives' burden: A meta-analysis', *Journal of Mental Health,* 8(3), 275-285.

Davis, DJ and Schultz, CL (1998) 'Grief, parenting and schizophrenia', *Social Science and Medicine,* 46(3), 369-379.

Deakin Human Services (1999) *Learning Together: Education and Training Partnerships in Mental Health,* Canberra: Department of Health and Aged Care

Department of Health (1999) *National Service Frameworks for Mental Health: Modern Standards and Service Models,* London: Department of Health.

Department of Health (2002) *Developing Services for Carers and Families of People with Mental Illness,* London: Department of Health.

Department of Human Services (1998) *Individual Service Planning,* Melbourne: Department of Human Services.

Dewees, M (2002) 'Contested landscape: The role of critical dialogue for social work in mental health practice', *Journal. of Progressive Human Services,* 13(1), 73-91.

Dixon, L, Krauss, N and Lehman, A (1994) 'Consumers as service providers: The promise and challenge', *Community Mental Health Journal,* 30(6), 615-625.

Dixon, L, McFarlane, WR, Lefley, H, Lucksted, A, Cohen, M, Falloon, I, Mueser, K, Miklowitz, D, Solomon, P and Sondheimer, D (2001) 'Evidence-based practices for services to families of people with psychiatric disabilities', *Psychiatric Services,* 57(7), 903-910.

Dixon, LB and Lehman, AF (1995) 'Family interventions for schizophrenia', *Schizophrenia Bulletin,* 21(4), 631-643.

Epstein, M (2004) *Deep Dialogue* (Unpublished Manuscript).

Evidence-Based Medicine Working Group (EBMWG) (1992) 'Evidence-based medicine: A new approach to teaching the practice of medicine', *JAMA,* 268, 2420-2425.

Ferguson, H (2003) 'Outline of a critical best practice perspective on social work and social care', *British Journal of Social Work,* 33(8), 1005-1024.

Filc, D (2004) 'The medical text: Between biomedicine and hegemony', *Social Science and Medicine,* 59(6), 1275-1285.

Furlong, M (1997) 'How much care and how much control? Looking critically at case management', *Australian Journal of Primary Health – Interchange,* 3(4), 72-89.

Furlong, M and Leggatt, M (1996) 'Reconciling the patient's right to confidentiality and the family's need to know', *Australian and New Zealand Journal of Psychiatry,* 30(5), 614-622.

Gilgun, JF (2005) 'The four cornerstones of evidence-based practice in social work', *Research on Social Work Practice,* 15(1), 52-61.

Godress, J, Ozgul, S, Owen, C and Evans, LF (2005) 'Grief experiences of parents whose children suffer from mental illness', *Australian and New Zealand Journal of Psychiatry,* 39(1-2), 88-94.

Goldstein, MJ and Miklowitz, DJ (1995) 'The effectiveness of psychoeducational family therapy in the treatment of schizophrenic disorders', *Journal of Marital and Family Therapy,* 21(4), 361-376.

Gournay, K and Thornicroft, G (2002) 'A UK perspective on case management (letter)', *Australian and New Zealand Journal of Psychiatry*, 36(5), 701-702.

Groom, G and Hickie, I (2003) *Out of Hospital, Out of Mind!: A Review of Mental Health Services in Australia – 2003*, Canberra: Mental Health Council of Australia.

Harding, C, Zubin, J and Strauss, J (1992) 'Chronicity in schizophrenia: Revisited', *British Journal of Psychiatry*, 161(18), 27-37.

Hatfield, A and Lefley, H (1993) *Surviving Mental Illness: Stress, Coping & Adaptation*, New York: Guilford.

Hemming, M and Yellowlees, P (1997) 'An evaluation study of clinical case management using clinical case management standards', *Journal of Mental Health*, 6(6), 589-598.

Holloway, W (2001) 'The psycho-social subject in "evidence based practice"', *Journal of Social Work Practice*, 15(1), 9-22.

Howgego, IM, Yellowlees, P, Owen, C, Meldrum, L and Dark, FL (2003) 'The therapeutic alliance: The key to effective patient outcome? A descriptive review of the evidence in community mental health case management', *Australian and New Zealand Journal of Psychiatry*, 37(2), 169-183.

Hromco, JG, Lyons, JS and Nikkel, RE (1997) 'Styles of case management: The philosophy and practice of case managers', *Community Mental Health Journal*, 33(5), 415-428.

Huxley, P and Thornicroft, G (2003) 'Social inclusion, social quality and mental illness', *British Journal of Psychiatry*, 182(4), 289-290.

Intagliata, J (1982) 'Improving the quality of community care for the chronically mentally disabled: The role of case management', *Schizophrenia Bulletin*, 8(4), 655-674.

Jones, DW (2004) 'Families and serious mental illness: Working with loss and ambivalence', *British Journal of Social Work*, 34(7), 961-979.

Kanter, J (1989) 'Clinical case management: Definition, principles, components', *Hospital and Community Psychiatry*, 40(4), 361-368.

Mari, JDJ and Streiner, DL (1994) 'An overview of family interventions and relapse on schizophrenia: meta-analysis of research findings', *Psychological Medicine*, 24(3), 565-578.

Marshall, M and Lockwood, A (1998) 'Assertive community treatment for people with severe mental disorders', *Cochrane Database of Systematic Reviews 1998*, Issue 2, Chichester, West Sussex: John Wiley & Sons.

Marshall, M, Gray, A, Lockwood, A and Green, R (1998) 'Case management for people with severe mental disorders', *Cochrane Database of Systematic Reviews 1998*, Issue 2, Chichester, West Sussex: John Wiley & Sons.

McCabe, R and Priebe, S (2004) 'The therapeutic relationship in the treatment of severe mental illness: A review of methods and findings', *International Journal of Social Psychiatry*, 50(2), 115-128.

McFarlane, WR, Dixon, L, Lukens, E and Lucksted, A (2003) 'Family psycho-education and schizophrenia: A review of the literature', *Journal of Marital and Family Therapy*, 29(2), 223-245.

Meaden, A, Nithsdale, V, Rose, C, Smith, J and Jones, C (2004) 'Is engagement associated with outcome in assertive outreach?', *Journal of Mental Health*, 13(4), 415-424.

Mental Health Branch (2004) *Caring Together: An Action Plan for Carer Involvement in Victorian Public Mental Health Services*, Melbourne: Mental Health Branch, Department of Human Services.

Mental Health Commission (1998) *Blueprint for Mental Health Services*, Wellington: Mental Health Commission

Mental Health Commission (2003) *Report on Progress 2001-2002*, Wellington: Mental Health Commission.

Morley, C (2003) 'Towards critical social work practice in mental health: A review', *Journal of Progressive Human Services*, 14(1), 61-84.

Mowbray, CT and Holter, MC (2002) 'Mental health and mental illness: Out of the closet?' *Social Service Review*, 76(1), 135-179.

Mueser, KT and Bond, GR (2000) 'Psychosocial treatment approaches for schizophrenia', *Current Opinion in Psychiatry*, 13(January), 27-35.

Murphy, A and McDonald, J (2004) 'Power, status and marginalisation: Rural social workers and evidence-based practice in multidisciplinary teams', *Australian Social Work*, 57(2), 127-136.

Mykhalovskiy, E and Weir, L (2004) 'The problem of evidence-based medicine: Directions for social science', *Social Science and Medicine*, 59(5), 1059-1069.

National Association of Social Workers (NASW) (1992) *NASW Standards for Social Work Case Management*, Washington DC: NASW.

Phillips, SD, Burns, BJ, Edgar, ER, Mueser, KT, Linkins, KW, Rosenheck, RA, Drake, RE and McDonel Herr, EC (2001) 'Moving assertive community treatment into standard practice', *Psychiatric Services*, 52(6), 771-779.

Pitschel-Walz, G, Leucht, S, Bauml, J, Kissling, W and Engle, RR (2001) 'The effect of family interventions on relapse and rehospitalization in schizophrenia: A meta-analysis', *Schizophrenia Bulletin*, 27(1), 73-92.

Psychiatric Services Branch (1994) *Victoria's Mental Health Services: Improved Access through Coordinated Client Care*, Melbourne: Department of Health and Community Services.

Rapp, C (1998) *The Strengths Model: Case Management with People Suffering from Severe and Persistent Mental Illness*, New York: Oxford University Press.

Rose, N (1998) 'Governing risky individuals: The role of psychiatry in new regimes of control', *Psychiatry, Psychology and Law*, 5(2), 177-195.

Rosen, A and Teesson, M (2001) 'Does case management work? The evidence and the abuse of evidence-based medicine', *Australian and New Zealand Journal of Psychiatry*, 35(6), 731-746.

Royal Australian and New Zealand College of Psychiatrists (2005) 'Clinical practice guidelines for the treatment of schizophrenia and related disorders', *Australian and New Zealand Journal of Psychiatry*, 39(1-2), 1-30.

Saleebey, D (1996) 'The strengths perspective in social work practice: Extensions and cautions' *Social Work*, 41(3), 296-305.

Sands, R (2001) *Clinical Social Work in Behavioural Mental Health*, Boston: Allyn & Bacon.

Sayce, L (1999) 'Parenting as a civil right: Supporting service users who choose to have children', in A Weir and A Douglas (eds) *Child Protection and Adult Mental Health: Conflict of Interest?* (pp 28-48), Oxford: Butterworth Heinemann.

Schaedle, RW and Epstein, I (2000) 'Specifying intensive case management: A multiple perspective approach', *Mental Health Services Research*, 2(2), 95-105.

Sheldon, B (2001) 'The validity of evidence-based practice in social work: A reply to Stephen Webb', *British Journal of Social Work*, 31(5), 801-809.

Sherman, PS and Porter, R (1991) 'Mental health consumers as case management aides', *Hospital and Community Psychiatry*, 42(5), 494-498.

Sherman, PS and Ryan, CS (1998) 'Intensity and duration of intensive case management services', *Psychiatric Services*, 49(12), 1585-1589.

Simpson, A, Miller, C and Bowers, L (2003) 'Case management models and the care programme approach: How to make the CPA effective and credible', *Journal of Psychiatric Mental Health Nursing*, 10(4), 472-483.

Singer, PA and Todkill, AM (2000) 'Bioethics for clinicians', *Canadian Medical Association Journal*, 163(7), 833.

Smith, M (2004) 'Parental mental health: Disruptions to parenting and outcomes for children', *Child and Family Social Work*, 9(1), 3-11.

Solomon, P (1994) 'Response to "Consumers as service providers: the promise and challenge"', *Community Mental Health Journal*, 30(6), 631-634.

Solomon, P and Draine, J (1995) 'Adaptive coping among family members of persons with a serious mental illness', *Psychiatric Services*, 46(11), 1156-1160.

Tanenbaum, S (2003) 'Evidence-based practice in mental health: Practical weaknesses meet political strengths, *Journal of Evaluation in Clinical Practice*, 9(2), 287-301.

Test, MA (1998) 'Community-based treatment models for adults with severe and persistent mental illness', in J Williams and K Ell (eds) *Advances in Mental Health Research* (pp 420-436), Washington DC: NASW.

Thyer, B (2001) 'Evidence-based practice and clinical social work', *Evidence Based Mental Health*, 5(1), 5-7.

Trevillion, S (1999) *Networking and Community Partnership*, Aldershot: Ashgate.

Wadsworth, Y (ed) (2001) *The Essential U & I*, Melbourne: VicHealth.

Walker, S (2005) 'Towards culturally competent practice in child and adolescent mental health, *International Social Work*, 48(1), 49-62.

Webb, S (2001) 'Some considerations on the validity of evidence-based practice in social work', *British Journal of Social Work*, 31(5), 57-79.

Westerman, T (2004) 'Guest editorial: Engagement of indigenous clients in mental health services: What role do cultural differences play?', *Australian e-Journal of the Advancement of Mental Health*, 3(3). Available at: <http://www.auseinet. com/journal/vol3iss3/westermaneditorial.pdf>.

Woodbridge, K and Fulford, KWM (2004) *Whose Values? A Workbook or Values-based Practice in Mental Health Care*, London: Sainsbury Centre for Mental Health.

World Fellowship for Schizophrenia and Associated Disorders (1999) *FPC (Families as Partners in Care) Goals and Principles.* Available at <http:// www.world-schizophrenia.org/activities/fpc/principles.html>

Wynne, LC (1994) 'The rationale for consultation with the families of schizo-phrenic patients', *Acta Psychiatrica Scandinavica*, 90(384), 125-132.

Wynne, LC, McDaniel, SH and Weber, T (1987) 'Professional politics and the concepts of family therapy, family consultation, and systems consultation', *Family Process*, 26(2), 149-166.

Ziguras, SJ and Stuart, GW (2000) 'A meta-analysis of the effectiveness of mental health case management over 20 years', *Psychiatric Services*, 51(11), 1410-1421.

Chapter 6

Disability

Lesley Chenoweth

Introduction

Providing services and supports to people with a disability and their families constitutes a major site for social work and human service practice. Practitioners are likely to meet people with disabilities in many practice contexts. For example, hospital social work and community health services, family support services and employment services all include people with disabilities. In other contexts, services and programs are provided specifically for people with disabilities and their families. These include for example, community living services for adults with disabilities, rehabilitation programs following accident or injury, family support and respite services for families of children with a disability and early intervention programs for young children with developmental disabilities.

This chapter provides an overview of practice in the disability field and presents a number of approaches which are well-established and acknowledged as best practice in this field. The chapter first outlines the overall context of disability practice in terms of policy and legislative frameworks and then elucidates the theoretical underpinnings of our understandings of disability, and the theories and meanings that influence service delivery and practice. The major issues confronting people with disability and families and the corresponding contexts of practice are then presented. Several key approaches widely adopted in disability practice: person-centred practice, family-centred practice and the strength perspective, are then covered. Finally, some conclusions about what constitutes best practice in this field are offered.

Policy and Legislative Context
of the Disability Field

Unravelling the web of policies and legislation that impact on the lives of people with disabilities and their families is an extremely complex task. Policy occurs at international, national and local levels, all of which have distinct features of operation and outcomes. Policies addressing disability issues also cover a number of portfolios and all levels of government in Australia.

International level policy and law on disability is best represented by the major instruments or covenants that have been developed by the United Nations. These are the International Declaration on the Rights of Mentally Retarded Persons, 1971, the International Declaration on the Rights of Disabled Persons, 1975 and Principles for the Treatment of People with Mental Illness, 1992. These instruments contain basic statements about the human rights of people with disabilities and have been developed through lengthy negotiation, discussion and debate by member nations. Member nations then sign these agreements in two stages, first as signatories to the covenant and subsequently as ratifiers by bringing national legislation into line with the international principles.

There are criticisms of these human rights instruments. It is argued that existing instruments about human rights generally should provide sufficient coverage for all people including people with disabilities and that having separate declarations for special groups further creates difference and segregation. There are also problems of implementation of these human rights. The United Nations instruments do not carry any obligations on the part of initial signatories to implement them or penalties for failure to execute them. The only safeguard lies in the public 'face' of member nations and the pressure for signatories to introduce legislative and policy measures in their own countries to reflect the human rights principles. Despite these criticisms, United Nations declarations have provided a powerful reference point for nations to consult in the development of disability policies and are often held up as standards by which to gauge these national policies. Currently, the United Nations is developing a new convention on the Rights and Dignity of People with Disabilities.

DeJong (1994) proposed a useful framework of disability law and policy around three aspects. These are: (1) legislation around protection of rights (for example, *Disability Discrimination Act 1992* (Cth)); (2) policies about programs or services for people with disabilities (for example, special education policies, vocational rehabilitation or disability services); and (3) policies about income maintenance or financial assistance (for example, pensions or benefits for people with disabilities and carers, medical insurance).

The framework underscores the broad scope of disability policy and is useful especially for those involved in service provision and practitioners, in that it highlights the poor synchronisation of these three policy arenas. In addition to disability specific policies, other aspects of broad public policy also impact on people with disabilities. These include for example health, transport, taxation, education and housing policies which may impact directly, for example the provision of wheelchairs through health policy or indirectly, for example a free trade agreement which might raise the cost of medications.

In Australia, all levels of government have different policy and program responsibilities for and responses to disability. The Commonwealth historically had carriage of the funding and provision of disability services, but handed over many programs to the States in the early 1990s. The Commonwealth provides pensions and benefits for disabled people and their families and carers, funds supported employment programs and some advocacy. Under regularly negotiated agreements between the Commonwealth, States and Territories, the Commonwealth States and Territories Disability Agreement, the States are funded to provide accommodation support, family support, respite, community access and post-school services. The States also have responsibility for the education of all children, including those with disabilities, health services that are particularly important for people with disabilities such as the provision of aids and equipment and accessible public housing. Local governments are more sporadic in their approaches to disability issues. Disability provisions by local governments include ensuring that public and civic amenities such as libraries, swimming pools and public transport are accessible. Social workers therefore can be involved at individual, family and community levels to achieve positive changes for people with disabilities.

Definitions of Disability

How disability is defined is crucial in terms of how or even whether we see the 'problem' of disability and therefore what services and interventions are deemed appropriate and most effective. The term disability has multiple meanings and definitions, and various pieces of legislation, policies and programs will define 'disability' in ways that reflect different goals and purviews. There are also quite contested theoretical and ideological debates around disability and different theoretical positions will determine the kind of interventions that practitioners employ. This can be very confusing for workers, policy makers and for disabled people trying to navigate their way through different programs.

International World Health Organization Definitions

Historically, the most commonly adopted definition of disability was that developed by the World Health Organization (WHO). The original definition incorporated three constructs as follows:

- *Impairment* – In the context of health experience, an impairment is any loss or abnormality of psychological, physiological or anatomical structure or function.

- *Disability* – In the context of health experience, a disability is any restriction or lack (resulting from impairment) of ability to perform an activity in the manner or within the range considered for a normal human being.

- *Handicap* – In the context of health experience, a handicap is a disadvantage for a given individual, resulting from an impairment or a disability, that limits or prevents the fulfilment of a role that is normal (depending on age, sex and social and cultural factors) for that individual (Wood, 1980: 27-29).

This framework, while adopted almost universally for many years, was problematic in that it fragmented the disability experience into categories that were not always so neatly divisible. It also assumed that there was a universal 'normal' experience and that the disabling process was a series of linearly progressive experiences. Addressing these limitations of the old definition, WHO revised a classification system for disability, the International Classification of Functioning, Disability and Health (ICF) which lays out different components of the disabling process in an integrated model comprised of several broad areas. This is depicted in Figure 6.1. Within this framework, the various components are defined as follows.

Figure 6.1 The ICF framework

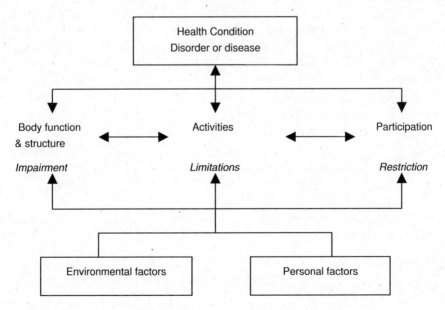

Source: World Health Organization (2002: 9)

1. Body functions and structures are classified by physiological functions (for example, mental, sensory, digestive, neuromusculo-skeletal) or anatomical parts of the body (for example, eye, ear, skin, limbs).

2. Activities are classified by person level tasks or actions (for example, learning, moving around, personal care).

3. Participation is classified by life situations (for example, work, school, community, leisure).

4. Environment is classified by the physical, social and attitudinal factors that form the background for a person's life (for example, natural surroundings, buildings, societal attitudes, government policies) (Lollar, 2002).

This expanded the constructs around the experience of disability and included a more comprehensive conceptual map for theory and practice in disability through a person-in-environment framework. It can be argued that this framework reflects a generic social work approach whereby interventions can be undertaken at personal and environmental levels either separately or in conjunction with each other.

Alternative Definitions

Many disabled people, however, regarded these frameworks as oppressive and place disability within the individual. Their critique argued that medical and individual models of disability fail to take sufficient account of the social barriers which constitute the real 'problem' of disability – that is, disabling environments, rather than individual or personal pathology. An alternative definition to the original WHO model developed by disabled people in Britain challenged the medical model inherent in the WHO definition. Oliver (1990), citing the UPIAS (Union of the Physically Impaired Against Segregation) 1976 classification, proposed a re-definition thus:

- *Impairment* – lacking part or all of a limb, or having a defective limb, organism or mechanism, of the body.
- *Disability* – the disadvantage or restriction of activity caused by a contemporary social organisation which takes little or no account of people who have physical impairments and thus excludes them from the mainstream of social activities.

These differing definitions reflect the different ways in which disability and impairment have been theorised.

Theories of Disability

Theories offer explanations for human behaviour and human problems. They also guide practice and allow, to a certain extent, the prediction of outcomes of interventions. We have seen that taking a different perspective on defining disability can profoundly change the sort of approach you would take in treatment or support. Similarly, the ways which disability is theorised informs how we understand the experience of disability and what kinds of interventions might be employed to provide support or solutions. There are numerous theories of disability which have informed disability services and practice with disabled people and families. These can be grouped into two broad theoretical approaches: individual models and social models.

Individual Models

Individual models adopt the position that disability is located within the individual person either as some form of tragedy, disease, flaw or moral failing. These models place responsibility for disability somewhere in the individual.

Personal Tragedy Theory

Personal tragedy theory suggests that disability is a tragic happening that occurs to unfortunate isolated individuals on a random basis. Responses to this 'personal tragedy' are therefore designed to compensate for the imperfection, to offer therapies to treat or cure it or to counsel and support the individual's adjustment to the tragedy (Borsay, 1986). The nature of the tragedy can be explained through religion, for example, as punishment for the 'sins of the father' or through medical science, for example as the result of a genetic flaw or infection. It has been argued that current disability services and policies are primarily based on this view of disability (Rioux, 1996).

This model came under criticism particularly from writers with disabilities (Morris, 1989; Oliver, 1990, 1996). The problem argued was that it was limited in its cultural and historic application. In many societies and in Western cultures at different times, disability or impairments are ascribed varied value status, ranging from very positive, through neutral to extremely negative. For the residents of Martha's Vineyard, an island off Massachusetts, for example, being deaf was not a personal tragedy since every member of the community used sign language (Groce, 1985).

The significant corollary to a personal tragedy perspective on disability is that the role of society is ignored and people with disabilities are marginalised, fragmented and dislocated. An alternative argument is proposed by supporters of the social model and is discussed later in the chapter.

The Medical Model

Medical explanations of disability and impairment began with the Enlightenment in the 18th century when advances in science and medicine began to be made. Medical understandings of the causes of disability and how we should treat it have progressed from that time for more than 200 years. The medical model has dominated disability policies and services for many decades and continues to influence disability services and rehabilitation programs.

A basic assumption of the medical model is that people with disabilities have some defect or lack of a vital bodily function, such as sight, hearing, mobility, speech or cognition. The fundamental focus is on a person's deficits in these realms. Such deficits may be related to a disease – for example unborn babies being exposed to German Measles in utero resulting in blindness at birth; or an accident, for example spinal cord injury in a motor vehicle accident resulting in paraplegia. Interventions based on the medical model are therefore focused on the processes of *diagnosis* – what is the cause of the deficit?, and *treatment* – how can we cure the deficit or reduce it to a level for normal functioning.

Another key feature of the medical model is the classification and measurement of disability. The search for causes has led to a vast array of tests and measures of levels of functioning in order to determine deficits and disability. These tests are widely used to determine the level and kind of vision and hearing impairments, for example, but also include the use of intelligence quotient (IQ) tests to determine intellectual disability. The currently used definition of intellectual disability includes a score of 70 or below on a standardised IQ test (American Association for Mental Retardation (AAMR), 2002). The use of medical tests to determine disability has now expanded into the realm of prenatal testing whereby many genetically based disabilities such as Down syndrome and other congenital disabilities such as spina bifida are diagnosed before birth. These developments have raised many ethical questions and dilemmas for practice but such tests are now almost universally used throughout the developed world. For example, you could be involved in supporting parents with one child with a congenital disability make decisions whether to test in a subsequent pregnancy.

Most people with disabilities have considerable contact with medical services and health professionals and many interventions based on this model have provided invaluable supports for people with disabilities and have contributed to improved quality of life. However, it has also been widely critiqued for its deficit orientation and failure to take into account the social aspects of disability – that is, how disability is viewed and constructed by society. The medical model is also a norm-based approach – it assumes that there is a normal or right way of doing things and that disabled people are therefore deviant from that norm.

Social Models

Social or societal models of disability were developed throughout the 20th century in response to the growing realisation that society had a key role in the defining and maintenance of disability (Rothman, 2003). These models adopt the standpoint that disability is socially constructed, that is, that disability is created, promoted and exacerbated by society and the environment.

Disability as Deviancy and Difference

A group of theories from the mid-20th century which addressed notions of individual difference and societal responses to that difference had implications for disability. Concepts of social roles, deviance and labelling suggested that individual differences in appearance and behaviour are regarded as negative by others in the social group who then exclude and marginalise those who exhibit these differences. The general theories of deviancy, labelling and stigma are especially relevant for disability.

Deviancy theories occupy a significant place in sociology and, while largely concerned with criminality, have been applied to the situation of people with disabilities. The most notable contributions addressing disability specifically have been those works on stigma (Goffman, 1963) and asylums and institutions (Goffman, 1961).

This work addressed the issue of stigma in the lives of people with disabilities and historically was important in that it made the first real challenges to the orthodox view of the times that the problems of disability were individually determined. Rather, this theory argued that the problems of disability were socially determined rather than the result of individual impairments.

> [A]n individual who might have been received easily in ordinary social intercourse possesses a trait that can obtrude itself upon attention and turn those of us whom he meets away from him, breaking the claim that his other attributes have on us. He possesses a stigma, an undesired differentness from what we had anticipated ... we believe the person with a stigma is not quite human. On this assumption we exercise varieties of discrimination, through which we effectively, if often unthinkingly, reduce his life chances. (Goffman, 1963: 5)

Their work was based on participant observation in institutions and in spending time with people with disabilities living in the community. For the first time, researchers began to experience at close hand the process of stigmatisation of those viewed as different. They described how people with impairments are aware of how those differences are deeply discrediting and will attempt to disguise or deny them, a process which Goffman called 'passing'. It is interesting to note that both Goffman (1963) and Edgerton (1967) found that to have an intellectual disability was the most stigmatised condition because it was impossible to remove that label once it was applied. To be judged as 'mentally retarded', as it was termed at that time, meant that one was viewed as incompetent in all areas of one's life and people so labelled would go to extreme lengths to avoid disclosing the fact.

Normalisation and Social Role Valorisation Theories

These theories provided another perspective on understanding the experience of disability from a societal perspective. They were also influential in the development of disability policies and services, and the closure of institutions in Australia.

Two formulations of normalisation were developed: one from Scandinavia (Nirje, 1969) and another by Wolfensberger (1980), initially in North America. Nirje advocated that people with intellectual disability should be able to live the patterns and conditions of everyday life which are as close as possible to the norms and patterns of the mainstream of society. Wolfensberger (1980) defined normalisation as:

> Utilization of culturally normative means (familiar, valued techniques, tools, methods), in order to enable a person's life conditions (income, housing, health services etc) which are at least as good as that of average citizens, and to as much as possible, enhance or support their behaviour (skills, competencies, etc), appearances (clothes, grooming etc), experiences (adjustment, feelings etc) and status and reputation (labels, attitudes of others etc). (p 80)

Inherent in this definition is an endorsement of the relationship between the individual (behaviour, skills, appearance) and society (housing, income, attitudes of others) though the emphasis is obviously towards the individual.

A central tenet of Wolfensberger's theory is what he termed the 'universal dynamics of societal devaluation' (1992: 2). This argument proposes the following process whereby people with disabilities experience devaluation. First, the perspective argues, all human perceptual processes are evaluative – it is impossible to have value free or neutral perception. This means that our perceptions of other people are also value laden and some people will be perceived and valued negatively, that is, devalued. When people are devalued in this way, they are more likely to be treated badly and experience what Wolfensberger calls 'wounds'. These wounds include: being rejected, separated and excluded from the mainstream; being denied or afforded poorer housing, healthcare and education; and being denied rights, autonomy and participation in the valued world. Wolfensberger then argues that when this devaluation takes place on the level of a social collectivity or even an entire society, devalued classes are created who systematically receive poor treatment 'at the hands of societal structures ... including formal, organized human services' (p 3).

Wolfensberger asserted that those most likely to be devalued in Western societies are people who are 'impaired or handicapped'; who are 'seriously disordered in their conduct or behaviour'; those who 'rebel against the social order'; the poor; people who have few or unwanted skills; and finally others who are unassimilated into the culture for other reasons (for example, the elderly, the unborn, racial and ethnic minorities).

Wolfensberger (1983) later developed social role valorisation theory (SRV) which he defined as 'the creation, maintenance and defense of valued social roles for people, particularly those at value risk, by the use, as much as possible, of culturally valued means' (p 234). The central construct of *social roles* forms the basis for Wolfensberger's theory. He postulated that people with disabilities are at serious risk of being cast into negative social roles, which include the following:

- *Other* – the person with a disability marginalised as other to the dominant social group;
- *Non-human* – to be regarded as either sub-human, animal, vegetable or object;
- *Menace* – to be regarded as a threat to be feared, an annoyance or an object of dread;
- *Object of Ridicule* – to be regarded as a something to be made fun of or as trivial;
- *Object of Pity* – to be regarded as a tragic victim;
- *Burden of Charity* – to be regarded as a drain on the goodwill of others or the public purse;
- *Diseased Organism* – that is, as sick;
- *Child* – to be regarded as either perpetually a child (in the case of people with intellectual disability) or as returning to childhood (the elderly or people with acquired brain injuries); and
- *Dead or Dying* – to be regarded as better off dead, nearly dead or as already dead

(adapted from Wolfensberger, 1992: 10-12).

The main critiques of normalisation and SRV include those within the feminist disability literature (for example, Brown and Smith, 1989) who drew parallels between the people with disabilities and women in our society. This thesis argues that normalisation, as an apolitical and individualistic principle or theory, does not take into account the advantages of the collective approach to enhancing the lives of people with disabilities.

Chappell (1992) argued that normalisation does not address the power relationship between able-bodied professionals and disabled service users. She claimed that normalisation reflects the views, concerns and values of professionals rather than those of the people with disabilities and as such fails to take into account how disability is socially constructed in the establishment of services and policies which effectively disempower and impoverish people with disabilities.

113

Normalisation has also been criticised for failing to celebrate difference, rather focusing on the requirement that people with disabilities need to change or modify their behaviours and images to appear 'normal' (summarised in Race, Boxall and Carson, 2005). Normalisation has been widely used by service planners and policy makers, though the tendency to 'hypernormalisation' has occurred. For example, some proponents of so-called normalisation might advocate imprisonment of offenders with intellectual disability as the normative response. There remains a question as to the universality of normalisation, that is, how far should its application be taken and to what extent does it imply an intolerance of difference. Wolfensberger (1998) offered a re-definition of SRV that addressed some of these concerns:

> SRV is a systematic effort to extract empirical knowledge that can be applied in service of the valuation of people's roles, so that they are more likely to have access to the good life, or the good things of life. Any action that accords with role-defense or role-upgrading can be said to be role-valorizing. (p 58)

What Wolfensberger appeared to be intending here is that SRV can be used universally in all cultures and that this formulation will not make any judgments about what is culturally valued.

Normalisation and SRV had a profound impact on policies and services for people with disabilities for at least two decades from the 1980s. As well as offering a theoretical basis for planning and delivering services, they also offered a framework for understanding the experience of disability as one of rejection and devaluation. In the past 10 to 15 years however, new theories of disability moved the focus away from the individual to the wider society and these are now discussed.

The Social Model of Disability

The social model of disability emerged initially in the United Kingdom and proposed that disability was the result of social barriers, not individual problems. The argument that disability is the result of social oppression rather than the limits of individuals forms the basis of a number of social theories of disability.

The developments in social models of disability occurred in the United States and in Britain but had different social and academic origins in each context. In the United States, social theories of disability have been a progression from functionalism and deviancy theories discussed earlier. In Britain, they have been drawn from materialist theories of Marx and Engels and 'suggest that disability and dependence are the "social creation" of a particular type of social formation; namely, industrial capitalism' (Barnes, 1996: 44).

Oliver (1990) argued that capitalism with its implicit valuing of productive people, played a powerful role in this construction of disability. Oliver used the term 'surplus population thesis' which subscribes to the idea that in economically vulnerable societies, any weak dependent members who threaten the survival of the majority will be abandoned or cast out. In capitalist societies, a core value is the capacity to work productively and participate in the market. People with disabilities are not regarded as productive and therefore more likely to be excluded from the economy and therefore society. Economic determinism is not the only factor here. Values and ideology influence social practices in relation to people with disabilities in capitalist societies (Wolfensberger, 1983; McKnight, 1988).

In the United States, an expression of the social model has been the *minority group approach* (Hahn, 1994). In this model, people with disabilities are seen as an oppressed group that needs to mobilise and become politicised. The disabled group is regarded as possessing the same characteristics of other minorities based on race, gender or ethnicity. This approach is associated with the growth of the disability movement in North America in which disabled people form a powerful lobby to government for resources to meet their needs. It differs from the British social model in that it has tended to opt for special measures that focus on the disability (for example, rights to physical access) rather than advocating for broader social changes that affect the entire community.

There are limits, however, to the extent to which the social model of disability can address some of the most complex issues that people with disabilities encounter. It has been argued that the social model is too formulaic and simplistic and therefore cannot adequately address the individual experiences of impairment (French, 1993; Corker and Shakespeare, 2002). These writers argue that there are many experiences of impairment that simply cannot be addressed through social manipulation. The social model has also been criticised for its failure to include experiences of people with intellectual disabilities. Many people with intellectual disability have been excluded from debates by proponents of the social model (Goodley, 2000, 2001).

Disabled Identity

From the shortcoming of the social model and as a development from the minority group approach, a shift has emerged towards discussions about disabled identity (Shakespeare, 1996; Peters, 2000; Putnam, 2005). In this approach, disability is viewed as an integral part of the person and thus should be accepted as part of that person's identity. Disability and identity theories operate in several important ways. Shakespeare (1996) has suggested that disability identification operates on three levels: the political (disability activism), the cultural (disability arts) and the personal (understanding one's own experiences).

The notion of the development of a normative social identity across the life course is potentially disrupted by the experiences that having an impairment brings to that process of identity formation. In this schema, being born with a certain impairment is said to have very different impact than acquiring a disability later along the life course (Barnes and Mercer, 2003). What is important is the establishment of one's identity that includes, but it is not limited to, one's impairments. For example, Shakespeare (1996) has argued that post-structural approaches to identity might provide better ways of understanding the complexities of the lived experiences of people.

The issue of identity politics has also made an important contribution to theories about disability. In this line of argument, the importance of the disability movement and collective political actions is viewed as a primary source of a strong disability identity (Barnes, Mercer and Shakespeare, 1999). The disabled identity is one adopted with pride just as activists in the women's and gay rights movements have done in previous social and political movements. Identity politics provide a means by which disabled people can become empowered and involved in directing their own agendas rather than being 'done to' by other experts. It also provides opportunities for young disabled people to identify with a collective group with purpose and solidarity.

It is clear that different theoretical approaches will offer different possibilities for practice. Practitioners have a number of options for their work based not only on what kind of theoretical approach best fits with their practice framework but also what theories inform and guide the organisations they work for. For example, working to support a self-advocacy organisation or with a group lobbying for improved access to transport will be best suited to social model approaches. On the other hand, working in a rehabilitation setting with people with spinal cord injuries will be more oriented to medical model approaches. The kind of experiences that many disabled people encounter in their lives will also direct and influence the theoretical approaches we might adopt in our practice.

Key Disability Issues and their Implications for Practice

Most disabled people's experiences are ones of social exclusion, across some or all of the major domains of one's life. Many people with disabilities typically seek the same things in life as everyone else at the corresponding life stage. Just as being part of a family, going to school, getting a degree, a good job, finding a life partner, socialising with friends, having a spiritual life and being part of one's society and culture might be what most people seek in life, so too do most people with disabilities.

Much social work and human service practice in this field involves providing support to access all of these life domains and practitioners may therefore be involved in assisting people and their families to achieve ordinary lives. This kind of practice can be viewed as aligned with theories of normalisation and social role valorisation. The practitioner works alongside the person to support them in attaining or defending ordinary social roles.

Having equity of access to education, employment, transport and other community services and facilities is an ongoing issue for many people with disabilities, many of whom face physical and attitudinal barriers to achieving this. For example, many forms of public transport are not accessible to people in wheelchairs so they have to rely on a sub-sidised but still expensive and inadequate taxi service. This means that disabled people often have to forgo outings or experiences simply because they cannot get to the venue. Many express frustration at not being able to spontaneously meet a friend for coffee or decide to stay on at a club or party until three in the morning because they are not able to simply call a cab or catch a bus when they want to.

Attitudinal barriers also limit work options for people with disabilities. Employers may be reluctant to hire a person with a disability even if they have the same qualifications as a non-disabled person because they think the person will not be a reliable or productive worker. Many people with disabilities are therefore unemployed or underemp-loyed in mundane jobs. This in turn continues the cycle of poverty for people with disabilities. Social workers therefore may be involved in advocacy on behalf of disabled people with employers, or involved in campaigns to lobby for equal rights for jobs.

Practice approaches addressing these issues can be more readily conceptualised through the social model approach. Coming to grips with the seemingly insurmountable barriers faced by many disabled people can be a challenging experience for practitioners. However, an analysis based on the social model can be a useful and practical way forward. It enables practice that aims to empower the person through offering an alternative framework – one which does not focus on individual deficits or blame. It can also seek to involve them in collective action for change.

Disability is regarded as a stigma in many societies and people can experience rejection, marginalisation, exclusion and oppression in a number of ways. Many people with disabilities, especially those with intellectual or cognitive impairments, are very socially isolated with few friends and relationships outside their families and paid service person-nel. Even when living in ordinary community settings many people may not participate in their local community in a real sense. Working in these situations may involve exploring the person's likes, dislikes and goals and locating opportunities and resources to support more participation in community life.

The majority of people with disabilities live with their families even well into adulthood, so practitioners work alongside families in many situations. This can be at the point of diagnosis supporting new parents who have been told their baby has a disability through to assisting families to plan for their adult son or daughter to move into independent living in their own home. Much of this work involves planning with families around support needs for their family member and then obtaining and coordinating services and supports to meet those needs. In most situations practitioners work in a climate of unmet need whereby the demand for services and supports for families far exceed the service systems' capacities to meet them.

Family members are also likely to be socially isolated because of the time taken with providing care and negotiating the various systems of services. The coordination of medical and therapy services, attending meetings to enrol and attend school, applying for aids and equipment and so on is usually undertaken by parents. Families express this coordination as a constant but vital task requiring advocacy on behalf of their family member (Chenoweth, 1996). Siblings of children with a disability experience a range of psychological and social impacts from having a brother or sister with particular needs.

Some people with disability (for example with severe intellectual disability and some forms of cerebral palsy) do not communicate verbally so establishing a relationship requires patience and learning new ways to communicate. Also many people with an intellectual disability may not be able to make decisions without assistance or may require a substitute decision-maker. This can involve legal processes or statutory authorities especially in decisions about medical treatments or financial matters.

Finally, people with disability have higher incidences of all forms of abuse. Those with no verbal communication are particularly vulnerable to sexual abuse and physical abuse is a fairly common occurrence in residential facilities (Sobsey, 1994). There are few services and supports available for victims of abuse, who are often traumatised by these events.

This section has explored some of the issues confronting people with disabilities and their families and considered the implications for theory and practice. The following section sets out in more detail some of the practice approaches used in the disability field.

Practice Approaches

Practitioners working in the disability sector adopt many practice methods working with individuals and families, group work, community work, policy practice, social action or political advocacy. Most social work practice approaches and methods are applied in this field of practice; however, there are several key approaches which are most commonly encountered and which most practitioners will work within. We first explore these through a broad distinction between macro and micro practice approaches, and then investigate three major approaches in more detail.

Macro Practice

Macro practice is work directed at bringing about change in organisations, policy and communities. Examples are as follows.

- *Advocacy* – arguing, debating and negotiating the environment to obtain necessary resources and supports for a client. Advocacy can also occur on a systems level – for example, advocating on behalf of a group of people with disabilities for better physical access.

- *Social and Political Action* – underpinned by social justice, working for change in attitudes, policies and behaviours. For example, being part of a movement to close institutions and establish community living options.

- *Community Development Work* – for example working within communities to raise awareness of disability issues, maximise inclusion or attitude change.

Micro Practice

Micro practice is intervention directed largely at the individual or group level. Examples are as follows.

- *Case Management* – This approach is widely used in disability programs, especially when the disability is severe and long term and where the person has little or no support systems. This usually adopts a person-in-environment perspective and provides individualised counselling to clients and links them to services and informal networks in the community. Case management involves both micro and macro practice (Rothman, 1991).

- *Group Work* – In many agencies group approaches can be effective, especially when there is an educational goal. For example working with a group of young women with intellectual disability to develop self-esteem and protective behaviours.

- *Crisis Intervention* – This approach can offer immediate intervention when disability is newly acquired or diagnosed and thus can be seen as precipitating the crisis or when other crises (such as divorce or natural disasters) impact on people with disabilities.

- *Family-centred Practice* – regarding the whole family as the focus of intervention rather than the person with a disability.

- *Working with Strengths* – strengths perspective (Saleeby, 2006) is now widely used in developmental disability practice.

Person-centred Practice

Person-centred planning arose from the shift to individualised program planning that came into vogue in disability services in the 1980s. This was a response to the paradigm shift to community living and as a way of breaking free from the congregate care models that existed in institutional settings. In institutional settings and congregated services, people were treated as one large group. People had to fit into the group program whatever their situation was. As services changed, it became apparent that individuals varied as to the kind of needs and aspirations they had and it was therefore necessary to determine what people as individuals needed and to plan supports and interventions around them.

Kincaid (1996) describes person-centred planning as a collective process in which service personnel involved with the person with a disability endeavour to learn more about the person, their capacities, hopes and wishes, and their family and plan a more positive future. There are many different models of individualised planning found in the literature and in different service contexts with a variety of names. Some of the terms you might encounter in the literature or in different agencies include: individual program plan, personal futures planning, individualised planning, person-centred planning, individual education plan or individual service plan. While there are many terms, all rest upon the same basic process of determining an individual's needs and goals, making plans for how those goals can be met, what resources are needed, who will be involved, by when this will occur and what outcomes will be achieved.

There are many benefits of this approach. First, it presents a positive view of people with disabilities. Second, the people involved are motivated to work towards a shared vision which can be both inspiring and motivating for all involved and thus allows for greater collaboration between the person with a disability their family and professionals. Third, this is a very empowering model for people with disabilities and family members and finally, it actively engages community members and other agencies.

Person-centred approaches have now had more than a decade of application, and problems, largely with implementation rather than the principles, have emerged. First, there is often too much emphasis on early planning and less on follow up. Human services are often driven by the need for 'the quick fix'. Secondly, and related to this first point, there is a tendency to fast track or standardise the process for efficiency. Having a standardised 'form' for every person with a disability defeats the purpose of person-centred or individualised plans. Thirdly, person-centred planning is often not well-linked to resources or implementing authority. The process may be well-facilitated but on its own will not achieve positive futures for people with disabilities. This usually requires changes in systems and organisations and a commitment of resources and supports. Fourthly, adopting this approach increases levels of complexity for disabled people, workers, families and agencies.

Family-centred Practice

Family-centred practice is an approach which emphasises the provision of family support in order to strengthen families (Briar-Lawson, 1998) and rests on the assumption that people can be best understood and helped in the context of their family of origin and current network of intimate relationships (Laird, 1996). While having a longstanding application in many spheres of practice, family-centred practice was developed largely in early intervention programs for children with developmental disabilities (Shannon, 2004). In more traditional approaches to 'treating' disability in children the focus is on the child and her or his problems. Within their specialist fields of expertise, therapists and professionals assessed the child, particularly their deficits and then developed interventions to address these difficulties. The family was usually not involved in these interventions or, only as an adjunct to the intervention – for example, undertaking therapy at home between visits to the professional although it was typically mothers who were involved in this way. In family-centred practice, the focus is shifted from the child as a separate entity to the child as a member of a family. Interventions tend to be family supportive rather than imposing demands on parents to fulfil professionals' requirements. The approach is based on a collaborative partnership between parents and professionals based on mutual recognition and valuing of their respective expertise (McBride, 1999).

Family-centred practice is founded on several important principles summarised by Carl Dunst et al (1993). These are: enhancing a sense of community; mobilising resources and support; sharing responsibility and collaboration; protecting family integrity; strengthening family functioning; and utilising proactive human service practices (Dunst et al, 1993).

Strengths Perspective

This perspective grew out of the mental health field from the work of researchers and educators at the University of Kansas (for example, Charles Rapp, Dennis Saleeby, Alice Leiberman, Ann Weick). It expanded internationally and is now widely adopted in many countries including Australia. While initially used in working with people with mental illness, the strengths approach is now adopted in many fields of practice including work with people with disabilities.

The strengths perspective represents an attempt to get away from the problem or deficit focus of much social work practice and shift to a focus on client strength. Saleeby (2006) argues that the strengths perspective asks the worker to be guided first and foremost by a profound awareness of and respect for clients' positive attributes and abilities, talents, and resources and aspirations. This approach seeks to understand how marginalised and oppressed people have survived in an oppressive catastrophic environment; such survival strategies are indicators of strength. The perspective incorporates the notion of niches or domains of the person's life where interventions may be focused and desired outcomes or goals determined by the client. These are influenced by personal and environmental factors. Rapp (1998) has related these elements into a holistic practice model as shown in Figure 6.2.

Figure 6.2 Elements of the Strengths Approach

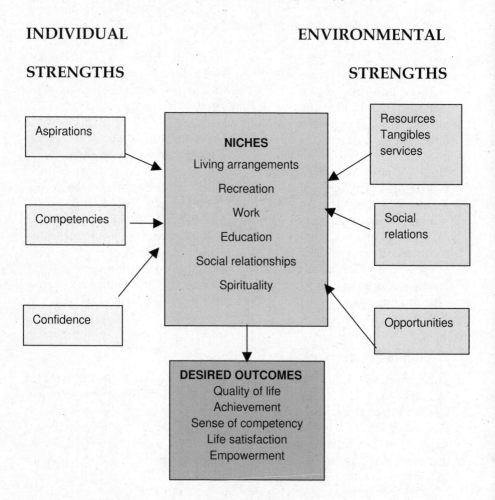

Source: Adapted and modified from Rapp (1998: 39)

Strengths-based approaches also rest on a number of important principles, which underpin all aspects of practice. These are:

1. quality of niches that people inhabit determines their achievement, quality of life and success in living;

2. people who are successful in living have goals and dreams;

3. people who are successful in living use their strength to attain their aspirations;

4. people who are successful in living have the confidence to take the next step;

5. people who are successful in living have at least one goal, one talent and confidence to take the next step;

6. people who are successful in living have access to the resources needed to achieve their goals;

7. people who are successful in living have a meaningful relationship with at least one other person;

8. people who are successful in living have access to opportunities relevant to their goals; and

9. people who are successful in living have access to resources and opportunities and meaningful relationship (Rapp, 1998: 43).

A strengths assessment involves working with the client in a systematic way exploring the strengths in each of the niches and setting out goals for the future. Both personal and environmental factors which may assist strength building or may act as barriers to achieving the goals are then explored with the client so that resources may be located and mobilised. Roles and tasks are assigned to both client and worker.

Conclusion

Social work practice in the disability field offers a wide range of contexts and possible approaches. There are several important aspects to practice in this field that novice practitioners need to be aware of and reflect upon if they are to be effective and purposeful in their work.

First, the disability field has been strongly influenced by values and ideologies for many decades. Disability became a human rights issue and the focus of social movements during the second half of the 20th century. Hence, practitioners may find themselves working in organisations with very definite views on what disability is and how it should be addressed. It is important to consider and become highly aware of your own values and beliefs about disability. Perhaps you have had personal experience of disability either yourself or a family or friend. Or maybe you have had little exposure to disabled people to date. It is essential to clarify your own assumptions and be open to challenge on them. As practitioners we need to be clear of where we stand on disability issues.

Second, the different theoretical approaches have translated into what is often seen as opposing forms of practice – through normalisation and SRV and the social model. We need to be aware of and utilise both approaches in practice. As Race et al (2005) have argued, there is much common ground across the two approaches in their shared focus on addressing oppression of disabled people. Through a focus on ideological differences, the opportunities for a dialogue for anti-oppressive practice have been missed to date.

Third, the disability field is extremely diverse. It covers practice possibilities across interventions – for example, working with individuals, groups, families, communities or in social action. Good practitioners need to have some expertise in more than one of these. Many practice situations will involve working perhaps with a person and their family or the local community. There are also wide variations in terms of age and class – impairment affects people of all life stages and all social groups. You may work with small toddlers with developmental delay, young people with acquired physical impairments or elderly people with Down syndrome. This requires knowledge and skills across many situations.

Fourth, disability practice usually means working with some of the most marginalised and vulnerable people in society. Practitioners will often have a duty of care to their clients as well as an ethical commitment to supporting them to take the ordinary risks and challenges of life. We need to understand the implications of extreme vulnerability and ensure we do not expose people for further exploitation, discrimination or abuse. Often we may need to stand alongside disabled people as allies in their dealings with other systems such as hospitals and the criminal justice system, where people with disabilities typically fare badly. We may find that we need to do this for our disabled colleagues as well as our clients.

There are also many difficult ethical issues within disability practice: for example, bioethical issues through genetic testing, the tensions of supporting the least restrictive options within the legal and organisation requirements to exercise duty of care and so on. Practitioners need to have well-developed procedures for ethical decision-making and a strong knowledge of their professional ethics as the basis for their practice.

Finally, there has been a push for a stronger evidence-based approach to practice and service delivery in recent years (Demsey and Nankervis, 2006). Developing this evidence base for social work disability practice is still in its early stages. Practitioners need to be part of that endeavour to ensure that our interventions are effective and have desired outcomes as well as reflecting the positive values about people with disabilities. Involving all disabled people including those of our colleagues with disabilities in research and evaluation of practice will make an important contribution to disability programs and practice for the future.

Review Questions

1. What are some of the major challenges faced by people with disabilities in meeting their needs?

2. Which theory of disability appeals to you most? Do you think you could use this theory effectively in your practice? How might you go about this?

3. What practice approach appeals to you most? In what situations would you use this approach? What might be its shortcomings and how would you adapt your practice to address these?

4. Do you think there are situations where it would not be good for a person to include being disabled as part of their personal identity? When might this be so? Or do you think that disability should always be integral to the person's identity? Give reasons for your position.

Useful Websites

People with Disabilities Australia	http://www.pwd.org.au/
Centre for Developmental Disability Studies at Sydney University	http://www.cdds.med.usyd.edu.au/index.html
International Classification of Functioning Disability and Health (WHO)	http://www3.who.int/icf/icftemplate.cfm
Disability Studies Unit at University of Leeds (UK)	http://www.leeds.ac.uk/disability-studies/
British Institute of Learning Disabilities	http://www.bild.org.uk/
The Center on Human Policy at Syracuse University (USA)	http://thechp.syr.edu/
National Center for the Dissemination of Disability Research (USA)	http://www.ncddr.org/
TASH (an organisation devoted to Equity, Diversity, Social Justice and Inclusion)	http://www.tash.org/

References

American Association for Mental Retardation (AAMR) (2002) *Definition of Mental Retardation*, Washington DC: AAMR. Available at: <http://www.aamr.org/Policies/faq_mental_retardation.shtml>.

Barnes, C (1996) 'The social model of disability: Myths and misrepresentations', *Coalition*, August, 25-30.

Barnes, C and Mercer, G (2003) *Disability*, Cambridge: Polity Press.

Barnes, C, Mercer, G and Shakespeare, T (1999) *Exploring Disability: A Sociological Introduction*, Cambridge: Polity Press.

Borsay, A (1986) 'Personal trouble or public issue? Towards a model of policy for people with physical and mental disabilities', *Disability, Handicap and Society*, 1(2), 179-194.

Briar-Lawson, K (1998) 'Capacity building for integrated family centered practice', *Social Work*, 43(6), 539-550.

Brown, H and Smith, H (1989) 'Whose "ordinary life" is it anyway?', *Disability, Handicap and Society*, 4(2), 105-119.

Chappell, A (1992) 'Towards a sociological critique of the normalisation principle', *Disability, Handicap and Society*, 7(1), 35-52.

Chenoweth, L (1996) 'Parents, professionals and practice: Twelve families' experience', in M Caltabiano, R Hil and R Frangos (eds) *Achieving Inclusion: Exploring Issues in Disability* (pp 117-128), Townsville, Qld: James Cook University Press.

Corker, M and Shakespeare, T (eds) (2002) *Disability/postmodernity: Embodying Disability Theory*, London: Continuum.

DeJong, G (1994) 'Toward a research and training capacity in disability policy', *Policy Studies Journal*, 22(1), 152-160.

Demsey, I and Nankervis, K (eds) (2006) *Community Disability Services: An Evidence Based Approach to Practice*, West Lafayette, IND: Purdue Press, and Sydney: University of New South Wales Press.

Dunst, C, Trivette, C, Gordon, N and Starnes, A (1993) 'Family-centered case management practices: Characteristics and consequences', in G Singer and L Powers (eds) *Families, Disability and Empowerment: Active Coping Skills and Strategies for Family Interventions* (pp 89-118), Baltimore: Brookes.

Edgerton, R (1967) *The Cloak of Competence*, Berkeley, CA: University of California Press.

French, S (1993) 'Can you see the rainbow? The roots of denial', in J Swain, V Finkelstein, S French and M Oliver (eds) *Disabling Barriers – Enabling Environments* (pp 69-77), London: Sage.

Goffman, E (1961) *Asylums: Essays on the Social Situation of Mental Patients and Other Inmates*, Harmondsworth: Penguin.

Goffman, E (1963) *Stigma: Notes on the Management of Spoiled Identity*, Harmondsworth: Pelican.

Goodley, D (2000) *Self-advocacy in the Lives of People with Learning Difficulties*, Buckingham: Open University Press.

Goodley, D (2001) '"Learning difficulties", the social model of disability and impairment: Challenging epistemologies', *Disability & Society*, 16(2), 207-223.

Groce, N (1985) *Everyone Here Spoke Sign Language: Hereditary Deafness on Martha's Vineyard*, London: Harvard University Press.

Hahn, H (1994) 'The minority group model of disability: Implications for medical sociology', *Research in the Sociology of Health Care*, 11(1), 3-24.

Kincaid, D (1996) 'Person-centered planning', in L Koegel, R Koegel and G Dunlap (eds) *Positive Behavioural Support: Including People with Difficult Behaviour in the Community* (pp 439-466), Baltimore: Brookes.

Laird, J (1996) 'Family-centered practice with lesbian and gay couples', *Families in Society*, 77(9), 559-572.

Lollar, D (2002) 'Public health and disability: Emerging opportunities', *Public Health Reports*, 117(2), 131-137.

McBride, S (1999) 'Research in review: Family centred practices', *Young Children*, 54(3), 62-70.

McKnight, J (1988) 'Regenerating community', *Social Policy*, 17(3), 54-58.

Morris, J (1991) *Pride Against Prejudice: Transforming Attitudes to Disability*, London: The Women's Press.

Morris, J (ed) (1989) *Able Lives: Women's Experience of Paralysis*, London: The Women's Press.

Nirje, B (1969) 'The normalisation principle and its human management implications', in R Kugel and W Wolfensberger (eds) *Changing Patterns in Residential Care for the Mentally Retarded* (pp 179-195), Washington DC: President's Committee on Mental Retardation.

Oliver, M (1990) *The Politics of Disablement*, Basingstoke, Hampshire: Macmillans & St Martins Press.

Oliver, M (1996) *Understanding Disability: From Theory to Practice*, Basingstoke, Hampshire: Macmillan.

Peters, S (2000) 'Is there a disability culture?: A syncretisation of three possible world views', *Disability and Society*, 15(4), 583-601.

Putnam, M (2005) 'Conceptualizing disability: Developing a framework for political disability identity', *Journal of Disability Policy Studies*, 16(3), 188-198.

Race, D, Boxall, K and Carson, I (2005) 'Towards a dialogue for practice: Reconciling social role valorisation and the social model of disability', *Disability & Society*, 20(5), 507-521.

Rapp, C (1998) *The Strengths Model*, New York: Oxford University Press.

Rioux, M (1996) 'Disability: The place of judgement in a world of fact', Paper presented at the *10th World Congress on the IASSID*, Helsinki, Finland.

Rothman, J (1991) 'A model of case management: Toward empirically based research', *Social Work*, 36(4), 520-522.

Rothman, J C (2003) *Social Work Practice Across Disability*, Boston: Allyn & Bacon.

Saleebey, D (2006) *The Strengths Perspective in Social Work Practice* (4th ed), Boston: Allyn & Bacon.

Shakespeare, T (1996) 'Disability, identity and difference', in C Barnes and G Mercer (eds) *Exploring the Divide* (pp 94-113), Leeds: The Disability Press.

Shannon, P (2004) 'Barriers to family-centered services for infants and toddlers with developmental delays', *Social Work*, 49(2), 301-308.

Sobsey, D (1994) *Violence and Abuse in the Lives of People with Disabilities: The End of Silent Acceptance*, Baltimore: Brookes.

Wolfensberger, W (1980) 'The definition of normalisation: Update, problems, disagreements and misunderstandings', in R Flynn and K Nitsch (eds) *Normalisation, Social Integration and Community Services* (pp 71-115), Austin, TX: ProEd.

Wolfensberger, W (1983) 'Social role valorization: A proposed new term for the principle of normalization', *Mental Retardation*, 21(6), 234-239.

Wolfensberger, W (1992) *A Brief Introduction to Social Role Valorization as a High-order Concept for Structuring Human Services* (Rev ed), Syracuse, NY: Training Institute for Human Service Planning, Leadership and Change Agentry, Syracuse University.

Wolfensberger, W (1998) *A Brief Introduction to Social Role Valorization as a High-Order Concept for Addressing the Plight of Societally Devalued People, and for Structuring Human Service* (3rd rev ed), Syracuse, NY: Training Institute for Human Service Planning, Leadership and Change Agentry, Syracuse University.

Wood, P (1980) International Classification of Impairments, Disabilities and Handicaps, Geneva: World Health Organization.

World Health Organization (2002) *Towards a Common Language for Functioning, Disability and Health ICF*, Geneva: World Health Organization. Available at: <www3.who.int/icf/beginners/bg-pdf>.

Legislation Cited

Disability Discrimination Act 1992 (Cth)

Chapter 7

Healthcare

Sandy Taylor

Introduction

Healthcare services are one of the most significant sites for the employment of social workers and human service workers in Australia (McCormack, 2001). According to the Australian Institute of Health and Welfare (AIHW) (2004), there were over 450,000 people employed in health occupations in Australia in 2000-2001, of whom almost 40,000 comprised health workers such as social workers and other allied health professionals; furthermore, this figure had increased by over 26 per cent since 1996. Professional healthcare workers such as social workers and human service workers are therefore an integral part of the system that delivers healthcare services in Australia and as such, according to Duckett (2004: 59), they help to 'define the very nature of [such] services'.

This chapter aims to provide an overview of professional social work and human service practice in Australia, particularly within the hospital and community health context. We will first examine different definitions of health and illness and their relevance for understanding how health-care services are organised and delivered. Two main frameworks of healthcare are then described, first, biomedicine, which includes the bio-psychosocial approach, and which is most relevant to hospital and acute care professional practice; and secondly, socio-ecology, which informs community-based health practice and emphasises wellness, health promotion and illness prevention within communities and populations. Current and emerging trends and developments in healthcare policy are examined next and their potential impact on hospitals and community health services as organisational sites of professional healthcare practice. An overview of theoretical and professional knowledge relevant to professional healthcare practitioners in hospitals and community health is presented and discussed, with brief reference to some of the main theoretical approaches relevant to professional healthcare practice. Finally, a chapter summary, key review questions and suggestions for further reading are presented.

Understanding Health and Illness

Access to quality healthcare is widely accepted to constitute a fundamental human right. In 1948, the General Assembly of the United Nations proclaimed and adopted the Universal Declaration of Human Rights which, in Article 25, states: '[T]he enjoyment of the highest attainable standard of health is one of the fundamental rights of every human being without distinction of race, religion, political belief, economic or social condition' (United Nations, 1948). The provision of quality, accessible healthcare services to all citizens of a country is fundamentally important: good health is not only a precious possession for us all as individuals, but a healthy population is the basis of a strong and prosperous society. As Hancock notes, 'Health is an essential component of active citizenship and participation in society' (1999: 6).

Most people can express direct opinions about health issues and the healthcare system as we all have had personal experiences of receiving healthcare services at one time or another in our lives. Within Australia, discussion and debate about healthcare issues, access to health services and the delivery of quality healthcare services are rarely absent from our television screens and daily newspapers. The health system and the quality of health services are also highly political issues; for example, healthcare policy has featured prominently in virtually every federal election in Australia since 1969 (Palmer and Short, 2000).

Most of us, upon reflection, would be able to define what 'good health' means to us personally. Health and illness can be defined in many different ways, however, and such definitions vary according to a person's age, gender, family history or personal experiences, as well as their cultural or ethnic background. Within traditional Australian Indigenous cultures, for example, O'Connor-Fleming and Parker (2001) tell us that there has been no single word for 'health' because such cultures are based on communal and collectivist values, rather than the individualistic ones that are often privileged in mainstream non-Indigenous culture. For Indigenous people, the health and wellbeing of a single individual cannot be separated from that of family and community; it also incorporates relationship and connectedness with traditional land or country.

How we define health and illness also changes over time. It is only in relatively recent times, for example, that 'new' conditions and diseases such as Human Immunodeficiency Virus (HIV) and Acquired Immunodeficiency Syndrome (AIDS), Attention Deficit Hyperactivity Disorder (ADHD), Post-traumatic Stress Disorder (PTSD), Chronic Fatigue Syndrome (CFS) and Severe Acute Respiratory Syndrome (SARS) have been defined and medically classified. How we define health and illness therefore is by no means fixed or static as it varies significantly across time, as well as across individuals, families, groups and cultures.

Perspectives of Healthcare:
From Biomedicine to Socio-ecology

In spite of the above qualifications, we almost universally associate health and illness with how well our physical bodies are functioning. This approach reflects a biomedical perspective which is dominant in defining health and illness in Australia and other developed countries. According to this perspective, health is defined as the 'absence of disease or pathology within an organism' (World Health Organization (WHO), 1946). Biomedicine emerged in conjunction with the rise of science, and the decline of religion, in Western Europe in the 18th and 19th centuries (Samson, 1999). It essentially views the human body as a machine: if a body part is not functioning well (as indicated by signs or *symptoms*), systematic investigations using scientific methods are undertaken to establish the specific biological or physiological cause of the dysfunction (the *specific aetiology*); once done, a *diagnosis* can be given and treatment can begin to restore the body to equilibrium and good functioning. The speed and accuracy of diagnosis and medical interventions have been increasingly supported by advances in medical and scientific knowledge regarding human anatomy, physiology, genetics, cellular and molecular biology and disease causing pathogens, as well as developments in medical technologies relating to surgery, pathology, anaesthesia, radiology and medical imaging.

Approximately 95 per cent of the total healthcare budget in Australia supports a biomedical approach to healthcare (Duckett, 2004), making it the dominant framework through which our healthcare services are structured and delivered. As Palmer and Short (2000), Duckett (2004) and others have noted, however, our 'healthcare' system is largely an 'illness care system' as the vast majority of healthcare resources support the treatment of those who are already ill. Hospitals alone constitute about 35 per cent of total recurrent healthcare expenditure and comprise the largest single component of overall healthcare funding (Australian Institute of Health and Welfare (AIHW), 2004). By contrast, public health and community-based health services, which aim to maximise the health and wellbeing of *all* citizens as well as prevent illness in the population, attract between 2 per cent and 5 per cent of total Commonwealth health funding (AIHW, 2004). State governments also contribute to funding community health and public health services but there too, such services constitute relatively minor items in healthcare budgets; in Queensland within 2003-2004, for example, 6 per cent of total funding went to providing public and community health services (Queensland Health, 2004a).

It is clear therefore, that most social workers or human service workers employed in delivering healthcare services within Australia will be located in sites that are informed and determined by biomedicine. These are generally multidisciplinary healthcare contexts, with medical and nursing professionals forming the two largest groups, while others, like social workers and allied health professionals, provide services to complement the biomedical focus (Duckett, 2004). As Healy notes (2005: 20), '[T]he biomedical discourse is one of the most powerful discourses shaping practice contexts, particularly in health services such as hospitals, rehabilitation services and mental health services'. The strengths of biomedicine are indisputable: its knowledge base is extremely well-supported through scientific research that is well-funded and highly esteemed within society and it provides effective treatment, care and life-saving interventions in many acute and chronic medical situations. Biomedicine is thus a dominant and pervasive model of healthcare in Australia. It exerts a significant influence on Australian society, on potential consumers of healthcare and also on healthcare practitioners and service providers.

Within biomedical settings such as public hospitals, the practice framework of most social workers and human service workers will be based on a derivative of biomedicine, known as the biopsychosocial per-spective. As its name suggests, this perspective takes into account not only biological factors that influence an individual's health or illness status, but psychological and social factors (Engel, 1977; Caltabiano and Sarafino, 2002). A widely used biopsychosocial definition of health which most of us will recognise was also proposed by the WHO (1946): 'Health is a state of complete physical, mental and social wellbeing and not merely the absence of disease and infirmity'. A strength of this definition is that it presents a *holistic* view of the individual by acknowledging that good health is more than just good *physical* health: it also encompasses mental, emotional and social wellbeing. Many people argue too that spiritual wellbeing should be included in holistic definitions of health and wellbeing (Payne, 2005).

The biopsychosocial perspective is conceptually attractive to social workers and other professional healthcare workers because it resonates strongly with holistic perspectives such as 'person-in-environment' and 'psychosocial' approaches. This model emanates from a systems-based framework in which the many, varied and complex interrelationships between an individual, his or her family, community, culture and society are acknowledged (Engel, 1977; Caltabiano and Sarafino, 2002). Hospital-based social workers and other professional health workers can work extremely effectively within a biomedical context by adopting a holistic biopsychosocial framework, by advocating on clients' behalf within the dominant biomedical context and by working towards maximising quality of life beyond the hospital ward for both patient and family. In so doing, practitioners can effectively resist the dangers of biological reductionism wherein the primary and institutionalised emphasis is on disease, pathology and deficit. It is important to remember, however, that the biopsychosocial model typically remains focused on achieving change or adaptation within the individual client and his or her immediate environment.

A second major perspective for understanding and defining health is based on a perspective that is broader than that relating to the biomedical or biopsychosocial status of any *one* individual; such a perspective involves a socio-ecological framework of health (Keleher and Murphy, 2004; Germov, 2005). Social workers and other human service workers will most likely encounter socio-ecological frameworks for healthcare delivery if they are employed in community health settings, public health services, health education or health promotion programs. In addition to acknowledging the biological and/or genetic determinants of health and illness in particular individuals, this approach focuses on the health status of groups, communities and populations. It is underpinned by a social determinants perspective and emphasises the role of social and environmental factors like income, education, housing, employment, working conditions and geographical location in determining the health status of whole groups or communities. The way health services are organised and how accessible they might be are also highly relevant issues within a socio-ecological framework. An underlying tenet of this approach is that, because individuals do not always have control over the broader factors that influence their health status, interventions are required at structural and policy levels to address social and other factors that contribute to health inequalities. Thus, while some people may appear to make poor or risky health choices like smoking, eating unhealthy foods or engaging in risky behaviours, there are, in addition, complex and influential factors outside of their control that significantly influence their health status. Examples of such factors include the opportunities people have to obtain adequate and secure income, to access free quality health services or to have sufficient resources to choose healthy foods that are often also more expensive. Equitable access to quality health services by people living in regional and rural communities is also of major interest within such a framework. The socio-ecological approach is concerned with maximising health and preventing illness in all community sectors and across all social groups; as such, it focuses on interventions at the 'upstream' or policy and structural level, rather than at the 'downstream' level after individuals have developed illnesses or diseases (Keleher and Murphy, 2004).

The socio-ecological framework for understanding health and illness has been increasingly supported by empirical evidence within Australia and other countries that indicate very strong relationships between socioeconomic status and health status. People who are most socioeconomically disadvantaged for example, experience poorer health for every major cause of mortality and morbidity; they live shorter lives and experience more illness than all others (AIHW, 2004). The impact of such disadvantage also appears to be cumulative over the life span (AIHW,

2004). In addition to the actual levels of disadvantage, the *meanings* that society attaches to such disadvantage can further exacerbate it, resulting in stigmatisation, marginalisation and exclusion. The relationship between poor health and low socioeconomic status is true not only at extreme levels of socioeconomic disadvantage but as a gradient across all levels of society (AIHW, 2004). A recent report by Queensland Health (Queensland Health, 2004b: 7) entitled *Health Determinants Queensland* argues strongly that 'social and economic disparities are one of the major public health challenges confronting Queensland'.

In 1986, the WHO developed the Ottawa Charter, to which Australia was a signatory, and this aims to promote and maximise the good health of communities and populations (Keleher and Murphy, 2004). As a result of WHO initiatives, several significant health policy frameworks were developed within Australia, including the *National Health Strategy 1988*, known also as *Health for All Australians*, as well as *Goals and Targets for Australia's Health in the Year 2000 and Beyond*. The Ottawa Charter proposes principles and practice strategies for healthcare practitioners working within a socio-ecological framework and these involve diverse and multilayered goals and interventions. They include working at the individual level through health education and support, facilitating community ownership of healthcare issues, building supportive and active communities, and working across institutional sectors at policy and legislative levels to promote environments that are sustainable for health and equality for all citizens and communities. These principles, and the focus of each, are as follows (Keleher and Murphy, 2004).

- Principle #1: To build public policies that support health – The focus here is on developing interventions beyond the health sector that aim to facilitate living and working conditions to be more conducive to health and equity;

- Principle #2: To create supportive environments – The focus here is on fostering sustainable support systems that promote safety and quality in social life;

- Principle #3: To strengthen community action – The focus of this principle is on consulting with communities and strengthening community participation in health related matters;

- Principle #4: To develop personal skills – The focus here is on health education of individuals, groups and communities; and

- Principle #5: To reorient health services – The aim here is to expand beyond a biomedical focus on disease and work towards illness prevention, holistic and culturally appropriate healthcare and collaborative partnerships between consumers, health professionals and communities.

The special emphasis of the Ottawa Charter on principles of social justice and strategies to address social and health inequalities resonates strongly with healthcare professionals such as social workers for whom social justice is professionally valued (Laverack, 2005). The education of social workers incorporates participatory and empowering approaches to professional practice, as well as skills and methods to facilitate such practice; as such, social workers are particularly well-equipped to work within socio-ecological frameworks of healthcare. There are also many other health-specific educational programs in Australian tertiary institutions that are incorporating socio-ecological frameworks of practice, including nursing, allied health and health sciences, community development, public health, health promotion, health research, healthcare policy and Indigenous healthcare; such programs emphasise a social determinants perspective and the development of knowledge and skills that are appropriate for professional healthcare practice using socio-ecological frameworks.

Having explored the main frameworks for defining health and illness and for delivering healthcare services, we will now examine key and emerging issues in Australian healthcare and their potential impact on hospital and community as sites of professional healthcare practice.

Current and Emerging Issues
in Australian Healthcare

Whether we are located within hospitals or community health settings, the nature and parameters of social work and professional human service practice will be determined by many aspects of the contexts within which we work, including the professional, organisational and policy contexts. As Karen Healy argues in regard to the social work profession, '[w]e need to take seriously the impact of institutional context for shaping our practice approaches, our knowledge base, our sense of purpose and even ourselves as social workers' (2005: 4). Healy goes on to state that this is not a simple or one way street of influence: 'we should recognize that we are active participants in, and creators of, the contexts and frameworks through which we practise' (2005: 4). We will now examine some of the current contextual features of the Australian healthcare environment as they influence and determine the practice contexts for social workers and other human service professionals in healthcare.

The Changing Health Policy Context: Healthcare as a Market Commodity

Over the past three decades or so, all areas of public and social policy, including that relating to healthcare, have been undergoing significant change and 'reform' in Australia as a result of the dominance of neo-liberal political and economic ideologies (O'Connor, Smyth and Warburton, 2000). Such ideologies privilege discourses related to economic rationalism, market forces, free choice and individual responsibility. As the conservative Coalition has now been in power in Australia since

1996, a significant period of time has elapsed in which these policy directions have been able to be implemented and consolidated across many sectors. Such policies have resulted in a substantial impact on many areas of the healthcare system, how services are organised and delivered and on professional healthcare practice. During this period, in Australia as in all developed countries, healthcare costs have continued to rise, largely driven by rising costs associated with medical technologies, medicine prescriptions and ever increasing consumer expectations of the healthcare system (Duckett, 2004; Hancock, 1999). Within such contexts, decisions about how to allocate and 'ration' limited healthcare resources are becoming increasingly critical an issue that is described by Leeder (1999) as 'the ethical challenge of the age'.

Healthcare policy in Australia is characterised by 'marketisation' and 'commodification' of healthcare, whereby market forces and the private sector are increasingly involved in funding and delivering healthcare services (Hancock, 1999; Duckett, 2004). Such developments mark a substantial shift from the principle that access to quality healthcare is a universal entitlement of all citizens to one where healthcare is a market commodity which can be bought and sold (Hancock, 1999). According to Judith Healy (1998 cited in Healy, 2005: 28), this philosophy is based on the belief that 'the market can deliver better and cheaper services than government'. All levels of government have withdrawn from providing direct healthcare services to contracting them out to both 'for-profit' and 'not-for-profit' organisations within the private sector. The healthcare system is thus increasingly described as 'two tier' in which public and private funding and service delivery co-exist. Support for private health insurance has also increased with government subsidies for the sector and approximately 49 per cent of Australians now hold some form of private health insurance to complement their access to public healthcare services (AIHW, 2004). In addition, and within many healthcare services, consumers have been increasingly called upon to supplement the funding of healthcare services through 'co-contributions' for services received; this is in keeping with 'fee-for-service' and 'user pays' principles that characterise a market system. Across all health services, a focus on efficiency, effectiveness and measurable outcomes has become 'the bottom line' for evaluating service delivery, although the rhetoric of universal and equitable access to quality healthcare services has continued (Hancock, 1999).

While the Commonwealth Government remains the principal funding source for the healthcare system, the relationship between the Commonwealth and State governments which largely administer the delivery of health services has also become increasingly complex and at times, volatile, as political imperatives can generate excessive bureaucratisation and administration, duplication of services and cost shifting between different government sectors (Hancock, 1999). For example, the increasing requirements to pay upfront for medical services provided by general practitioners and medical specialists, once managed through the universal bulk billing mechanism of the Medicare system, is resulting in significantly increased demand at Departments of Emergency Medicine (formerly known as 'Casualty' departments) in public hospitals, as people present for consultations because they can no longer afford to attend local medical practitioners. The global context is also impacting on health policy and service provision in Australia as the influence of multinational corporations such as those developing and promoting pharmaceutical products extends well beyond national boundaries. The recent Free Trade agreement between Australia and the United States is an example of this where changes to Australian policy regarding the Pharmaceutical Benefits Scheme were strongly promoted by the USA as part of the complex trade agreement between the two countries (Harvey et al, 2004).

Hospitals and Community Health: Changing Organisational Contexts of Healthcare

As a result of these significant trends in Australian healthcare policy, hospital and community health settings as sites of healthcare delivery and professional practice have experienced pressure and change. Most hospitals in Australia as well as other developed countries, in keeping with the imperatives of economic rationalism, are now financially administered via a 'casemix' funding model whereby all costs associated with each inpatient 'episode', or admission, are calculated (Cleak, 2002). Admissions to public hospitals have become highly 'streamlined', with shorter inpatient stays and supplementation by day hospitals, outpatient clinics, 'hospital-in-the-home' services and community-based services for post-acute follow-up (Duckett, 2004). These changes have also been facilitated by advances in medical procedures and technologies that allow greater diagnostic precision, less invasive treatment procedures, more rapid recovery and quicker discharge. Operations such as coronary bypass heart surgery, a major surgical operation in the past, is now routine and can be followed by discharge home within days, rather than weeks or months. Day hospitals also allow for surgical or medical procedures, such as the administration of chemotherapy or radiotherapy for cancer patients, to be administered routinely and without hospital admission. In short, hospital-based care has largely shifted from an 'institutional' to an 'ambulatory' mode of care, with non-inpatient care now constituting approximately 25 per cent of all hospital expenditure (Duckett, 2004). In view of these changes, issues regarding patient compliance with prescribed treatments have also become increasingly significant for clinicians, professional healthcare workers and service delivery organisations (Daly, Hughes and op't Hoog, 2002).

As a result of changes in hospital structures and service delivery models, public hospitals have become less likely to be 'sites of care' than sites of short term, expert medical and technical procedures and interventions: according to Draper (1999, cited in Hancock, 1999: 135) '[t]he modern perception of a hospital is a technological one, focussed on procedure as the rationale for patient stay'. Less than a decade ago in Australian hospitals, social workers might have facilitated 'social admissions' to public hospitals, as in the case of an elderly person with dementia being admitted to hospital while his or her primary carer underwent an inpatient medical procedure in the same hospital. Admissions of this nature are now highly unlikely, as the social context of illness is much less likely to be acknowledged within the hospital context. The large acute hospital context is complex and focused, often requiring social work assessments and interventions within short periods of time and in busy, pressurised medical contexts, and where effective communication across a range of medical and health disciplines is critical for good outcomes (Miller, 2001). While some greater flexibility in this regard may be possible at times in rural, rather than urban hospitals, rural and regional communities have also been significantly affected by these policy trends and in addition, have additional challenges for service coordinators, providers and consumers of health services that are associated with the distance factor (Chenoweth and Stehlik, 2001; Munn, 2003; McDonald and Zetlin, 2004).

Organisations that deliver community-based health services have also been markedly affected by these policy changes. Many community health centres, whose primary goals may include preventive health, education, health promotion and/or community development, are increasingly engaged in the post-acute follow-up of patients who have been discharged from public hospitals into the care of their families and communities (Smith, 1999). What might have been an emphasis on delivering healthcare services in the community from a socio-ecological framework is therefore at risk of being jeopardised by needs being generated within the biomedical healthcare system. As hospitals are more likely to discharge patients home 'quicker but sicker', the burden of care has been shifting back to the community and this in turn impacts not only on community health services, but on families, carers and women (Hancock and Moore, 1999). Further, with increased emphases on economic accountability, bureaucratic tasks involving administration, record keeping, funding re-applications and determination of consumer eligibility are likely to assume significantly greater time and importance for community-based organisations and their workers. Professional healthcare workers such as domiciliary nurses or allied health workers, for example, are now more likely to be involved in assessing client eligibility for services or advising patients about means tests, fees or required co-payments and are therefore required to know and be able to implement relevant organisational policies in this regard.

The Push for Evidence

Evidence-based practice (EBP) involves integrating, within the clinical context, the best research evidence, the clinician's expertise and the patient's values (Sackett et al, 1997). For the past decade or so, there has been an increasing emphasis on the importance for medical practitioners and associated healthcare professionals to have clear evidence on which to base clinical healthcare decisions and recommendations. Numerous factors have contributed to this trend. Within the health professions themselves, there has been growing recognition of the importance of having such evidence in order to make the most efficacious clinical decisions and treatment recommendations. Consumers too have become increasingly well-informed and articulate and are more willing to challenge the longstanding authority of doctors and healthcare professionals about treatment options that are being proposed to them. As an outcomes-focused approach, evidence-based healthcare is also consistent with current trends toward economic and clinical accountability, efficiency and effectiveness. Finally, from public health and health economics perspectives, the effectiveness of biomedicine in improving the overall health status of the population has been questioned; Palmer and Short claim, for example (as cited in Hancock, 1999: 94), that 'society has overestimated the effectiveness of curative medicine and underestimated its limitations'.

The evidence-based imperative remains a contested issue within the professional social work literature. According to Murphy and McDonald (2004), this contest represents an inherent clash between humanistic and scientific paradigms. Critics of EBP argue that the approach, while well-suited to disciplines such as medicine, nursing and those allied health professions with strong biomedical foundations in practice and research, fits less well with professions such as social work whose foundations lie in humanism and where the practice emphasis is on 'process' rather than 'outcomes' (Gibbons, 2001). According to this view, *relationship* and *process* underpin professional social work practice and it is difficult to quantify and 'reduce' such concepts to measurable outcomes and within an immediate post-intervention time period. Further, it is argued, social workers often deal with the most complex situations, clients or groups and their professional focus by its nature is typically holistic and overarching, rather than discrete, easily operationalised and time-specific. According to this perspective, the focus should be on 'process' rather than 'outcomes'; if this occurred, EBP frameworks would be more appropriate for professional social workers and human service workers to embrace.

On the other hand, others argue that it is critical for social workers and human service workers to find meaningful ways to engage with EBP and practice-based research in order to develop and test the scientific bases of professional practice, as well as retain professional relevance in healthcare (Reid, 1994 cited in Healy, 2005; Smith, 2002). Commentators such as Stoez (2000 cited in Healy, 2005: 33) argue that until social workers learn to effectively *engage* with economic rationalism as a determining paradigm for professional practice rather than simply *critique* it, we will confront 'political irrelevance and programmatic decline'. Similarly, Smith (2002) argues within the Australian context that 'it is imperative that social work researchers face the challenge of investigating the process factors impacting outcomes' (p 147). In one of the few Australian empirical studies to date that compared outcome and non-outcome directed models of hospital-based social work practice, Shapiro and her colleagues (2004) from the University of Queensland found that, while clients were satisfied with social work services they received within both models, clients who had experienced interventions from social workers using the outcome-directed model reported more favourable outcomes in various domains, including psychological wellbeing and social relationships.

Case Management

Case management, defined as 'a method of providing extended, continuing care to people with chronic and perhaps deteriorating life problems in community settings' (O'Connor, Wilson and Setterlund, 2003: 180), has become increasingly common in Australia as a model for managing and delivering human and healthcare services. It is a particularly common model for delivering healthcare services in the rehabilitation, mental health, disability and community-based health sectors; according to its proponents, the case management model facilitates greater efficiency in service provision and allows for priorities to be set and responded to systematically by professional workers. Commentators such as McDonald (cited in Kennedy, Harvey and Gursansky, 2001) argue that case management will become the *dominant* model of service delivery as health professions become more generic and less discipline-specific.

While the ideal model of case management is based on assumptions of a collaborative approach with clients around developing their care plans, social workers and other health professionals may experience tensions when working within a case management framework, between professional values that support the autonomy and empowerment of clients in decision-making on the one hand and the case management requirements of overseeing and planning on behalf of clients on the other (Netting, 1992; Ozanne, 1996; O'Connor et al, 2003). Numerous social work practitioners within the Australian healthcare context have evaluated management as a model within a range of practice contexts (Rapp and Chamberlain, 1985; Ozanne, 1996; Thornton and Battistel, 2001; Smith, 2002).

Discipline-specific versus Generic Healthcare Professions

The 'de-professionalisation' of the healthcare workforce has also been cited as a significant feature of the changing healthcare context in

Australia (McDonald, 1999; Healy, 2004) in recent times. Although hospitals continue to employ discipline-specific health professionals such as social workers and other allied health professionals, the demand for 'generic' health workers in a variety of other healthcare contexts has been increasing. Where this occurs, discipline-specific professional qualifications are not prerequisites for employment and thus generic healthcare workers are equipped with a wide variety of knowledge, skills and competencies. Such trends are particularly apparent in community-based and non-government health sectors, including mental health and disability service settings. Healthcare workers in these sectors are often employed under classifications and titles such as youth workers, mental health workers, case managers, crisis workers, disability support workers, Indigenous health workers, community health workers, health promotion officers and health education workers. The case management model supports this trend according to McDonald (1999: 30) as it has an outputs-based focus, rather than one that is based on differentiation of workers' professional qualifications.

Social Work and Human Services Practice in Healthcare

So far, we have examined the complexity and relativity of the concepts of health and illness, the biomedical and socio-ecological models of health that influence how healthcare services can be organised and delivered, and some of the main policy and organisational features of the current healthcare system in Australia. How do social work and human service practitioners fit into this complex picture and what knowledge and skills do they need in order to work effectively within these environments?

Knowledge from Biomedical and Public Health Disciplines

Professional social workers and human service workers in hospital and community health services draw upon a wide range of theoretical and professional knowledge. First, workers who are located within clinical health settings that are characterised by biomedical discourses will draw upon the specialised biomedical knowledge that relates to those settings. Whether acute inpatient or specialised community-based services, professional healthcare workers typically develop a substantial knowledge base in the relevant biomedical area and this provides a fundamental point of reference for professional assessments and interventions. Social workers regularly demonstrate such biomedical knowledge when they write professionally about their practice approaches within such specialised settings; for example, in traumatic brain injury (Simpson et al, 2002); adult (Thornton and Battistel, 2001), as well as paediatric, burn settings (Miller, 2001); spinal injury (Dorsett and Geraghty, 2004); clinical genetics (Richards and Taylor, 1997) and life threatening illness (Briton, 2000).

In community-based health services also, professional healthcare workers build upon specialised biomedical knowledge regarding conditions such as brain injury (Simpson et al, 2005); eating disorders (Black, 2003); orthopaedic injuries and trauma (Harms, 2004); inherited disorders such as Huntington's disease (Taylor, 1998); postnatal depression (Stone, 1997); and life threatening illness such as HIV/AIDS (Briton, 2000). Where community-based workers are employed to undertake community development, health education or health promotion, they will also access theory and knowledge from disciplines such as public health and epidemiology (see, for example, Gay, Herriot and May, 1995).

Psychological and Sociological Theories

A wide range of theoretical knowledge from cognate disciplines including psychology, psychiatry and sociology also informs professional healthcare workers' understanding of human growth, development and behaviour, as well as of the potential impact on, and response of, people regarding illness, disease or trauma (Jones, 2003; Healy, 2005). Psychology in general, and health psychology in particular, are substantive areas of psychological theory and practice that relate to normal and 'abnormal' human growth, development and ageing; learning, motivation and adjustment; human and social development, identity formation and role theories within the context of age and life stage; health related intentions, decision-making and behaviour; stress, coping, resilience and adaptation; mastery and self-efficacy; the nature of attachment to others; and the psychological challenge to individuals and families of sudden change, trauma or crisis events as well as grief and loss. These theories contribute significantly to the knowledge base of healthcare workers both during their professional education as well as their professional working lives, where they continue to draw on this knowledge as they encounter new situations involving the individuals, families or communities with whom they work.

Sociological theories also provide substantive frameworks for informing professional healthcare workers about health and illness within social, cultural and political contexts. Such theoretical frameworks allow us to understand the health and illness of individuals or groups as they are impacted upon by factors such as class, socioeconomic status, gender, race and ethnicity. They contribute also to our understanding of concepts such as power and influence, patriarchy, agency and structure, risk, medicalisation, stigma, labelling, difference and deviance as well as the social processes that facilitate the inclusion, or the exclusion and marginalisation, of individuals within society. Marxist and neo-Marxist theories, symbolic interactionism, feminist theory and many postmodern theories have contributed significantly to the analysis of social structure, processes and power within the healthcare context (Iphofen and Poland, 1998; Grbich, 1999; Germov, 2005). For social workers in every professional and healthcare context, theoretical knowledge about structural factors and social processes significantly underpins the nature and purpose of their practice and their commitment to social justice.

Theoretical and Practice Knowledge from Social Work and Human Service Professions

In addition to the theoretical knowledge from cognate disciplines, social workers and human service workers draw upon many theories of professional practice from within the context of their own professions. Fook (2002), Dominelli (2002), O'Connor, Wilson and Setterlund (2003), Chenoweth and McAuliffe (2005), Healy (2005) and Payne (2005), among others, provide comprehensive overviews of professional knowledge and skill for social workers and human service practitioners. At the heart of professional social work practice in healthcare, as in other fields, are humanistic traditions and values that promote the individual's autonomy and self-determination; collaborative, empathic and empowering relationships with clients and groups; and professional commitment to principles of social justice and to addressing disadvantage and inequity. According to O'Connor et al (2003: 11), 'the purpose of [social work and welfare] practice is to promote the development of equitable relationships and the development of individuals' power and control over their own lives, and hence improve the interactions between individuals and social arrangements'.

The relational connections between individuals, families or groups and their social environment is of fundamental interest to the social worker and provides a framework within which social work assessments and interventions are conducted. Assessments involve collaborative, ethical and respectful engagement with clients, families, groups and communities and have intrinsic goals of addressing relational inequities (O'Connor et al, 2003; Healy, 2005). Interventions can include individual and/or family counselling and collaborative problem solving, support, resource finding and referral, community development, lobbying and advocacy; practice research and policy analysis also constitute central intervention tools in healthcare and other human service sectors (O'Connor et al, 2003; Chenoweth and McAuliffe, 2005). Further, theories relating to critical and reflective practice (Ife, 1997; Fook, 2002) as well as ethical decision-making (McAuliffe and Armstrong, 2002; Chenoweth and McAuliffe, 2005) provide additional significant frameworks of professional knowledge.

Theoretical and Practice Knowledge with Specific Relevance to Healthcare

In addition to generic approaches to theory and professional practice, the following specific theoretical approaches are particularly relevant within acute hospital and community health settings.

Task- or Solution-focused Approaches

These approaches are based on structured, time-limited and problem-focused frameworks for assessment and intervention (Healy, 2005). As such, they are particularly relevant in healthcare contexts that require short or limited term assessment and intervention, such as in departments of emergency medicine, hospital wards or outpatient services characterised by high patient turn over and an outcomes focus. As Miller (2001) clearly articulates regarding social work practice within a large Australian paediatric teaching hospital, the worker needs to be able to 'establish a relationship with a child or parent or both, usually in a semi-public environment, to assess the situation ... [and] quickly formulate and implement a plan of intervention action' (p 5).

Crisis Theory and Intervention

This theoretical framework and model of intervention is related to brief intervention approaches (Payne, 2005). It informs our understanding of situations where individuals experience a state of crisis following a life event which typically, but not necessarily, has been of a traumatic nature (Roberts, 1990). As hospitals are sites of many potentially traumatic events including the diagnosis and treatment of sudden and/or life threatening illness, death, accident and other trauma, crisis theory and crisis intervention provide appropriate frameworks for regular use by many social work practitioners within these contexts. Such models are also highly relevant intervention approaches within community health where practitioners routinely encounter individuals, families or groups who are experiencing trauma or crises.

Systems Theories Including Family and Socio-ecological Systems Theories

Systems theories promote our knowledge and understanding of the inter-relationships between individuals, families and significant others, as well as between them and their broader social environments. They have constituted an important theoretical perspective within the education of all social workers and other human service professionals for many decades (Healy, 2005; Payne, 2005). Systems theories are especially important within trauma, illness and disability contexts as they facilitate a broader framework for assessment than reductionist frameworks of biomedicine wherein disease is characterised entirely in biological terms and where the main focus is on individual body and pathology (Germov, 2005; Healy, 2005). *Family* systems theories too have been particularly beneficial within the healthcare context as they facilitate our understanding of the importance of the interconnectedness between individual and family when illness or trauma is experienced (Rolland, 1994). In recent times, systems theories have strengthened the focus for professional healthcare workers on the importance of networks, community and social support (Payne, 2005; Rolland and Williams, 2005). Finally, systems theories underpin socio-ecological frameworks through which we understand the importance of social determinants of health, models of primary healthcare and the principles of the Ottawa Charter (O'Connor-Fleming and Parker, 2001; Keleher and Murphy, 2004).

Systems theories resonate strongly with social workers and human service workers within professional healthcare as they provide a valuable framework for assessment at individual, family, group and community levels. For both hospital- and community-based healthcare professionals, a systems theory framework legitimises an assessment focus beyond the individual or small group and allows the worker to engage with social, legal or policy factors that may be impacting on the wellbeing of clients, families, groups or communities or that may be disadvantaging or marginalising them. For hospital-based workers, systems theories promote the social worker's legitimate engagement with the patient's and family's life in the post-hospital context and emphasise the importance of continuity of care between hospital or health service, and community. For community-based workers as well, systems theories contribute to professional understanding and practice in community development and capacity building.

Strengths Perspective

The strengths perspective is a widely utilised practice approach within the social work profession (Saleebey, 2006) and is particularly relevant to healthcare work. The perspective is based on a consultative, supportive, enabling and empowering approach which builds on the resilience and inherent strengths of clients and their families, in contrast to framework such as biomedicine which focuses on deficits, 'abnormality' and 'pathology'. This approach also strongly resonates with social work and human service professions because of its implicit support for values such as self-determination, empowerment and respect for clients, as well as beliefs that clients are the experts within their own lives and experiential domains. Such an approach is in strong contrast to the biomedical framework in which 'patients' are regarded as passive recipients of complex and technical services that are delivered at the hands of biomedical experts (Samson, 1999).

Anti-oppressive and Empowerment Practice

Professional practice approaches that embody values relating to anti-oppression and empowerment are highly relevant to professional healthcare workers in hospital-based as well as community health sites. These approaches are underpinned by critical social theories that emphasise the structural determinants of inequality in society, as well as individual factors that influence health status (O'Connor-Fleming and Parker, 2001; Keleher and Murphy, 2004; Laverack, 2005); as such, they elevate social justice to a central position within the professional worker's practice framework (Healy, 2005; Payne, 2005). This approach has particular relevance for community-based social work and human service workers who aim to deliver health services based on empowerment models (for example, Black's 2003 description of a community-based health service using a feminist approach for women affected by eating disorders), as well as those referring more generally to healthcare services based on Ottawa Charter principles. In these contexts, a practice model will include health education, empowering individuals and communities and strengthening community capacity, as well as working towards policy reform and intersectoral collaboration in order to address social and health inequalities (Laverack, 2005).

Models of Ethical Decision-making

A well as healthcare *policies* that are dominated by economic principles and values and which can generate ethical dilemmas for social work and human service professionals, healthcare *settings* per se can be the sites of many (bio)ethical dilemmas and issues. Theories and models of ethical decision-making therefore assume central importance for the professional healthcare practitioner (Hugman and Smith, 1995; Loewenberg, Dolgoff and Harrington, 2000; Banks, 2001; Rothman, 2004; Chenoweth and McAuliffe, 2005). These theories and practice frameworks are essential professional tools for healthcare professionals who may experience a range of bioethical dilemmas, from questions about the rights of individuals to live or not live, to those involving right of access to limited healthcare resources (Leeder, 1999).

Summary

Best professional practice in healthcare, whether in hospital or community settings, is complex, challenging, exciting and rewarding. It involves successfully integrating a wide range of knowledge, skills and contexts so that the practitioner can work professionally, strategically and effectively. Of central importance is an understanding that the concepts of health and illness, while socially, culturally, politically as well as individually constructed, are largely defined in biomedical and biological terms. Also of significance is an understanding and appreciation of current trends and values in healthcare policy and how these shape and significantly impact on the organisational sites of service delivery and professional practice; effectively engaging with, communicating within and negotiating these complex environments within a social justice framework are primary goals of the professional healthcare practitioner. Within these complex contexts, professional workers also bring a wide range of theoretical and professional knowledge and skill in order to undertake assessments and interventions that are appropriate and effective in relation to individuals, families, groups and communities. While working in healthcare can be accompanied by trauma and stress for the worker, it can also be characterised by rich opportunities for effective and rewarding engagement, advocacy and change. Professional supervision, critical reflective practice, peer support and continuing professional education are essential, however, for the effective, evolving healthcare practitioner.

Review Questions

1. How would you define 'good health' in a way that is personally meaningful to you? How do you think factors such as your age, gender, family life and cultural background have influenced this definition?

2. What are the main differences between the assumptions and focus of biomedical and socio-ecological perspectives on health and illness?

3. Name some of the main current trends in Australian healthcare policy. What influences do you think these might be having on the way services are delivered in hospitals? In community healthcare settings?

4. With regard to Question 3 above, identify the potential influence that these trends could have on consumers, and professional healthcare workers such as social workers and human service workers.

5. Identify and discuss some of the main differences in context, and their implications, between professional healthcare practice within a large city hospital and a rural community health centre.

6. Name two theoretical frameworks that are relevant to social work or human service professionals in healthcare and explain how these could inform the assessment process in: (i) a hospital-based Department of Emergency Medicine; (ii) an oncology ward in a large teaching hospital; and (iii) a community health centre that offers group programs to maximise the health and wellbeing of teenage mothers in the local area.

Useful Websites

Australian Institute of Health and Welfare	http://www.aihw.gov.au/
'For Health Professionals'– Department of Health and Aged Care	http://www.dhac.gov.au/internet/wcms/publishing.nsf/Content/For+Health+Professionals-1
HealthInsite	http://www.healthinsite.gov.au/
Australian Association of Social Workers	http://www.aasw.asn.au/
HealthWeb	http://healthweb.org/
Medical Journal of Australia	http://www.mja.com.au/
Cochrane Collaboration regarding evidence in healthcare	http://www.cochrane.org/index0.htm

References

Australian Institute of Health and Welfare (AIHW) (2004) *Australia's Health 2004*, Canberra: AIHW. Available at: <http://www.aihw.gov.au/publications/index.cfm/title/10014>.

Banks, S (2001) *Ethics and Values in Social Work* (2nd ed), Basingstoke, Hampshire: Palgrave MacMillan.

Black, C (2003) 'Creating curative communities: Feminist group work with women with eating disorders', *Australian Social Work*, 56(2), 127-140.

Briton, C (2000) 'Themes on hope and living with a life-threatening illness', *Australian Social Work*, 53(1), 51-55.

Caltabiano, ML and Sarafino, EP (2002) 'Current perspectives on health and illness: The bio-psychosocial perspective', in ML Caltabiano and EP Sarafino (eds) *Health Psychology: Biopsychosocial Interactions: An Australian Perspective* (pp 22-26), Milton, Qld: John Wiley & Sons.

Chenoweth, L and McAuliffe, D (2005) *The Road to Social Work and Human Service Practice: An Introductory Text*, Melbourne: Thomson.

Chenoweth, L and Stehlik, D (2001) 'Building resilient communities: Social work practice and rural Queensland', *Australian Social Work*, 54(2), 47-54.

Cleak, H (2002) 'A model of social work classification in health care', *Australian Social Work*, 55(1), 38-49.

Daly, J, Hughes, E and op't Hoog, C (2002) 'Evidence-based health: Three cheers for non-compliance', in H Gardner and S Barraclough (eds) *Health Policy in Australia* (pp 261-274), Melbourne: Oxford University Press.

Dominelli, L (2002) *Feminist Social Work: Theory and Practice*, Basingstoke: Palgrave.

Dorsett, P and Geraghty, T (2004) 'Depression and adjustment after spinal cord injury: A three year longitudinal study', *Topics in Spinal Cord Injury Rehabilitation*, 9(4), 43-56.

Draper, M (1999) 'Casemix: Financing Hospital Services', in L Hancock (ed) *Health Policy in the Market State* (pp 131-148), Sydney: Allen & Unwin.

Duckett, SJ (2004) *The Australian Health Care System*, Melbourne: Oxford University Press.

Engel, GL (1977) 'The need for a new medical model: A challenge for biomedicine', *Science*, 196 (4286), 129-136.

Fook, J (2002) *Social Work: Critical Theory and Practice*, London: Sage.

Gay, J Herriot, M and May, A (1995) 'Primary health care beyond the city', in F Baum (ed) *Health for All: The South Australian Experience* (pp 375-392), Kent Town, SA: Wakefield Press.

Germov, J (ed) (2005) *Second Opinion: An Introduction to Health Sociology* (3rd ed), Melbourne: Oxford University Press.

Gibbons, J (2001) 'Effective practice: Social work's long history of concern about outcomes', *Australian Social Work*, 54(3), 3-13.

Grbich, C (1999) *Health in Australia: Sociological Concepts and Issues*, Sydney: Longman.

Hancock, L (ed) (1999) *Health Policy in the Market State*, Sydney: Allen & Unwin.

Hancock, L and Moore, S (1999) 'Caring and the state', in L Hancock (ed) *Health Policy in the Market State* (pp 265-287), Sydney: Allen & Unwin.

Harms, L (2004) 'After the accident: Survivors' perceptions of recovery following road trauma', *Australian Social Work*, 57(2), 161-174.

Harvey, KJ, Faunce, TA, Lokuge, B and Drahos, P (2004) 'Will the Australia–United States free trade agreement undermine the pharmaceutical benefits scheme?', *Medical Journal of Australia*, 181(5), 256-259.

Healy, K (2004) 'Social workers in the new human services marketplace: Trends, challenges and responses' *Australian Social Work*, 57(2), 103-114.

Healy, K (2005) *Social Work Theories in Context: Creating Frameworks for Practice*, Basingstoke, Hampshire: Palgrave MacMillan.

Healy, L (1998) *Welfare Options: Delivering Social Services*, Sydney: Allen & Unwin.

Hugman, R and Smith, D (eds) (1995) *Ethical Issues in Social Work*, London: Routledge.

Ife, J (1997) *Rethinking Social Work: Towards Critical Practice*, Melbourne: Longman.

Iphofen, R and Poland, F (1998) *Sociology in Practice for Health Care Professionals*, London: Palgrave MacMillan.

Jones, K (2003) *Health and Human Behaviour*, Melbourne: Oxford University Press.

Keleher, H and Murphy, B (2004) *Understanding Health: A Determinants Approach*, Melbourne: Oxford University Press.

Kennedy, R, Harvey, J and Gursansky, D (2001) 'The response of Australian universities to case management', *Australian Social Work*, 54(4), 29-38.

Laverack, G (2005) *Public Health: Power, Empowerment and Professional Practice*, Basingstoke, Hamsphire: Palgrave MacMillan.

Leeder, S (1999) 'Resource allocation: The ethical dilemma of our age', in S Leeder (ed) *Healthy Medicine: Challenges Facing Australia's Health Services* (pp 89-100), Sydney: Allen & Unwin.

Loewenberg, F, Dolgoff, R and Harrington, D (2000) *Ethical Decisions for Social Work Practice*, Itasca, ILL: FE Peacock.

McAuliffe, D and Armstrong, M (2002) 'Using the moral continuum: An activity for teaching ethics in social work?', *Perspectives in Social Work*, 17(3), 3-8.

McCormack, J (2001) 'How many social workers now? A review of census and other data', *Australian Social Work*, 54(3), 63-72.

McDonald, C (1999) 'Human service professionals in the community services industry', *Australian Social Work*, 52(1), 17-25.

McDonald, C and Zetlin, D (2004) '"The more things change ...": Barriers to community services utilization in Queensland', *Australian Social Work*, 57(2), 115-126.

Miller, J (2001) 'The knowledge, skills and qualities needed for social work in a major paediatric teaching hospital', *Australian Social Work*, 54(1), 3-6.

Munn, P (2003) 'Factors influencing service coordination in rural South Australia', *Australian Social Work*, 56(4), 305-317.

Murphy, A and McDonald, J (2004) 'Power, status and marginalization: Rural social workers and evidence-based practice in multi-disciplinary teams', *Australian Social Work*, 57(2), 127-136.

Netting, F (1992) Case management: service or symptom? *Australian Social Work* 37(2): 160-163.

O'Connor, I, Smyth, P and Warburton, J (eds) (2000) *Contemporary Perspectives on Social Work and the Human Services: Challenges and Change*, Sydney: Pearson Education.

O'Connor, I, Wilson, J and Setterlund, D (2003) *Social Work and Welfare Practice* (4th ed), Sydney: Pearson Education.

O'Connor-Fleming, M and Parker, E (eds) (2001) *Health Promotion: Principles and Practice in the Australian Context* (2nd ed), Sydney: Allen & Unwin.

Ozanne, E (1996) 'Case management applications in Australia', *Journal of Case Management*, 5(4), 153-157.

Palmer, GR and Short, SD (2000) *Health Care and Public Policy: An Australian Analysis* (3rd ed), Melbourne: MacMillan.

Payne, M (2005) *Modern Social Work Theory* (3rd ed), Basingstoke, Hampshire: Palgrave MacMillan.

Queensland Health (2004a) *Queensland Health Annual Report 2003-2004*, Brisbane: Queensland Health. Available at: <http://www.health.qld.gov.au/publications/corporate/annual_reports/annualreport2004/default.asp>.

Queensland Health (2004b) *Health Determinants Queensland 2004*, Brisbane: Queensland Health. Available at: <http://www.health.qld.gov.au/phs/ Documents/phpru/22418_glance.pdf>.

Rapp, N and Chamberlain, R (1985) 'Case management services for the mentally ill', *Social Work*, 30(5), 417-422.

Reid, W (1994) 'The empirical practice movement', *Social Service Review*, 68(2), 165-184.

Richards, F and Taylor, SD (1997) 'Social work and genetic testing: Ethical issues encountered in predictive testing for Huntington's Disease', *Australian Social Work*, 50(4), 61-67.

Roberts, A (1990) *Crisis Intervention Handbook: Assessment, Treatment and Research*, Belmont, CA: Wadsworth.

Rolland, J (1994) *Families, Illness and Disability*, New York: Basic Books.

Rolland, JS and Williams, JK (2005) 'Towards a biopsychosocial model for 21st century genetics', *Family Process*, 44(1), 3-24.

Rothman, J (2004) *From the Front Lines: Student Cases in Social Work Ethics* (2nd ed), Boston: Allyn and Bacon.

Sackett, DL, Richardson, WS, Rosenberg, W and Haynes, RB (1997) *Evidence-based Medicine: How to Practice and Teach EBM*, New York: Churchill Livingstone.

Saleebey, D (2006) *The Strengths Perspective in Social Work Practice* (4th ed), Boston: Allyn & Bacon.

Samson, C (1999) 'Biomedicine and the body', in C Samson (ed) *Health Studies: A Critical and Cross-cultural Reader* (pp 3-21), Oxford: Blackwell.

Shapiro, M, Setterlund, D, Warburton, J and O'Connor, I (2004) 'Testing an outcome-directed model of social work practice in the hospital setting', Paper presented at the Princess Alexandra Hospital Research Week, May 2004.

Simpson, G, Foster M, Kuipers, P, Kendall, M and Hanna, J (2005) 'An organizational perspective on goal setting in community-based brain injury rehabilitation', *Disability and Rehabilitation*, 27(15), 901-910.

Simpson, G, Simons, M and McFadyen, M (2002) 'The challenges of hidden disability: Social work practice in the field of traumatic brain injury', *Australian Social Work*, 55(1), 24-37.

Smith, J (1999) 'Shifts in community health care', in L Hancock (ed) *Health Policy in the Market State* (pp 169-186), Sydney: Allen & Unwin.

Smith, S (2002) 'What works for whom: The link between process and outcome in effectiveness research', *Australian Social Work*, 55(2), 147-155.

Stoez, D (2000) 'Renaissance', *Families in Society*, 81(6), 621-628.

Stone, C (1997) 'Medical diagnosis of postnatal depression: Help or hindrance?', *Australian Social Work*, 50(2), 49-56.

Taylor, SD (1998) 'A case study of genetic discrimination: Social work and advocacy within a new context', *Australian Social Work*, 51(4), 51-57.

Thornton, A and Battistel, L (2001) 'Working with burns survivors: A social work approach', *Australian Social Work*, 54(3), 93-103.

United Nations (1948) *Universal Declaration of Human Rights*. Available at: <http://www.un.org/Overview/rights.html>.

World Health Organization (WHO) (1946) *Preamble to the Constitution*. Available at: <http://www.who.int/hhr/en/>.

Chapter 8

Older People

Deborah Setterlund, Jill Wilson and Cheryl Tilse

Introduction

Social workers, human service practitioners and older people encounter each other in a range of settings and circumstances. Practice can involve such diverse activities as assisting older people in hospital to access services so they can continue to live in their own home, to facilitating social action by older people in a neighbourhood setting. It involves working with and on behalf of older people in family, neighbourhood and institutional contexts. In this chapter we present a framework for practice designed to enable practitioners working in different settings and circumstances to work with older people towards mutually agreed upon ethical outcomes.

Practice Framework for Social Work in the Field of Ageing

The framework prioritises older people's subjective experience of their circumstances and their preferred outcomes regarding their wellbeing within the limits and opportunities presented by the organisational and ethical context of practice. It promotes a critical gerontology perspective, and the importance of applying context specific knowledge, theories and skills to suit the unique circumstances presented by older people. People bring into old age a range of experiences, positive and negative, such as a history of abuse or separation from parents, having been a refugee, having a history of significant achievements – they are all survivors of a wealth of experiences.

A broad orienting social context provides the necessary background knowledge for workers to understand how older people are positioned in society. Topics explored here are social factors such as demographic change, health and retirement incomes and relevant policy and service delivery factors.

Practice is also embedded in the worker's employing organisation. Organisations and the service delivery systems provide opportunities and constraints on practice. An understanding of the broad social environment for older people and the social work practice context provides a base from which to develop assessments and devise and use a range of interventions to achieve social goals.

Social workers are required to work within an understanding of the individual in interaction with their social environment including informal networks, formal organisations and institutions. Core values, context specific knowledge, theories and skills are needed to deliver best practice. We now turn to explicate this framework.

Social Contexts of Ageing

Knowledge of social factors related to the aged population provides the basis for understanding the policy responses governments make regarding containing the cost and delineating and targeting care for older people. It also provides the basis for appreciating diversity of experience in old age.

Demographic Change

Populations are ageing worldwide, with the Asia Pacific region ageing most rapidly (Phillips, 2000). In 2001, 12.3 per cent of the Australian population of 19.4 million people were aged 65 years and over and this percentage is expected to grow to approximately 26 per cent of the population by 2051 (Australian Institute of Health and Welfare (AIHW), 2002: 4). The proportion of older people aged 80 years and over is expected to grow from 1.3 per cent of the population in 2003 to 5 per cent in 2051 (AIHW, 2002: 5). The average life expectancy at birth for Australians is now 80 years. Life expectancy at age 65 has increased with women aged 65 in 2001 expected to live to 85.2 years and men to 81.6 years (AIHW 2002: 30). While women will continue to outnumber men in old age, men's life expectancy is increasing more rapidly than women's. The gap is closing and this has implications for care delivery; for example, there may be proportionally more men in aged care facilities than is currently the case.

The number of older Australians from culturally and linguistically diverse backgrounds is expected to grow from 18 per cent of the older population in 1996 to 23 per cent by 2011, with an expected 165 per cent increase in those over 85 years (AIHW, 2002: 5). However, the 2001 census figures show that people of Aboriginal and Torres Strait Islander descent comprised 2.4 per cent of the Australian population and of these, only 31, 200 were aged 55 years and over (AIHW, 2002: 48). Life expectancy at birth for Indigenous people is estimated to be 59 years for males and 65 years for females (Australian Bureau of Statistics (ABS) and AIHW, 2005). Indigenous people remain disadvantaged across a range of areas of social concern including health, income and housing. This, in addition to cultural issues and, in some cases, rural and remote location will shape the experience of ageing and social work practice with this group.

Income

Older retired Australians are supported by a mix of public pensions, superannuation and voluntary savings (Minister for Ageing, 2001). In 2002, 1.8 million older people received the Age Pension and the majority of these recipients were women (AIHW, 2002: 20). The Australian government policy trend towards greater self-provision in old age and the introduction of compulsory superannuation schemes will mean that in future years fewer older people will be receiving a full Age Pension, resulting in savings to public expenditure on income support for older Australians (AIHW, 2002: 21). It will also mean more complex incomes for older people and their carers to manage.

Health

Diseases of the circulatory system, cancers and diseases of the respiratory system account for over three quarters of all deaths of people aged 65 years and over (AIHW, 2002: 30). These diseases are strongly linked to risk factors such as obesity, high blood pressure and cholesterol, cigarette smoking and lack of regular exercise. Disability levels, measured in terms of core activity restrictions (related to self-care, mobility or communication) show that one in five aged people report a profound or severe core activity restriction (AIHW, 2002: 38). Depression has been identified as an under-diagnosed health issue for older people (AIHW, 2002: 37). It can impact on older people's confidence and capacity to cope with the challenges of ageing. Rates of suicide for older men increase with age, peaking at age 85 and older and is an emerging health concern and a target for preventative strategies.

Cognitive impairments caused by mental health issues, acquired brain injury, stroke or dementia will increasingly be issues for older people, carers and service providers. In 2002 there were 162,000 Australians (0.8 per cent of the population) suffering from dementia (Access Economics, 2005: 2). Based on current prevalence rates the numbers of Australians with dementia is predicted to rise to 581,300 in 2051 or 2.3 per cent of the projected population (Access Economics, 2005: 2).

Living Arrangements

In 1999 almost three quarters of older Australians lived in private housing, with a spouse or partner (AIHW, 2002: 6). Those living alone are much more likely to be women and the chances of living alone increases with age. There is a trend away from institutional care in Australia, while only 8 per cent of older people currently live in non-private dwellings including residential aged care (AIHW, 2002: 6). However, a much larger proportion of cohorts of very old people do enter residential facilities.

Family Networks

The majority of older Australians enjoy 'small but rich' social support networks (Kendig, 2000). Despite changing family patterns, characterised by an increase in one parent and blended families, higher rates of female participation in the labour force and higher family mobility, statistics show that families continue to provide assistance to older members (AIHW, 2002). Care for older people often is a mix of family and friendship networks, state funded and private services. Of increasing concern to policy makers and families alike is the position of the 'sandwich generation', middle aged parents who have responsibilities for both their own children and older parents, and older people who provide primary care for grandchildren. In addition, the diversity of family and friendship networks, including same sex partners and families (Langley, 2001), needs to be recognised in policy and practice.

Against this backdrop of social factors related to ageing we now turn to discuss related policy responses and how these ultimately influence service delivery, professional practice with older people and the ways that older people view themselves. A key issue to be understood is that the variation in circumstances of individual older people reflect the opportunities and constraints of a life course. Workers will need to be able to work with a diversity of older people in a variety of social contexts.

Policy Responses

The Australian government policy on ageing is set out in the key document *National Strategy for an Ageing Australia* (Minister for Ageing, 2001) which outlines four key themes: (1) independence and self-provision; (2) attitude, lifestyle and community supports; (3) healthy ageing; and (4) world class care including a focus on ageing in place. To some extent, Australia's ageing policy reflects concerns with a perceived 'burden' of an ageing population, particularly health and income support costs. This is reflected in a concern to shift and share responsibility for income support, care and health from the state to the individual and family. However, Australia is likely to accrue benefits from an ageing population, including increased prosperity through 'baby boomer' wealth, an increased pool of volunteers, and market opportunities related to older consumers (Healy, 2004). Australia's policy on ageing and the messages it conveys about the role of older people in society influences attitudes to older people. It is important therefore for professionals to have a critical understanding of changing societal views on ageing and the impact of dominant assumptions and stereotypes on professional practice.

Societal Views on Ageing and Stereotypes of Ageing

Old age as a time of physical and mental decline and non-productivity has been a dominant assumption in Western societies. However, in the past two decades a critique of this assumption has emerged (Tirrito, 2003), increasing the range of possibilities about what it means to be old. Such changes are now appearing in popular culture where, for example, some American television shows portray 'mainstream older characters as powerful, healthy, active, admired, sexy and affluent' (Fitzgerald, 1999: 76).

The trend towards a more positive and less one dimensional view of old age is reflected in Australian ageing policy, where concepts of *healthy ageing, successful ageing, positive ageing, active ageing* and *well ageing* are now prominent in ageing policy discourse. The names of some older people's groups, for example, 'Older People Speak Out', and '60 and Better' suggest an active, more assertive role for older people in society.

However, these positive images of ageing coexist with historical, entrenched negative stereotypes of old age as a time of illness, senility and passivity. Media reports focus on the potential for abuse by fraudsters and caregivers. The professional challenge for practitioners is to understand how these diverse constructions of old age impact on older people, their families and professional interactions with older people. For example, constructions such as healthy and successful ageing can become a 'new orthodoxy' (Katz, 2000) which may suggest to those who do not fit this image that they are somehow unsuccessful and individually respon-sible for their health problems. Portrayals of older 'unsuccessful' people as high consumers of scarce health and welfare resources may engender guilt in older individuals needing extensive healthcare services.

Professionals who respond uncritically to these constructions of old age may act against the interests of older people – for example, by assu-ming that 'it's time' an older person may be moved to a nursing home, following multiple admissions to hospital or that older women should be able to manage domestic activities better and for longer periods than older men. Social workers need to be more aware of their own biases when working with older people (Richards, 2000) and employ critical reflective processes to question their decision-making in practice.

Theories of Ageing and Critical Gerontology

There are a wide range of biological, psychological, life course and social theories such as activity theory and life course theory (Baltes and Baltes, 1990) which can be used to guide assessment, intervention and evaluation of outcomes. Practitioners need to have a working knowledge of these and other theories, the impact they have had on professional practice and societal views of ageing and a critique of their relative strengths and weaknesses. Moody (2000) provides a useful overview of key theories on ageing. Theories on ageing need to be applied alongside problem and context specific theories such as dementia specific theories surrounding environmental modification and the importance of maintaining the older person's personal identity (Kitwood and Bredin, 1992). In this chapter we elaborate critical theory which focuses on the role of power in influencing interactions between individuals and their social arrangements.

Critical gerontology is concerned with 'identifying possibilities for emancipatory social change, including positive ideals for the last stage of life' (Moody 1993: xv). Applied to work with older people, critical theory guides practice towards exploring both the personal and structural factors that marginalise older people and interventions that assist older people to assert their views and preferences. Such interventions are also concerned with producing more equitable structures, such as fairer social policy and anti-discriminatory laws. It calls for critical reflective practice, where practitioners are aware of their own biases, question the basis for their decision-making and focus on clients' strengths and their differences in experience, rather than on deficits. Critical theory explores causes predominantly in relation to barriers to older people exercising their options. Being critically reflective means that the practitioner appraises and uses available knowledge in the form of research findings to guide assessment and make choices with clients about suitable interventions.

Postmodern theory contributes to critical theory an understanding of the ways in which some truths or knowledge come to be dominant and marginalise the experiences or 'voices' of those who exercise least power in society. In ageing studies, postmodernism highlights the importance of understanding the interaction of social structural factors such as class, ethnicity and sexual preference which shape human experience in unique ways, the ways in which power operates in society and the importance of listening to the voices of those most marginalised (see, for example, Bytheway, 1995; Bevan and Jeeawody, 1998).

Key Issues in Ageing

As part of the orienting context of ageing it is important for workers to have an understanding of the key issues in the field of ageing. These issue are broad and could include issues of housing, transport, poverty, super-annuation, quality in health and aged care services, social isolation, well ageing, user rights and relationship and family conflict. While these are important for social work practice we have chosen to focus on five issues that present significant challenges for practitioners: dementia, care giving, assisted and substitute decision-making, financial elder abuse and participation.

Dementia

Dementia is a 'term used to describe the symptoms of a large group of illnesses which cause a progressive decline in a person's mental functioning' (according to Alzheimers' Australia Fact Sheet) which 'affects higher cortical functions, including memory, thinking, orientation, calculation, learning capacity, language and judgment' (Brown, 1998: 253). It is progressive, chronic and insidious in onset, with no definitive cause or cure. It requires long term care that is costly financially and emotionally and challenges the individual, family members, care providers and health institutions.

In Australia there are a range of services to assist older people with dementia and their carers, largely provided by Home and Community Care, such as information provision, advocacy, transport assistance, community nursing, meals on wheels, home maintenance and respite care (day care, in home and residential care) (Brown, 1998). Older people with dementia can access long term residential care where they may be placed in specially designed safe units which can cater for people who wander and who have behaviour difficulties. Social workers play a variety of roles in supporting older people and their carers. These include advocacy for services, assistance with organising community and residential care, arranging substitute decision-making mechanisms, support for caregivers, assessment and referral for specialised services.

Caregiving

The most recent available Australian statistics show that in 1998 there were approximately 200,000 unpaid people providing care for people aged 65 years and older (AIHW, 2002: 42). Caregiving networks provide essential support for older people with disabilities. Family members are the largest source of caregiving in Australia and the majority of formal and informal care work is carried out by women, mostly spouses and daughters. An extensive research study on family caregivers conducted in Victoria, Australia showed that carers reported poorer health and wellbeing than non-carers and that stress was associated with being of younger age, living with the care-recipient, being single, unemployed, and caring for a person with mental disabilities and associated behaviour problems (Schofield et al, 1998). While caregiving is by no means uniformly burdensome and can be emotionally rewarding, the carer role remains largely invisible and undervalued in society. Social work with older people frequently involves working with family members, friend, neighbours and formal paid carers who care for older people.

Caregivers from culturally and linguistically diverse backgrounds may experience additional specific difficulties related to lack of information about services available, care recipients' dislike of formal services, feelings of obligation to continue caring at all costs and the need for greater involvement by other family members (Schofield et al, 1998: 53-

54). The difficulties of caregiving in rural and remote areas may be exacerbated by problems of access to health and aged care services (AIHW, 2002: 22, see also Chapter 9 of this volume).

In Australia caregivers are Home and Community Care clients in their own right and the Commonwealth funds services and information networks to provide support. Social work with carers involves timely access to information, respite services and practical, emotional and financial support. They mediate where the needs of older people and their carers may be in conflict.

Assisted and Substitute Decision-making

Increased longevity and physical and cognitive impairment in older age means that more older people will need assistance with decision-making and/or carrying out their decisions, in relation to their finances, accommodation and health matters, including decisions around treatment at end of life. Family members and partners are most likely to be assisting older people with such decision-making.

Practitioners need to be aware that while the majority of families will strive to protect the interests of their older members, there is the potential for difficulties to arise and conflicts of interests or abuse to occur (Setterlund, Tilse and Wilson, 1999, 2002). As a result older people may feel disempowered in the decision-making process, and caregivers may find assisting with decisions adds to the stress of caregiving.

In order to assist older people and their caregivers in problematic situations surrounding decision-making, practitioners need a thorough understanding of relevant legal provisions, namely *Powers of Attorney* and *Guardianship and Administration* legislation and the *Aged Care Act 1997* (Cth) (Setterlund et al, 2002) which sets out rights and responsibilities in relation to accommodation and service delivery.

Financial Elder Abuse

Financial abuse is one form of elder abuse (other forms are physical, psychological, social, sexual) that appears to be increasing (Rabiner, O'Keefe and Brown, 2004: 54). It may include theft of money or material belongings, coercion or undue influence towards an older person to relinquish money and fraudulent use of an older person's money. Research into the management of the assets of older people within families shows that decision-making regarding older people's assets is an emerging and contested issue and that risky practices regarding older people's assets may in some instances lead to abuse (Tilse et al, 2005). While it is difficult to accurately estimate the degree of financial abuse of older people from the available studies, one study revealed that elder abuse affects some 4.6 per cent of older people, of whom 1.1 per cent reported financial abuse (Kurrle, Sadler and Cameron, 1992).

Research shows that mostly financial abuse of older people is conducted by close family members and relatives (Kurrle et al, 1992; Podneiks, 1992; Brill, 1999). In this position of relative trust, family members have the capacity both to safeguard and to misuse an older person's assets. Social workers need to work with older people and their carers on issues of accountability and transparency in dealing with money, the need to balance trust within families with prudent practices and to increase financial literacy generally in the community to reduce the incidence of financial elder abuse.

Participation in Community Life

Participation of older people is defined by the United Nations (1991) as involvement in policy development, sharing knowledge and skills, serving as volunteers and forming movements and associations. The concept of participation is strongly represented in Australian government healthy ageing policy goals (AIHW and Commonwealth Department of Health and Aged Care, 1997) and in the *Aged Care Act 1997* (Cth) (Care Standard 3 – Resident Lifestyle). Participation involves a personal dimension, for example, volunteering, and a political dimension, such as the need to reduce discrimination against older people.

The concept of participation has been critiqued for its capacity to be interpreted conservatively as, for example, older people taking responsibility for their own health and becoming targets of government strategies to 'activate' them (Katz, 2000). Nevertheless, the ideal of increasing the participation and inclusion of groups who are readily marginalised by society, and the notion of highlighting the contributions and strengths of older people resonates with social work's concerns with social justice, and social change. Furthermore, social work's expertise in community work can provide the theoretical and skills base needed to facilitate the participation of older people in community life and civil society and extend the scope of social work with older people beyond a concern with dependency and disability.

In summary, social workers entering the field of ageing require orienting knowledge which helps develop a broad understanding of the societal trends in relation to older people, commonality and diversity of experience in older age and key issues, all of which impact on practice. Equipped with this background knowledge, practitioners are then in a position, within their organisational context, to work with older people to understand and intervene in a range of situations. The following section explores the practice context, which includes the framework for assessment and intervention.

The Practice Context in the Field of Ageing

We begin this section by briefly discussing the influence of the organisational context and the core of social work (including purpose, values and ethics and theory) on practice and then proceed with a more detailed discussion of assessment processes and interventions in the field of ageing.

The Influence of the Organisational Context

While older people may access human services of all kinds, social workers are most likely to encounter older people in community and hospital health settings, and specific settings such as respite, dementia services and residential aged care services. Each setting provides opportunities and constraints for innovative practice. Social aspects are often obscured by recent trends towards managerialism, targeting of services and privatisation of services. High workloads, and complex and competing organisational demands have also led to increased emphasis on risk assessment and management, formal assessment protocols for service, a reduced emphasis on professional judgment and more routinised approaches to problems.

In this context it is essential that social workers have an understanding and critique of socioeconomic policies and how social work is positioned within these policies. Practitioners must be able to articulate outcomes sought and ways of achieving these. They need to take account of what constitutes best practice, put accountability systems in place, advocate for alternative, socially just ways of providing welfare and use discretion in applying policy in practice. The challenge for practitioners and administrators is finding a balance between meeting organisational demands and using professional discretion and judgment (O'Connor et al, 2003).

Purpose

In human service work, a clear sense of purpose is needed to guide ethical practice. From a social work perspective, the purpose of human service work may be viewed as assisting people to have more equitable relationships with their social arrangements and having more power and control over their own lives (O'Connor et al, 2003). That power is constrained by the extent that it infringes on the wellbeing of others. The role of the practitioner is to ensure that the interests of older people are prominent, particularly when older people lack capacity to assert their own interests, while seeking outcomes that take account of the interests of others, for example, the wellbeing of family carers. Ethical decision-making in circumstances of competing interests is central to work with, and on behalf of, older people.

Values and Ethics

As with all professional practice, core values and ethics underpin practice with older people. In addition to generic professional social work values and ethics (Australian Association of Social Workers, 1999), there is an argument that work with older people requires particular vigilance around issues of consent, confidentiality and conduct (Tinker, 2003: 207). Tinker's view is based on concerns that older people may suffer cognitive impairments which affect their decision-making, may be in dependent relationships with others who may be making decisions on their behalf and may have more difficulties than do other groups of people with processing information.

Practitioners, often in consultation with other health professionals, need to carefully assess the older person's decision-making capacities, particularly variations in their capacity around different matters. They need also to ensure that older people are not being coerced into decisions by caregivers and that information is provided in a way that they can process. The trend towards consumer participation in service delivery has highlighted the importance of mutuality in decision-making between professionals and clients, to the full extent of each individual's capacity. Given the stereotypes that surround getting old, workers need to reflect carefully on their own ageist attitudes and those reproduced in their organisation (Bytheway, 1995) which limit and constrain decision-making and choices for older people.

Assessment and Intervention

Assessment

Assessment involves both processes and an end point of agreements about client led outcomes. Supportive, relational processes facilitate mutual understanding of the problematic situation and negotiation of agreed outcomes or changes that clients want in their lives as a result of interventions. Our guide for assessment involves attention to process, understanding individual and social factors, analysing the interactions between these factors, particularly power imbalances, and establishing agreed outcomes.

The Process of Assessment

An accurate assessment necessitates listening attentively to the older person's construction of their own experiences (Richards, 2000) and effective communication skills. 'Communication predicaments' occur when professionals make generalisations about the communicative capacities of older people based on negative stereotypes of incapacity and dependency rather than on an assessment of an individual's skills (Ryan et al, 1995). Generalising can lead to uncalled for speech modifications such as a slower speaking rate, exaggerated intonation, high pitch and overly simplified language and grammar. This type of communication may have a negative impact on the older person's self-esteem and further attempts to communicate.

Ryan et al (1995) suggest a communication enhancement model in which professionals assess the older person's individual capacity, adjust their communication style accordingly and where necessary, positively modify the communication environment through strategies such as improved acoustics or more effective hearing devices.

In many organisations, in particular in health and Aged Care Assessment Team settings, practitioners are expected to use formal assessment protocols, consisting of set questions categorising physical, cognitive, emotional and functional capacity (for example, activities of daily living). Some protocols may include scaled item tests such as the mini-mental state. Where formal protocols are used the worker must be sensitive to the potential negative impact of routine questioning on the older person's self-worth and anxiety levels regarding their health limitations. Formal protocols can be used creatively in a conversational manner, covering categories in a non-linear way and seeking information through both closed and open-ended questions, where the latter invites the older person to express their subjective views and experiences.

Assessing Individual Factors

We suggest a focus on four aspects of individual experience: basic needs, physical health, psychological health and life course experiences. Basic needs includes level of income, adequacy of housing, restrictions that may limit capacity to meet basic needs, such as lack of information, and mobility problems. Physical health includes functional capacities and impairments and their impact on activities of daily living such as dressing, feeding, showering. Practitioners need to be alert to the physical signs of elder abuse such as suspicious bruising or physical injury and the older person appearing uncomfortable talking about these injuries (McInnes-Dittrich, 2002: 90). Psychological wellbeing refers to an individual's general satisfaction with life and specifically whether dementia or depression are indicated and further expert assessment needed. Life course experiences refers to experiences over time that older people identify as important and the meaning of those experiences then and now. For example, an individual's reconstruction of living through historical events such as the Second World War and 'the Depression', and particular events such as loss of loved ones, experiences of abusive or nurturing relationships, work achievements and disappointments, are all likely to impact on a person's current wellbeing.

Assessing Social Arrangements

To understand the social arrangements with which individuals engage, Monkman's (1991) four outcome domains have been adapted. 'Informal networks' refers to the density and quality of relationships with family, kin, friends, coworkers and others who are available to the older person for emotional support, advice and physical assistance if needed. 'Formal and societal resources' involves mapping the individual's interactions with formal organisations such as clubs and service groups through to societal institutions such as the health system, the legal system, income security and so on. 'Expectations' refers to obligations and duties grounded in societal structures (especially those related to class, gender and culture) and expressed as roles and tasks. Patterned behaviour around roles may be empowering or disempowering of older people or others, for example, cultural expectations that grandparents should make themselves available to care for grandchildren while adult children work may disadvantage some older people. 'Laws, policies, customs and rules' explores the impact of regulations and policies as well as customs held by society or family. For example, earlier in this chapter we outlined a range of changes in welfare provision towards user pays and individual responsibility for wellbeing in old age, which have an impact on people's access to resources in later life.

Analysing the Interactions Between Individual Factors and Social Arrangements

Once the practitioner has an understanding of these content areas of assessment, it is possible to critically analyse the transactions or tensions within these arrangements that are contributing to the problematic situation. Where the practitioner is working as part of a team, this process will involve hearing and evaluating the perspectives of other team members, and integrating different perspectives to form a multidimensional understanding of the older person's situation. It will also involve advocating where relevant to ensure the perspectives of the older person and their family are heard. Protecting the interests of older people in teams requires skills in effective communication, conflict resolution and advocacy.

A critical gerontology theory is useful to understand the role of power in shaping relationships between older people and others in their social environment. Does, for example, the older person who is experiencing severe mobility limitations have informal resources to draw upon and are these resources supportive? Is the older person feeling overly controlled or disempowered by services that do not match needs or by the way in which services are delivered? Is the older person expecting a level of care from a relative that is impossible to provide, based on cultural expectations surrounding the role of family and their obligations to elders? Is the situation such that the older person is not cognitively competent to express their needs directly? In these situations practitioners will be relying on relatives and others close to the older person to provide information and interpret observed behaviour.

In analysing the nature of these transactions it is crucial to identify both strengths and constraints. The enabling or disabling effects of the environment on older people's life choices and chances need to be carefully considered. Once a mutual understanding of the client's situation has been obtained, the next step in assessment involves establishing agreed outcomes.

Establishing Agreed Outcomes

Client outcomes are identifiable client related events or changes as a result of intervention. See Nicholas, Qureshi and Bamford, *Outcomes into Practice* (2003) for comprehensive practice guidelines for outcome directed practice with older people and their carers. They must be client directed as far as their personal and situational resources allow, agreed upon by the worker, particularly in relation to professional ethics and worker competence and negotiated within the expectations, constraints and opportunities of the organisational context. Preferred outcomes are not always easy to voice and the practitioner must be skilled and creative in facilitating thinking beyond the confines of what is known. Outcomes need to be expressed in measurable terms as far as possible (for example, we will know what form of support all family members can offer at this time) and in language familiar to the client. Once outcomes have been agreed upon, the next practice phase involves choosing interventions that are both acceptable to clients and most likely to achieve the outcomes desired.

Choosing Interventions

We favour an empowerment approach (Harvey, 2001; Langley, 2001) to intervention. This approach supports social work's aim to increase older people's power and control over their own lives. It requires skills in a range of strategies capable of changing both intra/interpersonal and social conditions. Advocacy, policy work, action research and organisational work are all relevant. In this chapter we have focused primarily on a case study where the focus was on an individual. We have also included brief examples of group work and community intervention.

Interpersonal Work

A case study of interpersonal work is drawn from a community health centre, where social workers work with a team of allied health professionals, with the overall aim of improving and maintaining an individual's health and wellbeing. Practitioners are able to make home visits, provide needed interventions and/or referral to relevant services.

Mrs Bresky, aged 80 years, assessed as physically frail but mentally alert, living alone and receiving minimal personal care services, was referred to a social worker working in a community health centre, by a domiciliary carer, who reported that Mrs Bresky appeared unusually anxious, afraid to go out and generally very 'down'.

The worker had established a good relationship with Mrs Bresky in assessing her circumstances six months previously. She knew that she had survived internment during the Holocaust in Poland, had lost most of her immediate family members during that time and had subsequently forged a fulfilling life in Australia. She misses her husband who died five years ago, but has a small circle of friends with whom she is in phone contact, but sees infrequently due to their respective mobility problems. Mrs Bresky is extremely proud of her daughter, a successful accountant and gets on well with her son-in-law and her two primary school aged grand-daughters.

Using principles of empowerment related to the older person as experts in their own lives and the need to understand individual and social circumstances (Cox and Parsons, 1994) in a home visit, the worker began by listening to Mrs Bresky's view of her current situation. She was upset following several incidents of harassment by local youngsters who rang her doorbell late at night as these events awoke the fear and dread she had felt during the Holocaust years and she feared something 'bad' happening to her daughter. Mrs Bresky had not discussed these matters with her daughter fearing to 'put too much pressure on her'.

As part of the assessment process, the worker reflected on her use of theories and knowledge in shaping her understanding of Mrs Bresky's circumstances (Gibbs and Gambrill, 1999). She took time to learn more about the impact of the Holocaust in later life and depression in older age and realised she needed to explore more deeply with Mrs Bresky any changes in sleeping, appetite and negative thoughts, as disturbances in these areas can be indicative of a depressive illness (Beavan and Jeeawody, 1998: 177). The worker also learned that the use of an empowerment approach was highly effective when working with Holocaust survivors (Giberovitch, 1995: 281). The worker found that it is common for Holocaust survivors to experience a rekindling of past fears as a result of a traumatic event such as the 'doorbell' incidents and that 'some survivors lapse into states of anxiety and depression. Many live with a fear of harm befalling their children' (Giberovitch, 1995: 285).

Social isolation, experienced by Mrs Bresky as increased inability to visit friends, can also lead to depression and an increased focus on past horrific experiences by the older person (Giberovitch, 1995). The worker was alerted therefore to the need to consider the quality of Mrs Bresky's social networks as well as the more obvious factor of the harassment by local youngsters.

After deeper exploration of the connections between individual issues, past experiences and current social circumstances, the worker and

Mrs Bresky agreed that together they could work on three outcomes: Mrs Bresky feeling safe in her own home, feeling more positive about life and being able to communicate better with her daughter.

The first step in helping Mrs Bresky feel more positive was to discuss referral for a medical assessment of depression, based on Mrs Bresky's reported lack of energy and appetite and persistent feelings of dread. The specialist concluded that Mrs Bresky had mild clinical depression and discussed the positive and negative aspects of a short term course of antidepressants. This enabled Mrs Bresky to make an informed choice about medication which she declined in favour of 'supportive talking'.

Using a strengths and empowerment approach, the worker suggested that they make a list of all the things that she valued and felt good about in her life. While this was difficult the worker gently reminded her of the many events which she had mentioned such as her work success as a journalist, her survival skills, and her strength of character, not only in relation to the Holocaust but as an immigrant to Australia, and as a giving parent, wife and friend to others. Mrs Bresky, who tended to downplay what 'ordinary people do', was able to acknowledge that she had achieved much in her life and to recall how she had coped with feeling 'down' in the past.

It transpired that Mrs Bresky had relied on talking to her husband, and she did not feel comfortable talking to anyone else, including her own daughter, about the war years and her losses at that time. Although the worker said she would be honoured to talk with her about her feelings in relation to these past events, Mrs Bresky was adamant that younger people 'should be spared these horrors'. After exploring a number of possible solutions, it was agreed that Mrs Bresky would contact a Polish friend. Because she was housebound she was unable to use this support and the worker agreed to explore taxi vouchers for reduced fares to assist Mrs Bresky to visit her friend. Transport is an example of structural barriers which reduce participation in community life (Setterlund and Abbott, 1995).

In relation to feeling safe, Mrs Bresky and the worker organised an electrician to attend to improved house lighting and a visit from a police liaison officer to discuss recent community initiatives with young people in the area. The worker also discussed with Mrs Bresky a resource of an older people's action group who met at the local neighbourhood centre, where one of the concerns was safety for all age groups in the community. The worker suggested that Mrs Bresky's journalistic skills could be very valuable to the group. As Mrs Bresky felt uncertain about the group, the worker arranged for one of the members of the group to visit and discuss the group with Mrs Bresky, so she could make an informed choice about joining. Mrs Bresky gradually joined the older people's action group, at first by agreeing to assist them from her own home and eventually by attending group sessions on a flexible basis.

To communicate better with her daughter, Mrs Bresky took up the worker's suggestion that they rehearse telling her daughter about her current issues and actions. Mrs Bresky talked to her daughter as planned and was surprised to learn her daughter had longed to hear more about her mother's past but had always felt it was a taboo subject. They reported that their communication improved.

In essence the worker's interpersonal helping interventions involved strengths building, reframing and normalising experiences, expanding social networks and linking the client with services. Interactions between personal and social factors were addressed in a way that provided Mrs Bresky with information, choices and control. Critical reflection and use of evidence in practice assisted the worker to consider a range of possible explanations and interventions and to share these with Mrs Bresky to come to mutual agreements about suitable actions for change. As a result, Mrs Bresky began to feel safer, more confident to go out, more positive about life and stronger emotionally to talk more openly with her daughter.

Group Work

As with all group work intervention, groups can provide older people with an opportunity to increase social networks, provide mutual support, engage in meaningful activities, participate in social action and contribute to their own emotional healing (Corey and Corey, 2006) for example, through dealing with grief. Types of groups often associated with older people include physical therapy, therapeutic life review (Molinari, 1994), reminiscence, remotivation and reality orientation, preplacement (preparing older people for a move to a residential setting) and health education. Less emphasis has been placed on social action groups for older people. Family carers, including those who may have a relative living in residential care settings, can also benefit from the support, information sharing and opportunity to take social action provided by group work.

Particular issues related to group work with older people focus on avoiding stereotypes that could limit meaningful activity, building on strengths and compensating for physical and cognitive deficits, validating strong emotions and acknowledging both negative and positive life experiences. One of the author's experiences of group work with older people concerns a residents' newspaper described in detail in O'Connor et al (1998: 121-127). A group of residents in an aged care facility in conjunction with a student social worker had formed a group to produce a residents' newsletter. The group experienced conflict regarding control over the activities and decision-making. The hierarchical structure of the home and stereotypes of women as subordinate meant that women in the group were expected by senior nursing staff to defer to the sole male in the group. While the women resented being placed in this position they felt unable to challenge the hierarchy. The social work student's involvement centred around developing the women's conflict resolution skills, empowering them to speak up for themselves while avoiding marginalising the contribution of the male participant.

Community Work

Community work has the potential to address the structural barriers that create individual difficulties for older people such as isolation, lack of participation in community life, access to information regarding services and negative attitudes to ageing. A program named '60 and Better' is one such intervention (Shapiro, Cartwright and MacDonald, 1994). It started as a demonstration program in a lower socioeconomic suburb of Brisbane where the community of 60 years and over comprised approximately 800 people. Today the program exists in a range of locations across the State, funded by the State government. The goal for the program was to identify the physical, social and attitudinal factors which made mobility for older people difficult and to improve the health status regarding the physical mobility of people over 60 years in the community. A community development approach where community development was viewed as a continuum, which ranges from individual casework to collective political action (Jackson et al, 1989), was used with all sectors of the community.

An important factor in the success of the demonstration project was that an active community support group of older people provided the impetus to seek funding for the community development project and worked alongside a university researcher evaluating the program and a fulltime social worker employed to develop the program. A variety of methods were used to determine the issues of specific concern to older people, including whole of community surveys and focus groups to uncover the concerns of older community members and key members of the community such as health professionals, teachers and members of the police force.

A number of community change strategies were initiated by older people in partnership with professional and other workers in the local community. These strategies included activities such as gentle exercise, Tai Chi and general fitness classes, health information workshops, safety awareness workshops, daily telephone link for isolated older people, 'walk abouts' by volunteers to identify infrastructure hazards (poor street lighting, uneven pavements, dangerous road crossings), intergenerational interaction through involvement of older people in schools and a home maintenance scheme. A newsletter was used to reach older people in the community to gain their ideas for health/safety/fitness workshops, discussions or classes and to provide information on health, safety, fitness, local news, available services and coming events.

Evaluations of the program strategies showed evidence of the creation of a supportive health environment, increased skill development for older people, improved inter-sectoral cooperation and sustainability of the project through active committee membership and ownership of some activities by local groups independent of the main project and cost effectiveness (Shapiro et al, 1994). The project demonstrated that community work has the capacity to build a healthy environment, increase older people's participation in their community and improve their physical and social health.

Working With and on Behalf of Older People: What Works Best?

Good practice in the field of ageing involves the successful integration of a number of key dimensions of practice and a capacity to work within and between multiple contexts. To be effective in the contemporary human service environment, workers need to understand the broad structural context of ageing and be able to understand the tensions between the broad context, the immediate context and the experiences of individuals and families with whom they work.

Processes of critical reflective practice and a focus on identifying and working towards outcomes assist the worker to question their own decision-making, seek and evaluate alternative explanations and to facilitate choices around interventions that are based on the best available knowledge about what works best under which conditions. A clear understanding of ethics and purpose and a commitment to hearing the experiences and voices of older people underpin the entire practice process. The integrative capacity of social workers to attend to both social and personal factors that affect older people, their commitment to social justice and capacity to intervene at different levels of experience, means they are well-placed to provide effective practice for the growing numbers of older people who may require their assistance.

Review Questions

1. Drawing on social factors relating to ageing, what are some of the key common and diverse experiences of the older population that practitioners need to understand?

2. On a piece of paper draw two columns, one labelled 'older women are …'; the other 'older men are …' and write down all the common ways each gender is described. What stereotypes emerge? Are older women perceived differently to older men?

3. What are the likely constraints and opportunities for work with older people afforded by the organisational context of practice in the contemporary human service environment?

4. What is meant by an empowerment approach to practice?

5. How does critical reflection and working towards outcomes enhance practice? What are some of the limitations of these processes in practice?

Useful Websites

Australian Department of Health and Aged Care	http://www.health.gov.au/
Alzheimer's Australia	http://www.alzheimers.org.au/
Policies and Programmes on Ageing (UN database)	http://www.seniorweb.nl/un/start.asp
Age Concern England	http://www.ageconcern.org.uk/
The National Center on Elder Abuse (NCEA)	http://www.elderabusecenter.org/default.cfm
Mature Age Gays (Sydney Australia)	http://www.magnsw.org/

References

Access Economics (2005) *Dementia Estimates and Projections: Australian States and Territories, Report for Alzheimer's Australia*, February.

Australian Association of Social Workers (1999) *AASW Code of Ethics*, Barton, ACT: Australian Association of Social Workers.

Australian Bureau of Statistics and Australian Institute of Health and Welfare (2005) *The Health and Welfare of Australia's Aboriginal and Torres Strait Islander Peoples*, Canberra: Commonwealth of Australia.

Australian Institute of Health and Welfare (AIHW) (2002) *Older Australia at a Glance 2002* (3rd ed), Canberra: AIHW and Department of Health and Ageing.

Australian Institute of Health and Welfare and Commonwealth Department of Health & Family Services (1997) *Healthy Ageing: Older Australia at a Glance*, Canberra: Australian Institute of Health and Welfare.

Baltes, P and Baltes, M (1990) *Successful Aging: Perspectives from the Behavioural Sciences*, New York: Cambridge University Press.

Bevan, C and Jeeawody, B (1998) 'The phenomenon of depression in elderly people', in C Bevan and B Jeeawody (eds) *Successful Ageing: Perspectives on Health and Social Construction* (pp 170-207), Sydney: Mosby.

Brill, D (1999) *Safeguarding the Financial Interests of Vulnerable Seniors: A Research Project by the Office of the Public Advocate*, Perth: Office of the Public Advocate.

Brown, P (1998) 'The challenge of dementia', in C Bevan and B Jeeawody (eds) *Successful Ageing: Perspectives on Health and Social Construction* (pp 250-300), Sydney: Mosby.

Bytheway, B (1995) *Ageism*, Buckingham: Open University Press.

Corey, MS and Corey, G (2006) *Groups: Process and Practice* (7th ed), Belmont, CA: Brooks/Cole.

Cox, E and Parsons, R (1994) *Empowerment Oriented Social Work Practice with the Elderly*, Pacific Grove, CA: Brooks/Cole.

Fitzgerald, T (1999) 'The elderly at the millennium: Courting the consumer', *Ageing International*, 12(Summer), 72-86.

Gibbs, L and Gambrill, E (1999) *Critical Thinking for Social Workers: Exercises for Helping Professions*, Thousand Oaks, CA: Pine Forge.

Giberovitch, M (1995) 'Social work practice with aging survivors', in J Lemberger (ed) *A Global Perspective on Working with Holocaust Survivors and the Second Generation* (pp 277-288), Jerusalem: JDC-Brookdale Institute of Gerontology and Human Development.

Harvey, G (2001) 'The rights of elderly people in a nursing home – A little creativity, a lot of respect, a taste for adventure, and an allergy to bureaucracy', in L McCall, M Heumann and D Boldy (eds) *Empowering Frail Elderly People* (pp 155-174), Westport, CT: Praeger.

Healy, J (2004) *The Benefits of an Ageing Population* (The Australia Institute Discussion Paper Number 63), Canberra: The Australia Institute.

Jackson, T Mitchell, S and Wright, M (1989) 'The community development continuum', *Community Health Studies*, 13(3), 66-73.

Katz, S (2000) 'Busy bodies: Activity, aging, and the management of everyday life', *Journal of Aging Studies*, 14(2), 135-152.

Kendig, H (2000) 'Family change and family bonding in Australia', in W Liu and H Kendig (eds) *Who Should Care for the Elderly? An East-West Value Divide* (pp 107-125), Singapore: Singapore University Press.

Kitwood, T and Bredin, K (1992) 'Towards a theory of dementia care: personhood and well-being', *Ageing and Society*, 12(3), 269-287.

Kurrle, S, Sadler, P and Cameron, I (1992) 'Patterns of elder abuse', *Medical Journal of Australia*, 157(10), 673-676.

Langley, J (2001) 'Developing anti-oppressive empowering social work practice with older lesbian women and gay men', *British Journal of Social Work*, 31(6), 917-932.

McInnes-Dittrich, K (2002) *Social Work with Elders: A Biopsychosocial Approach to Assessment and Intervention*, Boston: Allyn & Bacon.

Minister for Ageing (2001) *National Strategy for an Ageing Australia: An Older Australia, Challenges and Opportunities for All*, Canberra: Commonwealth of Australia.

Molinari, V (1994) 'Current approaches to psychotherapy with elderly adults', *Directions in Mental Health Counselling*, 4(3), 3-13.

Monkman, M (1991) 'Outcome objectives in social work practice', *Social Work*, 36(3), 253-258.

Moody, H (1993) 'Overview: What is critical gerontology and why is it important?', in R Cole, A Achenbaum, P Jakobi and R Kastenbaum (eds) *Voices and Visions of Aging: Towards a Critical Gerontology* (pp 1-2), New York: Springer.

Moody, H (2000) *Aging: Concepts and Controversies* (3rd ed), Thousand Oaks, CA: Pine Forge.

Nicholoas, E, Qureshi, H and Bamford, C (2003) *Outcomes into Practice*, York: Social Policy Research Unit (SPRU), The University of York.

O'Connor, I, Wilson, J and Setterlund, D (1998) *Social Work and Welfare Practice* (3rd ed), Melbourne: Longman.

O'Connor, I, Wilson, J and Setterlund, D (2003) *Social Work and Welfare Practice* (4th ed), Sydney: Pearson Education.

Phillips, DR (2000) 'Ageing in the Asia-Pacific region: Issues, policies and contexts', in DR Phillips (ed) *Ageing in the Asian-Pacific Region: Issues, Policies and Future Trends* (pp 1-34), London: Routledge.

Podneiks, E (1992) 'National survey on abuse of the elderly in Canada', *Journal of Elder Abuse and Neglect*, 4(1/2), 5-58.

Rabiner, D, O'Keefe, J and Brown, D (2004) 'A conceptual framework of financial exploitation of older persons', *Journal of Elder Abuse and Neglect*, 16(2), 53-73.

Richards, S (2000) 'Bridging the divide: Elders and the assessment process', *British Journal of Social Work*, 30(1), 37-49.

Ryan, E, Meredith, S, MacLean, M and Orange, J (1995) 'Changing the way we talk with elders: Promoting health using the communication enhancement model', *International Aging and Human Development*, 4(2), 89-107.

Schofield, H, Bloch, S, Herrman, H, Murphy, B, Nankervis, J and Singh, B (1998) 'Supports for the carer and care-recipient', in H Schofield, S Bloch, H Herman, B Murphy, J Nankervis and B Singh (eds) *Family Caregivers: Disability, Illness and Ageing* (pp 123-168), Sydney: Allen & Unwin.

Setterlund, D and Abbott, J (1995) "Older women participating in the community: Pathways and barriers", *Community Development Journal*, 30(3), 276-284.

Setterlund, D, Tilse, C and Wilson, J (1999) 'Substitute decision making and older people' *Trends and Issues in Crime and Criminal Justice*, No 139, Canberra: Australian Institute of Criminology.

Setterlund, D, Tilse, C and Wilson, J (2002) 'Older people and substitute decision making legislation: Limits to informed choice', *Australasian Journal on Ageing*, 21(3), 128-133.

Shapiro, M, Cartwright, C and MacDonald, S (1994) 'Community development in primary health care: An Australian experience', *Community Development Journal*, 29(3), 222-231.

Tilse, C, Wilson, J, Setterlund, D and Rosenman, L (2005) 'Older people's assets: A contested site', *Australasian Journal on Ageing*, 24(1), 51-56.

Tinker, A (2003) 'Older people and ethics', *Australasian Journal on Ageing*, 22(4), 206-210.

Tirrito, T (2003) *Aging in the New Millennium: A Global View*, Columbia, SC: University of South Carolina Press.

United Nations (1991) *Principles for Older Persons* (General Assembly resolution 46/91 16th December), Geneva: United Nations.

Legislation Cited

Aged Care Act 1997 (Cth)
Guardianship and Administration Act 2000 (Qld)
Powers of Attorney Act 1998 (Qld)

Chapter 9

Rural and Remote Communities

Bob Lonne and Ros Darracott

Introduction

Social work in rural and remote locations is about context, practice being shaped by the unique geographic, economic, political and social characteristics of the community and its members. Practising effectively with, and within, these communities entails working in a community embedded manner that respects, embraces, utilises and fosters local values, abilities and capacities. In this chapter we explore definitional criteria for rural and remote communities, examine a conceptual framework for understanding the special characteristics, contexts and issues that practice in these locations involves and outline best practice approaches.

Increasingly, empirical research and practice driven literature has been defining, describing and examining the nature of practising and living within rural and remote communities. Moreover, a growing body of international research and literature is establishing the significance of rural practice as an emerging field worldwide (Pugh, 2003; Turbett, 2003, 2004; Bodor et al, 2004; Saltman et al, 2004). While some researchers have argued for rural and remote practice to be recognised as specialist fields because of the demands and practice roles when both working and residing within a small community (Martinez-Brawley, 1986), the general view is that urban and rural practice share many methods and models, but with local contextual variations (Cheers, 1998; Ginsberg, 1998; Krieg Mayer, 2001; Pugh, 2003).

Due to its contextually driven nature, rural practice varies both within the Australian context and from that in other countries. Identified features of rural practice include, first, that the social worker typically has a much closer relationship with their community than do their urban counterparts (Lonne and Cheers, 2000; Green 2003a). Secondly, the worker commonly uses generic methods in generalist practice across many practice fields

(Lonne and Cheers, 2000). Thirdly, a variety of issues stem from personal and professional isolation (Lonne and Cheers, 2004a). Finally, the marginalisation of rural communities and their human services from society's dominant power structures has contributed to many structural and resource inadequacies, and organisational staffing issues (Cheers and Taylor, 2001).

Rural and Remote Communities

Definitions of 'rural' and 'remote' communities affect decision-making about social policy, planning and resource allocation for the roughly one third of Australians living there (Wakerman, 2004). These notions of rurality are constructed differently in different societies. By acknowledging the diversity among rural and remote communities we can avoid stereotyping and treating them as all the same. Significant differences occur in population sizes, proximity to large commercial centres, economic bases and infrastructure, wealth and political influence, histories, Indigenous, ethnic and other demographic characteristics, social systems, values and aspirations and social care needs.

Social workers use various definitions of 'rural' and 'remote' practice, but all tend to entail a notion of small community practice that is geographically distant and isolated from urban centres. Various definitions based on population sizes have been developed, but the concept of a population continuum may be more useful than setting an arbitrary figure, as relative degrees of rurality can be determined. Factors other than population size and distance from metropolitan centres have also been used, including economic activity, socio-cultural criteria and access to services (Cheers, 1998; Zapf, 2001), but no definition of either 'rural' or 'remote' is universally accepted. Remote communities are generally seen as having a smaller population (less than 2500 people) and significant disadvantage due to poor access to services, resources and political influence (Cheers, 1998; Wakerman, 2004). In either event, it is necessary for social workers to differentiate these unique community contexts, because requirements for successful practice can differ substantially.

The Macro Context

Australia's small economy is particularly vulnerable to the global economy's free market forces (Cheers, 2001). The substantial economic restructuring and social change that occurred during the latter part of the 20th century adversely affected many rural communities, particularly smaller agriculturally based ones with narrow economic bases and poor access to services and innovations (Pugh, 2001). Commodity prices trended downwards; production costs increased; migration from smaller communities to larger regional ones occurred; many large businesses and government services were closed or reduced; family farming businesses rationalised to survive in competitive international markets; many rural unskilled positions disappeared; and drought and mounting debt forced many to leave the land (Alston, 2000, 2002; Chenoweth and Stehlik, 2001). However, many communities thrived, particularly those based on mining and tourism, and administrative and regional centres (Cheers, 1998).

Overall, these economic changes compounded the longstanding social disadvantage of rural citizens. When compared to their urban counterparts, rural citizens generally experience significantly poorer outcomes across a range of health, educational, housing and financial indicators. For example, they tend to die younger, experience serious illness more often and have decreased access to high quality medical care, have lower education standards, higher rates of unemployment and poverty, lower incomes and poorer housing (Cheers 1998; Alston, 2000). Furthermore, they have higher rates of social and emotional problems including suicide and domestic or family violence (Alston, 1997; Wendt, Taylor, and Kennedy, 2002), and have significantly decreased access to formal social care services (Cheers 1998, 2001; Human Rights and Equal Opportunity Commission (HREOC), 1996, 1999). It is a travesty that Indigenous Australians are worse off than others on nearly every economic, health and social indicator, a direct consequence of dispossession and colonisation and the destruction of their familial structures and connections (Lonne, Theunissen and Clapton, 1997).

Ideologically conservative policy agendas and governments have rationalised and regionalised human services, and imposed privatisation to force inappropriate marketised, competitive tendering processes on rural communities (McDonald, 2002; Cheers, 2003). Further, the proliferation of case management and managerialist practices, along with increased accountability measures, has led to decreased professional autonomy (Fook, Ryan and Hawkins, 2000). These changes have placed rural and remote practitioners under pressure to alter their community-oriented practices towards less responsive approaches to local needs, issues and aspirations. Despite this, rural or remote practice is characterised by innovative and creative responses and interventions (Green and Mason, 2002; Bodor et al, 2004).

Understanding the Factors Influencing Practice

'Domain location' is an important conceptual framework for understanding the factors shaping the diversity of social care practice in rural communities (Cheers, 2003; Cheers, Darracott and Lonne, in press). The eight practice domains are as follows:

1. *The society domain* – the dominant values and beliefs of the broader society.
2. *The structural domain* – the policies, legislative and organisational contexts that shape practice.
3. *The geographic domain* – the economic and physical environment, including distance from supports.

4. *The community domain* – the dynamics, narratives and characteristics of the community in which the social worker is based.

5. *The personal domain* – the social and cultural contexts of the practitioner (for example, age, gender, culture).

6. *The professional domain* – the professional knowledge, skills, ethics, training and values that the social worker holds.

7. *The practice field domain* – discrete areas of practice being undertaken (for example, disability, child protection).

8. *The practice wisdom domain* – the practice wisdom relevant to the situation gained through experience by the individual social worker (Cheers 2003; Cheers et al, in press).

A social worker's location within each domain influences his or her practice. Thus, each practitioner's approach to rural practice will differ because of variations and shifts within particular domain locations. Social workers who change jobs and towns adjust their locations within their structural, practice field, geographic and community domains. For example, a small agriculturally based community that is vibrant and resilient with a low transient population and strong community narratives valuing locally based workers is a substantially different practice context to that of a drought affected grazing town which welcomes outside professionals and whose dominant narrative is about survival against the odds.

Rather than thinking of domains as linear continuums, it is more helpful to conceptualise practitioners in relation to each domain's central location, which corresponds with them embracing that domain's dominant narratives (see Figure 9.1 for an example). Alternatively, they may be more peripherally located and less influenced by these discourses. Positioning in each domain varies over time, and a practitioner's awareness of their location within a domain positively or negatively influences their practice.

Figure 9.1 An Example of a Domain Location – The Structural Domain

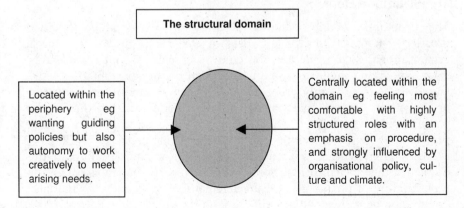

The structural domain

Located within the periphery eg wanting guiding policies but also autonomy to work creatively to meet arising needs.

Centrally located within the domain eg feeling most comfortable with highly structured roles with an emphasis on procedure, and strongly influenced by organisational policy, culture and climate.

Practitioners identify more strongly with some domains than with others. For example, a practitioner may feel comfortable embracing the dominant narratives of the structural domain but be quite marginalised in the practice wisdom domain. There are also discontinuities between some domains, that is, strong identification with one can make identification with another domain difficult. For instance, there is discontinuity between the professional domain with its quite rigid academic values and language, and the community domain with its common narratives of strong relationships and practicality (Cheers, 2003). The key characteristics and issues of each domain will now be explored.

The Society Domain

Centrally located within the society domain in Australia are the dominant values of a competitive, individualistic, socially conservative ideology that generally devalues Indigenous people and culture. Elsewhere it may be socialism, collectivism, a dominant religious system or the value of cooperation (Cheers, 2003). These dominant values influence societal resource distribution and greatly affect decisions such as urbanisation and participation in the global economy. The broadly held belief in the self-reliance of rural communities also belongs in the societal domain, which then translates into the community domain as a dominant local narrative.

Dominant societal discourses directly lead to poor service infrastructure and limited resources in rural communities. For social workers this can mean working in environments with inadequately funded and limited services available across broad areas of need, including social care services, transport infrastructure, medical services and commerce. These discourses have resulted in continuing disadvantage and institutionalised racism for Indigenous people. The dominance of urban-centric power and decision-making processes continues to lead to the imposition of policies and service delivery systems which are contextually inappropriate, further marginalising rural people (Cheers and Taylor, 2001).

The Structural Domain

The structural domain includes all those organisational factors and broader systems shaping practitioners' approaches to their jobs. Internal organisational factors include the culture, climate, the place of status, roles, power and the history and authority of the organisation. Is it legislatively based? Or highly procedural without much room for innovation or individual decision-making? Is authority hierarchical? Is the field of practice narrowly defined? Positive responses to these questions place practitioners centrally within this domain. Mandated service delivery agencies often require practitioners to have a central location in this domain. Other structural issues can influence practice, such as part-/full-time funding of positions, case management systems and managerialist domination of service delivery discourses (Fook et al, 2000; Parton, 2004).

Systemic structures include issues such as competitive funding, narrowly targeted funding and service planning, and increasing requirements for formal qualifications (McDonald, Harris and Wintergreen, 2003; Healy and Meagher, 2004).

Generally speaking, the Australian social welfare system is embedded within the structural domain with care being increasingly formalised and institutionalised (Cheers, 2003; McDonald et al, 2003; Parton, 2004), which can lead to a number of practice dilemmas. Balancing the tension between the social care and social control functions of a highly structured role such as child protection can be very difficult, particularly as community members may have strong views about service delivery matching local expectations (Cheers et al, in press). Strictly legislated procedures leave little room for contextualising a localised service. The transposing of urban practice models into rural communities by an organisation creates a similar issue. What works well in an urban area might not work in a rural community, for example, increasing specialisation or narrow case management roles. The dominance of the structural domain with its emphasis on procedure, formal qualifications and processes can devalue informal care processes, which are a crucial component in the network of social care in rural areas (Cheers, 1998).

The Geographic Domain

The geographic domain includes the physical, environmental, economic and spiritual nature of the community as a place. The economic basis of the community, relative wealth and its distribution, resource and infrastructure availability and climate are factors within this domain. A community's geographical characteristics influence how practitioners relate to it, their access to support networks and how they practice. If workers have their supports in a nearby community, they will often not invest themselves in their own community but, instead, will frequently commute elsewhere to their existing supports. Geographical isolation can increase feelings of isolation.

Geographic places have spiritual connections for many people, which influence practice (Zapf, 2003). For example, the practitioner who is spiritually connected to an area is likely to stay longer and be passionate about their 'place'. The physical environment, whether it is hot and dry or always raining, also influences practitioners' feelings about a place. Practitioners newly arrived to a rural community often experience culture shock and may have profound reactions to living and working in a different physical and cultural environment (Zapf, 1993; Lonne and Cheers, 2001). Culture shock may entail feelings of uncertainty, disorientation and mild anxiety as the practitioner adjusts to their new surroundings (Lonne, 1990). The geographic domain significantly impacts on the community domain.

The Community Domain

The community domain concerns the local community characteristics, including its history, dynamics, people, values and narratives about that community, such as seeing itself as robust, resilient, hopeful or depressed (Cheers, 2003). Practitioners who are centrally located in this domain subscribe to the community's dominant narratives, and value the strengths of the community and work with the community and its informal structures in a community embedded way. Those who embrace subversive narratives are located on the periphery.

Being closely aligned to the professional and structural domains can create difficulties with developing a central location within the community domain (Cheers et al, in press). Genuinely valuing and respecting the community, working from a position embedded within it, yet still retaining social work's social justice and ethical values framework and resisting induction into unhelpful community processes and narratives, can be challenging. The social conservatism commonly encountered in rural communities increases this challenge. The community domain also entails discovering and working with local dynamics, factions and gate-keepers. The more centrally aligned the practitioner is within the community domain, the more they are exposed to multiple relationships and require strategies to manage these with integrity.

The Personal Domain

Practitioners' personal backgrounds affect the way they view and experience the world and consequently influence their practice and the way the community experiences them (Cheers et al, in press). Characteristics like their age, background, urban/rural roots and the extent to which they embrace the dominant Western Anglo culture or another cultural group influence practice approaches. Individual life cycles affect practitioner's rural community practice and living experiences. For example, having a partner and children, and their ages, will influence experiences within a community. The central point in this domain would be the stereotypical white, middle class social worker.

Culture shock can result when there is a significant difference between the social worker's previous experiences and those encountered in their new community (Lonne and Cheers, 1999, 2001). It takes time to adjust to the high public profile, lack of anonymity, networking and multiple relationships (Lonne, 1990). Anti-provincial sentiment in academia hinders practitioners' preparations for, and valuing of, small rural communities, making adjustment more difficult (Martinez-Brawley, 1990). Social workers from culturally marginalised groups can also experience increased isolation in some communities.

The Professional Domain

For social workers, the professional domain entails their university training and personal identification with the profession, its values and ethics and the ongoing acquisition of formal knowledge and skills. It also includes the broader professional issues such as social work's declining power, and increasingly blurred professional boundaries (Healy and Meagher, 2004). The professional domain has many advantages but, as Indigenous cultures have taught us, it is not the only way of knowing (Cheers, 2003). If practitioners relate closely to the profession and its 'professionalisation' agenda, they are more centrally located in this domain. Professional elitism, a major barrier to service coordination, is a difficulty that can arise from a central location within this domain (Munn, 2003). Urban-centric training inadequately prepares professionals for the demands of rural practice and hinders them joining with the local community (Martinez-Brawley, 1990).

The Practice Field Domain

Practice fields include the various discrete forms and areas of social work practice including mental health, youth justice or corrections and child protection, with each having its own discourse and language (Cheers, 2003). The more tied practitioners are to one particular field, the more centrally they are located within that domain. The generalist practice field is commonly recognised as particularly appropriate for small rural communities where large gaps in service infrastructure exist (Lonne and Cheers, 2000). A tension exists between the trend towards specialisation and the rural community contextual imperatives that require generic and generalist approaches. When a generic, generalist service is unavailable the specialist will be expected, or pressured, by the community to work outside of their job description and address the service need (Cheers et al, in press). Some organisations recognise this and allow some latitude, while others do not. Generic, generalist practice is a challenge to the 'silo mentality' often dominant in the structural domain, because it requires integrative thinking rather than narrow, disconnected conceptualisations.

The Practice Wisdom Domain

Practice wisdom guides practitioners in their immediate practice situations and involves iterative, developmental processes that bring together their formal and informal learning experiences, knowledge and skills (Fook et al, 2000; Martinez-Brawley, 2002). It entails creative, intellectual and intuitive responses that are pulled from a combination of theory, practice experience, life experience and values, in order to address complex and uncertain environments and issues (Fook et al, 2000). Practitioners who are centrally located within the structural domain, with its proceduralism, are unlikely to be comfortable in the practice wisdom domain. Novice practitioners tend to rely on being centrally located within the structural and professional domains, while their more experienced counterparts will increasingly utilise practice wisdom to facilitate and develop their ever evolving practice frameworks (Fook et al, 2000). The central point in this domain is illustrated when practitioners have a high comfort level using and articulating their own practice wisdom, and contextualising their practice using reflective processes (Martinez-Brawley, 2002). Practice wisdom must be integrated, well-grounded, and not just an uncritical subscription to dominant community narratives or a relaxing of ethical standards to conform to community expectations.

Best Practice in Rural or Remote Communities

There are some ways of practising that are more likely to be effective across the diverse contexts and practice fields found in rural or remote communities. The first step towards best practice is practitioners genuinely valuing rural communities and wanting to be in their community of practice. The practitioner must work in a manner that is congruent with the context of that particular community. Community embedded practice, which is working from within, rather than 'doing to' a community, is achieved over time. It is important to know the particular issues within the community and region, including the economic base, the vulnerability to global forces and the impact on the community, and to understand the various narratives about the community's history and the current issues. Understanding the historical and contemporary experiences of the local Indigenous community is vital. Appreciating how various groups perceive you and your position makes it possible to find ways of being respectful, accessible and responsive to them all (Cheers et al, in press).

Rural people tend to emphasise relationships and networks, and social work practice should reflect this (Cheers et al, in press). Hence, strong networks need to be developed and maintained within the community across various fields, not just social care. Also, services should be indigenised, reflecting the local culture and needs, and where possible, being managed locally (Cheers and Hall, 1994). There is a significant role for social work in promoting organisational respect of local communities – best practice entails advocating for local needs and perspectives within policy and service delivery systems.

While practice should be community embedded and indigenised, best practice also requires the retaining of the meta-framework provided by formal training. An understanding of community dynamics and processes, a commitment to social justice principles and a systemic view of interactions are required to be part of, yet outside, dominant community discourses. Best practice requires social workers to challenge, in ways that will be heard by the community, narratives that marginalise groups or ignore significant social problems. This can be a source of great tension and difficulty as those discourses that require challenging can often relate to highly emotive issues such as racism, child abuse, homophobia and violence. Practitioners are best positioned to challenge these discourses where they are known for their credibility and participation within the community and take a respectful and collaborative position.

Practice needs to be collaborative to make the best of the limited infrastructure generally available in rural communities. Informal systems of care already in place need to be recognised and valued rather than disparaged, irrespective of the level and type of the training (or lack thereof) of those involved. It is important to maintain a broad view of social care and remember social work's relative place within these complex social care processes. Ideally, practice should be both generalist and generic to reduce gaps in the formal social care system. Collaboration can, and should, extend to creative problem solving such as aggregating several part-time positions across agencies to create one sustainable position. Skills in identifying the various community sub-groups and gatekeepers enables practitioners to develop strategies to work with them and ensure that services meet the whole community's needs.

Effectively working with, and within, a small community requires developing networks with many people and having multiple relation-ships with many individuals that facilitate community capacity building. This can be somewhat daunting, but is necessary to build credibility and robust helping networks. Multiple relationships are complex and skill is required to differentiate the layers of interaction and negotiate how they will work. Multiple relationships with colleagues and clients are vital to effective practice and must be managed with integrity (Bodor, 2004).

Being open and flexible aids professional credibility. Integrative thinking, the ability to 'integrate the various elements of a human encounter – the physical context, the history, the culture, the tangible and intangible components of relationships' fosters best practice (Martinez-Brawley, 2002: 296). It allows practitioners to pull together the know-ledges and perspectives of different domains in a reflective and reflexive manner for the development of practice wisdom.

Best Practice in Fields

Issues particular to individual practice fields have ramifications for a practitioner's work. For example, there may be domestic violence or child abuse incidents where best practice entails the social worker respectfully challenging local values and systems that support sexist beliefs and behaviour, misuse of power and perpetuating violent acts. The worker must champion a different value framework to that of their community, perhaps bringing them into dispute with local power structures. We shall now examine best practice approaches across practice fields.

Generalist Practice

Generalist practice using generic methodologies is considered to be a key practice approach for rural communities (Lonne and Cheers, 2000). The ability to work with all members of the community with any presenting issue using a range of methods ensures that people and issues do not fall through the gaps between limited services. For example, the same worker can assist a 65-year-old domestic violence victim through casework, and tackle child protection responses through community education and development projects. Generalist practice across diverse fields presents many challenges. It requires contemporary knowledge in many practice fields and well-developed skills in generic practice methods in order to work with individuals, groups and the whole community (Lonne and Cheers, 2004a). Because generalist practice requires flexibility and systemic thinking, it can be quite difficult for practitioners centrally located within the structural domain.

Good networks with skilled practitioners able to provide a consultancy role around specialist issues is vital, along with knowledge of one's professional limitations (Cheers et al, in press). Practice wisdom and a central location within the community domain are required for generic and generalist practice. In this particular practice field, a practitioner's embeddedness in community allows them the flexibility to be accessible to all groups and use all methodologies. Practitioners cannot use community development principles if they are not already embedded in the community.

Child Protection and Family Violence

Child protection and family violence practice in rural or remote locations has many benefits for practitioners' professional development, but also entails particular difficulties and stresses because the nature of these social problems and practice interventions are significantly different to urban contexts. Evidence indicates that rural communities commonly experience a higher incidence and seriousness of child abuse and neglect in comparison to urban ones (Lonne et al, 1997). A combination of factors are influential including poverty, social isolation and higher proportions of Indigenous people who suffer profound disadvantage. Also contributing are the commonly held beliefs and attitudes of rural citizens that condone violence such as tolerance of physical punishment of children, patriarchy and regarding family matters as private (Macklin, 1995). Hostility toward government and welfare interventions may also contribute towards abusive and neglecting situations remaining hidden and unreported (Manning and Cheers, 1995).

For similar reasons, family and domestic violence in rural communities is also said to remain largely hidden, exacerbated by poor access to support systems and resources (Alston, 1997). Rural contextual and cultural factors are significant influences preventing many women from escaping violent and abusive relationships, with fear of community responses compounding their predicament (Wendt and Cheers, 2002; Wendt et al, 2002). While, generally speaking, there are accessible natural helping networks, these may not be as available for abused children and women in remote communities (Cheers, 1985).

With child protection systems widely perceived as failing to be well-linked to community (Lonne and Thomson, 2005) rural social work offers opportunities to practise in a community embedded way with the whole community sharing real responsibility for women's and children's safety and wellbeing. Rural and remote work entails interagency and interdisciplinary communication, collaboration and coordination (Munn, 2003), and linking with the community to provide support, assistance and protective networks for families and children at risk (Taylor et al, 2004). The strong sense of community responsibility adopted by most rural citizens allows social workers considerable latitude to be innovative in responding and intervening (Clapton, Lonne and Theunissen, 1999). Moreover, protective and helping networks can usually be quickly accessed, assisting the family to acquire the sorts of support and help they need, and sometimes enabling early detection of problems (Clapton et al, 1999).

On the other hand, there are a number of issues, such as protective interventions focusing on removal rather than support, that stem from the generally poor access to local resources and formal human services such as alternative care placements, therapeutic counselling and support and accommodation services (Crago, Sturmey and Monson, 1996; Cheers, 1998). In addition, confidentiality pressures arise because the worker may be only one of many people who are aware of sensitive private information (Green, 2003a). Furthermore, some community members hold strong conservative views about the sanctity of the 'family' and 'parent's rights', and patriarchal and racist attitudes that condone violence, abuse and misuse of power by males. The legitimacy of state legislated intervention into family life can be seriously challenged and resisted. Community members who are aggrieved with social work protective interventions may well take matters into their own hands and threaten the safety of workers and their family members, with the resultant stress contributing to job dissatisfaction and staff turnover (Green, Gregory and Mason, 2003; Lonne and Green, 2004).

So how can social workers achieve best practice in these environments? First, by embracing and utilising the community embedded nature of rural and remote practice rather than problematising it (Wendt et al, 2002; Bodor, 2004). Reconceptualising how we perceive and understand social issues in these communities is important. It facilitates listening to the voices of those who are affected and providing assistance in accordance with their needs and aspirations (Wendt et al, 2002; Taylor et al, 2004). While there may be significant limitations maintaining confidentiality when 'half the town knows', opportunities present to creatively link with, and utilise, informal support and social care systems (Clapton et al, 1999; Green, 2003a; Bodor, 2004). A key feature of best practice is the appropriate use of power and authority that facilitates change processes by encouraging people to change, rather than merely reinforcing conservative beliefs and attitudes by becoming critical, judgmental and overbearing. Respectfully challenging dominant paradigms that support abusive behaviours and using community education and development strategies are beneficial ways for social workers to reshape the macro influences and viewpoints (Taylor et al, 2004).

Healthcare Systems – Aged, Mental Health, Health and Disability

Social work practice in the various healthcare systems such as aged care, disability services and mental and general health provides considerable rewards and challenges. Healthcare systems in rural or remote communities are often sparsely located across large geographical areas. They frequently entail visiting specialist service delivery models, including social workers and other allied health professionals, based in one rural centre providing outreach services to outlying areas, sometimes by flying in and out. A major disadvantage of these visiting specialist models is the lack of connection with the community being visited (Smith, 1989). Social workers can overcome this potential disadvantage by creating local networks in each community and becoming as embedded as possible within them. Hence visiting services can be appropriately contextualised and oriented to isolated communities.

Accessing healthcare can lead to people being displaced from their own community to access appropriate care, for example nursing home or supported accommodation. Creating new, and sustaining old, networks for displaced people is a critical need. Assessment services for people with aged care, disability or mental health needs are also often difficult, or impossible, to access, for example, geriatric psychiatry. Telemedicine has gone some way towards addressing these assessment needs, but can also lead to a de-contextualised service. Thus, social work has an important role in providing the missing context to ensure accurate assessments and care plans are made. Given the relocation issues involved in healthcare and the transient nature of some patients of disability and mental health services, practitioners need a good understanding of, and relationship with, local and regional services, such as the public trustee and regional advocacy services.

Social care services are often very flexible and responsive to health needs in rural and remote areas. Policies tend to be seen as guidelines, rather than dictates that must be slavishly followed. For the social worker who is well-networked across the service region, this can be a great advantage as incredibly creative responses to need can result. Rural practice encourages practitioners to be flexible and innovative.

Social work services in rural or remote hospitals or community health centres often take on the more generalist nature expected of rural practice. Practitioners are more likely to gain extensive experience across a broad range of presenting issues, diverse client groups and groupings. Best practice in this work is dependent upon being willing to be a generalist, knowing personal limitations and having good links to supervision and consultation when specialist knowledge is required. In smaller communities, the hospital social worker is often also required to provide inpatient and outpatient services across a large region.

The ability to work in a multidisciplinary environment is vital, and respect for all social care disciplines is required. For example, a Director of Nursing of a remote outpatient clinic undertakes more than a strict nursing role and this should be respected and supported, even if they are practising differently to how a social worker might. Professional elitism is a major barrier to service coordination (Munn 2003) and, therefore, best practice. Crisis response and management is an important aspect of hospital social work and the practitioner is generally needed in a crisis but is often not present on that particular day. This can place unrealistic demands upon the worker, and clear proactive planning and boundaries with realistic timeframes for response need to be established early (see Chapter 7 of this volume).

Young People, Youth Justice and Corrections

While many young people in rural or remote communities enjoy a satisfying life that revolves around work, family, church, drinking and occasional substance abuse and sports, others can find this boring and stultifying (Bone, Cheers and Hil, 1993; Furze, 1988). Furthermore, many rural communities have poor access to quality secondary education (HREOC, 1999). Limited educational opportunities frequently require young people to leave their home town in order to access higher and tertiary education in the larger cities. Some return to rural living while others do not. Generally speaking, there are inadequate opportunities for young people to take up local traineeships and employment. Many young people in rural or remote communities face difficulties, but Indigenous young people have it even tougher due to racism, poor educational outcomes and other consequences of social and economic disadvantage.

Youth development work in rural locations tends to take a community orientation that tries to address the recreational, social, training and personal needs of young people, as well as responding to those whose behaviour brings them into contact with police and other authorities. Evidence indicates that crime and violence are often experienced at higher levels in many rural areas, and there is a strong racialised component to its social construction (Hogg and Carrington, 1998). Young people in trouble with the law are often highly visible in the community and may face criticism, judgment and stigma from a conservative community. If a young person from a 'bad' family is offending there will be subtle as well as explicit pressure for authorities to 'do something about it', such as sending them to urban secure custody facilities geographically isolated from family and support structures.

Best practice in rural or remote communities involves balancing competing interests and perspectives. On the one hand practitioners have to understand and empathise with the young person's predicament and, on the other hand, they need to respect and respond to community expectations of safety and respect for the rights of all (Green and Mason, 2002). Despite the stigma attached to offending behaviour, rural communities typically respond well to interventions that exercise a balanced approach – providing both care and control. Rural citizens are generally prepared to go a long way providing assistance to a young person with difficult circumstances and extend a good deal of sympathy and understanding for victims of abuse and neglect. However, there are limits to tolerance for local young people who show little respect for others, and they may be socially ostracised and economically excluded. Outsiders may well be treated more harshly.

Working in the adult corrections field involves dealing with harsh and judgmental community attitudes, and the worker has to ethically manage relationships with community members wanting to share sensitive information and gossip. Merely ignoring these approaches is unwise because the worker is embedded within mutual and reciprocal relationships in their community. Confidentiality and privacy are central tenets of social work ethics but current professional and organisational codes tend to be urban-centric and incongruent with rural or remote contexts that involve dual and multiple relationships (Bodor, 2004). A more proactive and responsive approach usually delivers better outcomes for all. The dilemmas of client rights and community safety have to be addressed and this may well result in increased anxiety for the worker (Green and Mason, 2002). Rural community members are generally willing to help offenders to adopt pro-social attitudes and social workers have key roles in facilitating this assistance to encourage individuals to change problematic behaviours.

Organisational Support and Self-care

Sadly, little has been done to properly train graduates despite long-standing calls for rural perspectives to be incorporated into social work undergraduate curriculum (Green, 2003b). Generally speaking, social workers receive little tuition about best practice in rural/remote contexts (Lonne and Cheers, 2000). Rather than blindly applying the often urban-centric models and approaches advocated by many academics and university programs, best practice in rural or remote communities entails social workers critically analysing their context and then responding to its uncertainties and complexities (Cheers, 1998; Fook et al, 2000).

Poor preparation contributes to the high staff turnover commonly found in rural and remote positions (Lonne and Cheers, 2004b) and rural social workers generally experience higher stress levels and lower job satisfaction than their urban counterparts (Dollard, Winefield and Winefield, 1999; Lonne, 2003). In a longitudinal study of rural and remote social workers, Lonne and Cheers (2004b) found that roughly one third respectively left their positions in the first year, and between 12 and 24 months, and stayed more than two years. Employer related factors were the critical influences on premature departure whereas workers' and community characteristics tended to increase retention. When employers provided regular social, emotional and financial support, social workers tended to stay and develop local connections and enjoy the lifestyle and practice attractions. Those who were unsupported usually departed early. Governments have introduced specific strategies to address these longstanding staff recruitment and retention problems in rural and remote locations, but much more needs to be done (Department of Human Services, 2003; Australian Health Ministers Conference, 2004).

Social workers who relocate to take up rural or remote positions typically experience a U-curve of adjustment over a 12-18 month period involving phases of disorientation, honeymoon, grief and loss, withdrawal and depression and adjustment, with key aspects affecting their lengths of stay (Lonne and Cheers, 2001). Some workers experience profound culture shock and depressive reactions and leave early (Zapf, 1993). However, adequate preparation and the early and regular provision of social support can be powerful moderators of adverse reactions. If supervisors, colleagues and family members support workers through this adjustment period, it becomes increasingly likely that they will bond to their community and stay for lengthy periods (Lonne and Cheers, 2001).

Different approaches from employers, educators and staff could redress problematic staff turnover. Training on rural communities and practice is essential in degree programs and needs to be indigenised (Bodor and Zapf, 2002; Gair et al, 2003). A range of employer strategies is required including preparatory briefings on the position, community and adjustment issues, better targeted recruitment and incentives, regular and useful administrative supervision and support to monitor the adjustment process, increased training and staff development opportunities, mentoring to assist staff to balance their relationships within the community, their visibility and their involvement in community activities, and placing limits on the amount of after hours work and interruptions (Lonne and Cheers, 1999, 2004b). Finally, further research is required to examine the complex and dynamic practitioner-community relationship and its effect on adjustment, and to determine the relative effectiveness of employer strategies.

Summary

Rural Social Work is a contextually based practice field with the macro and micro levels intricately linked. Best practice requires an understanding of the social, structural, geographic, community, personal, professional, practice field and practice wisdom domains and how they impact on the interface between a particular community and a particular practitioner. It is this contextualisation of practice that is required in each and every community that differs rural social work from urban practice. Developing best practice in rural social work requires an ongoing commitment to developing practice wisdom through integrative thinking and reflective processes, as well as training and professional development opportunities. In rural practice contexts, regular, quality supervision from an experienced colleague is critical and assists practitioners to manage the complexities of living and working in the same community and managing the resulting multiple relationships with integrity. While beginning practitioners typically align more readily with the structural domain, the journey towards a central location within the practice wisdom domain is required to achieve best practice in the diverse and complex practice and living contexts found in rural and remote communities.

Review Questions

1. What are the particular features and issues that social workers deal with when living and working within the same small rural and remote community?
2. What are the eight domains for analysing and understanding rural and remote practice?
3. Identify the characteristics of best practice in rural and remote communities. How might these be applied to a specific practice field?
4. What sorts of systemic, organisational and personal practitioner strategies might be useful in addressing the high work stress and staff turnover typically experienced by social workers in rural and remote positions?

Useful Websites

Centre for Rural and Remote Area Studies at University of South Australia	http://www.unisa.edu.au/crras/
Centre for Rural Social Research at Charles Sturt University	http://www.csu.edu.au/research/crsr/index.html
National Rural Health Alliance	http://www.ruralhealth.org.au/nrhapublic/Index.cfm?Category=Welcome
Rural Social Work Action Group of the Australian Association of Social Workers	http://www.aasw.asn.au/about/specialinterest/rural.htm
International Journal of Rural and Remote Health	http://rrh.deakin.edu.au/home/defaultnew.asp

References

Alston, M (1997) 'Violence against women in a rural context', *Australian Social Work*, 50(1), 15-22.

Alston, M (2000) 'Rural poverty', *Australian Social Work*, 53(1), 29-34.

Alston, M (2002) 'From local to global: Making social policy more effective for rural community capacity building', *Australian Social Work*, 55(3), 214-226.

Australian Health Ministers Conference (2004) *National Health Workforce Strategic Framework*, Sydney: National Health Workforce Secretariat.

Bodor, R (2004) *Understanding the Experience of Dual and Multiple Relationships in Rural and Remote Social Work Practice*, Unpublished Doctoral Dissertation, Faculty of Social Work, University of Calgary, Calgary.

Bodor, R and Zapf, MK (2002) 'The learning circle: A new model of rural social work education from Canada', *Rural Social Work*, 7(2), 4-14.

Bodor, R, Green, R, Lonne, B, and Zapf, MK (2004) '40 degrees above or below zero: Rural social work and context in Australia and Canada', *Rural Social Work*, 9, 49-59.

Bone, R, Cheers, B and Hil, R (1993) 'A view from the margins: Perceptions of youth need in a rural community', *Rural Social Work*, 1, 23-34.

Cheers, B (1985) 'Aspects of interaction in remote communities', *Australian Social Work*, 38(3), 3-10.

Cheers, B (1998) *Welfare Bushed: Social Care in Rural Australia*, Aldershot: Ashgate.

Cheers, B (2003) 'The place of care – Rural human services on the fringe', Keynote Address presented at the *International Conference on Human Services*, Halifax, Canada.

Cheers, B 2001, 'Globalisation and rural communities', *Rural Social Work*, 6(3), 28-40.

Cheers, B and Hall, G (1994) 'Rural social planning and welfare services', in D McSwan and R McShane (eds) *Issues Affecting Rural Communities* (pp 275-280), Townsville, Qld: Rural Education Research and Development Centre, James Cook University.

Cheers, B and Taylor, J (2001) 'Social work in rural and remote Australia', in M Alston and J McKinnon (eds) *Social Work: Fields of Practice* (pp 206-219), Melbourne: Oxford University Press.

Cheers, B, Darracott, R and Lonne, B (in press) *Social Care Practice in Rural Communities*, Sydney: Federation Press.

Chenoweth, L and Stehlik, D (2001) 'Building resilient communities: Social work practice and rural Queensland', *Australian Social Work*, 54(2), 47-54.

Clapton, S, Lonne, B and Theunissen, C (1999) 'Multi-victim sexual assault: A case study in rural Australia', *International Child Abuse and Neglect*, 23(4), 395-404.

Crago, H, Sturmey, R and Monson, J (1996) 'Myth and reality in rural counselling: Towards a new model for training rural/remote area helping professionals', *Australian and New Zealand Journal of Family Therapy*, 17(2), 61-74.

Department of Human Services (2003) *Victorian Rural Human Services Strategy: Final Report for Consideration by the Project Advisory Board*, Melbourne: Victorian Government.

Dollard, MF, Winefield, HR and Winefield, AH (1999) 'Burnout and job satisfaction in rural and metropolitan social workers', *Rural Social Work*, 4, 32-42.

Fook, J, Ryan, M and Hawkins, L (2000) *Professional Expertise: Practice, Theory and Education for Working in Uncertainty*, London: Whiting and Birch.

Furze, B (1988) 'Rural youth work: Some considerations', *Youth Studies*, 5(3), 25-28.

Gair, S, Thomson, J, Miles, D and Harris, N (2003) 'It's very white, isn't it?: Challenging monoculturalism in social work education', *Advances in Social Work and Welfare Education*, 5(1), 37-55.

Ginsberg, L (1998) 'An overview of rural social work', in L Ginsberg (ed) *Social Work in Rural Communities* (3rd ed) (pp 1-26), Alexandria, VA: Council on Social Work Education.

Green, R (2003a) 'Social work in rural areas: A personal and professional challenge', *Australian Social Work*, 56(3), 209-219.

Green, R (2003b) 'Only in exceptional circumstances!: Education in Australia for rural social work and welfare practice', *Rural Social Work*, 8(1), 50-57.

Green, R and Mason, R (2002) 'Managing confidentiality in rural social welfare practice in Australia', *Rural Social Work*, 7(1), 34-43.

Green, R, Gregory, R and Mason, R (2003) 'It's no picnic: personal and family safety for rural social workers', *Australian Social Work*, 56(2), 94-106.

Healy, K and Meagher, G (2004) 'The reprofessionalisation of social work: Collaborative approaches to achieving professional recognition', *British Journal of Social Work*, 34(2), 243-260.

Hogg, R and Carrington, K (1998) 'Crime, rurality and community', *Australian and New Zealand Journal of Criminology*, 31(2), 160-181.

HREOC (1999) *Bush Talks*, Canberra: Commonwealth of Australia.

Human Rights and Equal Opportunity Commission (HREOC) (1996) *The Human Rights of Rural Australians*, Canberra: Commonwealth of Australia.

Krieg Mayer, AG (2001) 'Rural social work: The perceptions and experiences of five remote practitioners', *Australian Social Work*, 54(1), 91-102.

Lonne, B (1990) 'Beginning country practice', *Australian Social Work*, 43(1), 31-39.

Lonne, B (2003) 'Social workers and human service practitioners', in M Dollard, A Winefield and H Winefield (eds) *Occupational Stress in the Service Professions* (pp 281-310), London: Taylor and Francis.

Lonne, B and Cheers, B (1999) 'Recruitment, relocation and retention of rural social workers', *Rural Social Work*, 5, 13-23.

Lonne, B and Cheers, B (2000) 'Rural social workers and their jobs: An empirical study', *Australian Social Work*, 53(1), 21-28.

Lonne, B and Cheers, B (2001) 'Adjusting to rural practice: A national study', Paper presented at the *Australian Association of Social Workers National Conference*, Melbourne, Victoria, 3-26 September.

Lonne, B and Cheers, B (2004a) 'Practitioners speak – A balanced account of rural practice, recruitment and retention', *Rural Social Work*, 9, 244-254.

Lonne, B and Cheers, B (2004b) 'Retaining rural workers: An Australian study', *Rural Society*, 14(2), 163-177.

Lonne, B and Green, R (2004) 'The public eye: Rural human service workers' personal experiences of their visibility and safety and the impact on job stress', Paper presented to *Global Social Work Conference "Reclaiming Civil Society"*, Adelaide, South Australia, 2-5 October.

Lonne, B and Thomson, J (2005) 'A critical review of Queensland's CMC inquiry into abuse of children in foster care: Social work's contribution to reform', *Australian Social Work*, 58(1), 86-99.

Lonne, B, Theunissen, C and Clapton, S (1997) 'Child abuse in rural Australia: Explanations and implications', *Rural Society*, 7(1), 3-13.

Macklin, M (1995) 'Breaching the idyll: Ideology, intimacy and social service provision in a rural community', in P Share (ed) *Communication and Culture in Rural Areas* (pp 71-86), Wagga Wagga, NSW: Centre for Rural Social Research.

Manning, C and Cheers, B (1995) 'Child abuse notification in a country town', *Child Abuse and Neglect*, 19(4), 387-397.

Martinez-Brawley, E (1986) 'Beyond cracker-barrel images: The rural social work specialty', *Social Casework*, 67(2), 101-107.

Martinez-Brawley, E (1990) *Perspectives on the Small Community: Humanistic Views for Practitioners*, Washington DC: NASW.

Martinez-Brawley, E (2002) 'Putting 'glamour' back into practice thinking: Implications for social and community development work', *Australian Social Work*, 55(4), 292-302.

McDonald, C, Harris, J and Wintersteen, R (2003) 'Contingent on context?: Social work and the state in Australia, Britain, and the USA', *British Journal of Social Work*, 33(2), 191-208.

McDonald, J (2002) 'Contestability and social justice: The limits of competitive tendering of welfare services', *Australia Social Work*, 55(2), 99-108.

Munn, P (2003) 'Factors influencing service coordination in rural South Australia', *Australian Social Work*, 56(4), 305-317.

Parton, N (2004) 'Post-theories for practice: Challenging the dogmas', in L Davies and P Leonard (eds) *Social Work in a Corporate Era: Practices of Power and Resistance* (pp 31-44), Aldershot: Ashgate.

Pugh, R (2001) 'Globalisation, fragmentation and the analysis of difference in rural social work', *Rural Social Work*, 6(3), 41-53.

Pugh, R (2003) 'Considering the countryside: Is there a case for rural social work?', *British Journal of Social Work*, 33(1), 67-85.

Saltman, J, Gumpert, J, Allen-Kelly, K and Zubrzycki, J (2004) 'Rural social work in United States and Australia', *International Social Work*, 47(4), 529-545.

Smith, B (1989) 'Welfare service delivery: Options for remote areas', in E Van Dissel (ed) *Meet the Challenge! Creative Remote Area Practice – Proceedings for the National Conference of Rural and Remote Areas Social Welfare Practitioners* (pp 5-17), Adelaide: South Australian Department for Community Welfare.

Taylor, J, Cheers, B, Weetra, C and Gentle, I (2004) 'Supporting community solutions to family violence', *Australian Social Work*, 57(1), 71-82.

Turbett, C (2003) 'Rural social work in Scotland and Canada – A comparison between the experience of practitioners in Victoria County (Cape Breton, Nova Scotia), Port Au Port (Western Newfoundland), Aviemore (Highland, Scotland) and Isle of Arran (North Ayrshire, Scotland)', Paper presented at the *International Conference on Human Services*, Halifax, Canada.

Turbett, C (2004) 'A decade after Orkney: Towards a practice model for social work in the remoter areas of Scotland', *British Journal of Social Work*, 34(7), 981-995.

Wakerman, J (2004) 'Defining remote health', *Australian Journal of Rural Health*, 12(5), 210-214.

Wendt, S and Cheers, B (2002) 'Impacts of rural culture on domestic violence', *Rural Social Work*, 7(1), 24-35.

Wendt, S, Taylor, J and Kennedy, M (2002) 'Rural domestic violence: Moving towards feminist poststructural understandings', *Rural Social Work*, 7(2), 27-36.

Zapf, MK (1993) 'Remote practice and culture shock: Social workers moving to isolated northern regions', *Social Work*, 38(6), 694-704.

Zapf, MK (2001) 'Notions of rurality', *Rural Social Work*, 6(3), 12-27.

Zapf, MK (2003) 'Urban and rural perspectives on spirituality and social work: Profound connections between person and place', Paper presented at the *International Conference on Human Services*, Halifax, Canada.

Chapter 10

Aboriginal Australians

Joanna Zubrzycki and Bindi Bennett
in partnership with an Aboriginal reference group

Introduction

Contemporary work in the human services needs to encompass so many diverse opinions, knowledge, values, lifestyles and cultures that it can be confusing to know which path to take and how to respond. Many human service workers practice within a social justice paradigm that challenges them to try to respond equally to all aspects of social disadvantage that they encounter. However, this objective can be experienced as overwhelming and unattainable. We have ourselves struggled with feelings of uncertainty, especially in an area that is neither clearly nor comprehensively taught or discussed in our schools, universities or in our professional communities, that is, how to work effectively with our first nation, the Aboriginal people.

Australia has a history of invasion and colonisation of its Indigenous population. Due to the impact of this history on Aboriginal people and on Australian society as a whole, many non-Aboriginal people may feel stuck, guilty, angry, overwhelmed and confused when confronted with the numerous and complex social, health and economic problems that impact on the lives of Aboriginal Australians. In response, human service workers may either choose to avoid taking an active role in addressing these issues or decide that it is better to leave them up to Aboriginal people to resolve. For those human services workers who aim to make a difference in the lives of Aboriginal Australians many may be uncertain about how to develop their practice alongside Aboriginal people and their communities. The experience of Aboriginal workers working with their own communities can also be difficult and confronting, challenging them to think about their roles and identities (Bennett and Zubrzycki, 2003).

The aim of the chapter is to provide ideas that will facilitate different ways that both groups of workers can begin or indeed continue the journey of developing a culturally courageous and collaborative practice. This is a form of practice that is underpinned by a commitment and an ability to develop and apply the knowledge, skills and values that incorporate both Aboriginal and non-Aboriginal ways of understanding and working. We argue that an individual who can work with cultural courage is a worker who has examined their particular beliefs and values and has an ability to be reflective about their practice. In doing so, they have formed an understanding of racism and actively challenge its existence as an individual and as a professional.

The chapter develops three main ideas that we propose are the building blocks in the process of developing cultural courage. First, human service workers cannot expect to work effectively with Aboriginal people without a sound knowledge of the history of Aboriginal Australia and the Australian experience. This involves recognising the historical and political context as well as the privilege of whiteness in our society and how this impacts on practice. The second idea arises from the premise that the problems impact on everyone, and that a focus on the 'Aboriginal problem'(Young 2004: 5) takes away notions of collective responsibility and a shared humanity. Understanding this distinction requires human service workers to adopt a human rights perspective. Focusing on human rights supports the need to understand social issues such as trauma, family violence, alcohol abuse and loss and grief as interdependent. That is, they are experiences that inform and shape human behaviour as a whole (Atkinson, 2002). Many of these problems have at least in part evolved from the aforementioned history, and indeed by the historical and contemporary roles played by human services and government institutions. Confronting and resolving these problems requires mutual responsibility and action. Lastly, in order to become an active worker in this area it is important to recognise and attend to the processes and meaning of the work at both the personal and professional level. This means that workers need to continually reflect on how and why they are working with Aboriginal people and communities, what is the purpose of their involvement, what values underpin their practice and what impact does the work have on them personally and professionally? Embarking on this journey is as much about reflecting on process as it is about becoming a competent and responsible practitioner.

This chapter has been jointly created by a non-Indigenous social worker and an Aboriginal (Kamalaroi) social worker, with input from a national consultative group comprising of Aboriginal social workers and human service workers. This consultative process is an example of how to work in a respectful manner with the Aboriginal community. The process is briefly described in a postscript at the end of the chapter.

We presume that the readers of this chapter will be of both Aboriginal and non-Aboriginal heritage. We will use the term Indigenous to be inclusive of all first peoples, and Aboriginal to indicate first Australian people. (For a current demographic profile of Aboriginal Australians, see Australian Institute of Health and Welfare (AIHW) and Australian Bureau of Statistics (ABS), 2003). It is important to note that this chapter does not encompass Torres Strait Islander people, traditions and perspectives. Due to the experience and background of the authors and reference group members the focus of this chapter is on Aboriginal Australians.

Developing Ways of Understanding

The Historical Context

To understand the history of Indigenous Australia it is essential to recognise and understand the impact of colonisation on the contemporary experience of Aboriginal peoples, in particular their interaction with the welfare system (Gilbert, 2001; Haebich, 2003):

> The legacy of colonization has been the breaking down of our culture, laws, families, ceremonies, economic independence and the kinship system. In other words, all those things that gave us our identity, our strengths and our humanity. (King, 2003: 2)

Prior to non-Aboriginal contact Australia comprised a large number of Aboriginal communities – over 500 nations. These nations were neither heterogeneous nor uniform with some commonalities existing between communities, in particular in the relationship between their Laws and spiritual beliefs. However, the coming of others radically changed Aboriginal societies, bringing overt racism, the undermining of culture and the forcible removal of Indigenous Australians from their land as well as disease and death (Baldry and Green, 2002). According to Markus (1994: 203), 'Aboriginal Australia underwent a rape of the soul so profound that the blight continues in the minds of most blacks today' (cited in Gilbert, 2001: 53).

Aboriginal people first encountered welfare workers around 1814, a period when Australian social policy was strongly influenced by the concept of Social Darwinism. The notion that European people were superior was reflected in such welfare practices as the development of institutions, missions, slavery and the dispossession and removal of half-caste children (Gilbert, 2001: 43). The National Inquiry into the Separation of Aboriginal and Torres Strait Islander Children from their Families estimated that between 1788 and 1997 up to 50,000 Indigenous children had been removed from their families and placed in institutions or white foster homes (Baldry and Green, 2002: 4). The inquiry (Human Rights and Equal Opportunity Commission (HREOC) 1997) detailed the history of the Stolen Generations and its long term impact on the contemporary experience of Indigenous Australians:

The individuals I have seen lack of sense of personal identity, personal worth and trust in others. Many have formed multiple unstable relationships, are extremely susceptible to depression, and use drugs and alcohol as a way of masking their personal pain. (Dr Brent Waters submission 532 page 2 cited in HREOC, 1997: 189)

The rates of imprisonment of Indigenous Australians are one indicator of the individual and social impact of this severe trauma and dislocation. Indigenous Australians are '27 times more likely to be in police custody and 15.8 times more likely to be imprisoned than non-Aboriginal people' (Baldry and Green, 2002: 8). The Royal Commission into Aboriginal Deaths in Custody (1991) confirmed the link between deaths in custody and the removal of Aboriginal children from their families (p 8). This link has been reinforced by a recent study on the social and emotional wellbeing of Aboriginal children (Western Australian Aboriginal Child Health Survey (WAACHS), 2005). The survey found that children of Aboriginal carers who had experienced forced separation from their natural families and traditional homelands by a mission, the government or the welfare removal were

2.3 times more likely to be at high risk of clinically significant social and emotional or behavioural difficulties and had levels of both alcohol and other drug use that were approximately twice as high as children whose Aboriginal primary carer had not been forcibly separated from their natural family. (WAACHS, 2005: 26)

The Political Context

The political and community response to Australia's colonial history has been mixed. Committed non-Aboriginal Australians have worked along-side Aboriginal people for Aboriginal rights in campaigns. For example the 1967 referendum culminated in a solid majority of non-Aboriginal Australians voting 'Yes' to give Indigenous Australians the right to vote. A contemporary example of positive political initiative was the 1992 Redfern speech by Paul Keating, the then Labor Prime Minister of Australia. Keating's Redfern speech was regarded by many Indigenous Australians as a milestone in the recognition by non-Aboriginal Australians of their role in the disintegration of Indigenous culture:

We took the traditional lands and smashed the traditional ways of life. We brought disease. The alcohol. We committed the murders. We took the children from their mothers. We practised discrimination and exclusion ... It might help us if we non-Aboriginal Australians imagined ourselves disposed of land we had lived on for over 50,000 years, and then imagined ourselves told that it had never been ours. Imagine if ours was the oldest culture in the world and we were told it was worthless. Imagine if we had resisted settlements, suffered and died in defence of our land and then were told in history books that we had given up without a fight ... Imagine if we had suffered the injustice and then were blamed for it. (Keating, 1992 in Gilbert, 2001: 54)

In contrast to these sentiments, Australia's most recent political history (from the mid-1990s) has been increasingly influenced by the rise of right wing neo-liberal political ideology (Reynolds, 2000). The 'history wars' are one example of the ideas expressed by individuals and groups influenced by this ideology. This is the view that the documentation of Australian colonial history, as one marred by the massacre and dispossession of Indigenous Australians, is a fabrication (Reynolds, 2000). This debate has polarised public opinion regarding the level of responsibility that Australians should take for their colonial history. Most recently the conservative Federal government has taken retrograde steps in the area of Indigenous self-determination and land rights by amending the *Native Title Act 1993* (Cth) and denigrating and defunding many Aboriginal services such as the Aboriginal and Torres Strait Islander Commission (ATSIC) (see Horton, 1994), as well as mainstreaming others, for example the Aboriginal Legal Service.

It is important to recognise that the Aboriginal political landscape is also complex, with Aboriginal people holding a range of political viewpoints. This is reflected in the participation in all political parties of Aboriginal people and on a community level with the existence of various political factions. An understanding of the historical and political context also requires acceptance of the shared experience of historical disadvantage. Welfare professionals need to recognise that their roles, professional identities and actions are historically and socially constructed. Their presence in the welfare system is tainted by the acts of their predecessors, in particular the legacy of the Stolen Generations. This means that the process of establishing trust in communities where there is widespread suspicion of the welfare system is complex and requires sensitivity and commitment (Gilbert, 2001; Bennett and Zubrzycki, 2003; Zon et al, 2004).

The Privilege of Whiteness

A lot of non-Aboriginal people are scared of Aboriginal people. Why is that?

A lot of non-Aboriginal people feel great shame in relation to Aboriginal people. Why is that?

A lot of non-Aboriginal people feel great arrogance towards Aboriginal people. Why is that?

Those are not questions about Aboriginality, those are questions about whiteness, so for me the foundation for reconciliation is wadjellas [that is, White people in the Noongar language of the Australian south-west] reflecting on their own culture in their own heart about what's going on. (Muirhead, 2001 cited in Young, 2004: 104)

In the process of working with Aboriginal people, non-Aboriginal human service workers bring with them the privilege of personal and professional power that comes with being a member of the dominant race. This section explores this privilege by using the framework of Whiteness. Frankenburg (1993) defines Whiteness as having a number of linked dimensions:

> First Whiteness is a location of structural advantage, or race privilege. Second it is a standpoint (or worldview) a place from which white people look at ourselves, at others, at society. Third Whiteness refers to a set of cultural practices that are usually unmarked and unnamed. (Frankenburg, 1993: 1)

All of these aspects of Whiteness influence the work of human services workers. For non-Aboriginal workers being race privileged means that they need to reflect on how being a member of the dominant race imparts status and advantage. It is important to also consider what Whiteness means for those workers whose cultural heritage includes non-Anglo or Celtic dimensions. For example, workers who migrate to Australia from Africa, or who arrive as refugees, may experience the contradictory identities of being a member of a minority group in Australia as well as being a member of the dominant non-Indigenous culture. Research about the self in practice and the construction of personal and professional boundaries (Zubrzycki, 2004) indicates that these workers share with Indigenous Australians a strong desire to engage their cultural self in practice. For some workers this means that they may have a stronger capacity to engage with Aboriginal Australians in a shared experience of being the 'Other' (Zubrzycki, 2004).

Another group of workers who may experience Whiteness as a complex and contradictory privilege are those Aboriginal workers who have fair skin. For these workers skin colour can provide a mixed message to their non-Aboriginal peers and to their Aboriginal communities. Fair skin can be seen as a major barrier because it does not reinforce the stereotype of an Indigenous person – 'colour, lifestyle and heritage become the markers of authenticity' (Young, 2004: 9). While it is acknowledged that skin colour does result in difficulties about how one is perceived it is important to stress cultural disconnection is not based on skin or colour tones alone but also on experience and socialisation.

The cultural practices that are often unnamed and unmarked that reflect the privilege of Whiteness in human services work stem from the historical underpinnings of the welfare profession. Young (2004) argues that social work models of practice, for example, have been moulded by British and American culture and tradition. This means that under-standings about the helping process reflect various cultural practices and expectations that are regarded as the norm. These values and assumptions often reinforce stereotypes about Aboriginal people as dark skinned, belonging to an identified singular culture and being in need of someone else's help. These stereotypes also support a view that 'all people are equal and that cultural, social and historical difference and influences are unimportant' (Dudgeon, 2000: 255).

It is crucial for human service workers not to feel discouraged by the naming of Whiteness as an inherent privilege. Having the capacity to critically reflect on privilege, identity and the cultural construction of welfare practice is an essential part of the process of developing cultural courage because it means that workers are prepared to take responsibility for who they are and what they represent:

> Whiteness theorising complements critically reflective practice in ensuring that practitioners focus on their racial and ethnic identification as a crucial factor in their relationships with clients, their under-standings and interpretations of the issues and the resulting strategies used in their work. (Young, 2004: 1)

It is also important to stress that there are other markers of identity such as gender, class, age and ability and that these aspects of individual identity also shape personal and professional experiences. Gaining know-ledge about identity facilitates an ability to work respectfully in a way that acknowledges the differences and works towards developing trust.

So far we have focused on the importance of developing a knowledge base that is informed by the history of colonisation, an understanding of the political context of practice and the privilege of Whiteness. The second building block in the development of a culturally courageous and collabo-rative practice is the recognition that the problems impact on all of us. This means that social issues such as trauma, family violence, alcohol abuse, loss and grief can only be understood and resolved if they are recognised as interdependent, that is, they impact on the lives of both Aboriginal and non-Aboriginal Australians.

The Problems Impact on All of Us

Human Rights

> The struggle for human rights takes place across cultural boundaries; by saying that human rights are universal we imply that they are issues for people in all cultural contexts, and that it is a common, global struggle of which we can all be a part. (Ife, 2001: 70)

The process of recognising that the issues confronting Aboriginal people are human rights issues gives human service workers a strong mandate from which to practice. It frames the problems as universal struggles while also alerting human service workers to the fact that human rights can be realised, guaranteed and protected differently in different contexts (Ife, 2001). For example the right to an education is universal but is realised and experienced differently across rural and urban Australia.

The key challenge for human service workers is to maintain a strong human rights perspective while also understanding that there are diverse culturally appropriate ways in which those rights are realised (Ife, 2001). For this reason a pivotal aspect of the development of a human rights perspective is the need to recognise that culture gives meaning in life and underpins all human experience. The notion of cultural relativism, or culturalism can be a common misconception made by human services workers as they struggle to value diversity and develop knowledge about Aboriginal society.

> [Cultural relativism is] the assumption that if something is a cultural tradition this makes it above criticism and somehow sacrosanct. Culturalism reifies culture, and in effect allows for the continuation of the most abusive and oppressive practices, all in the name of cultural integrity. (Ife, 2001: 68)

Atkinson and Pease (2001) addresses this issue when he talks about the importance of keeping people safe versus allowing culturally appropriate interventions to occur and to take their course (p 183). A good example here is the concept of 'black love', that is, the acceptance by some non-Aboriginal workers that physical violence is the cultural way to express love. This is not cultural; it is a myth. Another example of culturalism is the process of theorising that the problem of child abuse is a form of culture normalised violence:

> This leads to acceptance of its inevitability and to restricted and sub-standard child protection activity through fear that any proposed intervention is racist in so far as it necessarily insults or injures culture. (Zon et al, 2004: 291)

In this example a mistaken understanding of cultural norms and behaviour masks the right to cultural safety for Aboriginal children. Atkinson and Pease (2001) argue that being aware of the universality of human rights facilitates the need to maintain cultural safety: 'Aboriginal people are entitled to the preservation of their human rights. So safety is paramount in that context' (Atkinson and Pease, 2001: 183). Hunter (2001) takes this understanding of safety further by asserting that while human rights abuses must be addressed on a national level, 'communities and families must be empowered to take their measure of responsibility for the abuses and injustices that are currently being perpetrated on the most vulnerable' (p 581).

For workers an understanding of cultural issues is essential and needs to encompass recognition that cultural norms and values are always evolving and are not universal in any cultural group (Ife, 2001). In Aboriginal society this diversity in part reflects the variable impact of colonisation on Indigenous Australians. The process of learning about Aboriginal culture needs to take into consideration regional (Horton, 1994), gender, age, class and other differences. Each characteristic shapes experience and opportunity.

Exploring the Problems

> Too often all that Australians know of the blackfella circle are the statistics of over representation on negative social indicators. They see high levels of public outlays which appear not to be reaching targets in health, housing, education, employment or economic development. Australians rarely hear of the life and aspirations of the people. Aboriginal people are denied their humanity in the face of statistics … it is the lives of people that are at issue, and it is their lives that need to be understood if we are going to turn the corner. (Dodson, 1998: 12)

It is universally recognised that the majority of Australia's Aboriginal people are experiencing significant disadvantage in areas such as employment, housing, income and education. In the areas of health and wellbeing Aboriginal people are significantly worse off than non-Aboriginal Australians (see AIHW, 2003). Yet according to Pat Dodson (1998) we need to understand the lived experience of Aboriginal people and not be focused on indicators of social disadvantage. Atkinson (2002) argues that developing knowledge of these statistics is also problematic because they frame the problem as an Indigenous issue:

> Knowing and naming the statistics does not change painful situations. In fact, much research work has been centered on putting statistics together, while Aboriginal pain continues, often defined as an "alcohol problem", a suicide problem, a "juvenile offending problem", a violence problem. And so on. (p 14)

It is important not to compartmentalise the 'Aboriginal problem' and to recognise that the social and psychological issues that face Indigenous Australians need to be understood in relation to non-Indigenous issues and to the impact of colonisation (Atkinson, 2002).

Young (2004) develops this idea further by emphasising 'the fine line between having a problem to solve and becoming the problem' (p 7). Practice in the human services often supports the view that the people experiencing the problems need to come up with their own solutions as a way of ensuring that responsibility and initiative is taken by those who have firsthand experience of the issues. These values underpin the development of specialised services staffed by designated Aboriginal workers. While such services can lead to the crucial delivery of often appropriate and sensitive practice they cannot survive in a white welfare system without support (Young, 2004). In order to avoid a dumping of responsibility there needs to be willingness from both Aboriginal and non-Aboriginal people to develop solutions which can make a universal difference to the lives of all Australians.

Atkinson (2002) applies these notions of interdependence and reciprocity in her research on the trauma that is experienced by many Aboriginal people. She argues that it is important to develop an understanding of the experience of trauma as complex, cumulative, intergenerational and interdependent with the trauma experienced by non-Aboriginal people:

For example it is not possible to know Aboriginal people's, or women's full experience of violence without also knowing non-Aboriginal people's, or men's full experience of violence and how these separate experiences inform and shape human behaviours as a whole. (p 17)

Layered trauma that results from colonisation is often expressed as violence that re-traumatises the individual and their community:

> People subjected to prolonged, repeated trauma develop an insidious progressive form of post-traumatic stress disorder that invades and erodes the personality. While the victim of a single acute trauma may feel after the event that she is "not herself", the victim of chronic trauma may feel herself to be changed irrevocably, or she may lose the sense that she has any self at all. (Hermann, 1992: 86 cited in HREOC, 1997: 195)

Layered trauma is further compounded by the complex and narrow bureaucratic response that often compartmentalises the problems and in doing so dismantles natural community support. One example of how a broader cultural perspective of trauma has been applied to practice is the development, in a South Australian community, of the understanding that family violence is holistic and a whole of community problem. This means that family violence is regarded as an issue that is interconnected with a range of community issues and problems that impact on everyone in the community, Aboriginal and non-Aboriginal. The issues that have been identified most strongly in this community include: shame and grief, undermining of culture, disruption to and weakening of family structures, intergenerational transmission of violence, hopelessness and despair, unemployment and poverty, anger and frustration, alcohol and drug misuse, gambling, boredom, dispossession and racism (Taylor et al, 2004).

Taking this approach Taylor et al (2004) argue that services need to be developed to address violence and trauma in a way that recognises the interdependence of socioeconomic disadvantage, mental wellbeing, welfare dependence and trauma. This entails challenging the current funding models to ensure that welfare services provide safety and support for families experiencing violence as well as opportunities for members of the community to develop independence from the welfare system. Non-Aboriginal workers have a role to play in the delivery of these services as long as they are committed to working alongside their Aboriginal peers and do not leave the problems to the communities to solve without adequate resources.

The Process of Developing Cultural Courage

Working Collaboratively

So far the emphasis of the chapter has been on identifying a number of key building blocks in the development of a culturally courageous and collaborative practice. These include understanding the historical and political context, the need to recognise the privilege of Whiteness, the human rights of Aboriginal people and the interdependence of the problems. This section brings these areas of knowledge together and presents a number of ideas and possibilities for practice with emphasis given to the processes and meaning of the work at the personal and professional level. The final part of this section has been written specifically for Aboriginal workers.

Lilla Watson, a Brisbane-based Aboriginal activist, identifies poignantly the challenges that confront all human services workers:

> If you have come to help me you are wasting your time. But if you have come because your liberation is bound up with mine then let's work together. (cited in Young, 2004: 118)

Lilla Watson is delivering a clear message to human services workers – if they are prepared to engage in the process of working with Aboriginal people as a journey of mutual transformation, then this will lead to lasting change as well as personal and professional growth. Developing the knowledge and skills to work collaboratively is one of the fundamental elements in this practice. The following example of service delivery encompasses many of the critical dimensions of collaboration.

The Mount Theo Petrol Sniffing Program in Yuendumu (Campbell and Stojanovski, 2001) is a powerful example of the development of services that incorporate culturally significant practices in dialogue with mainstream welfare and other services. This program was established by the Yuendumu community in the early 1990s as a community response to the crisis of petrol sniffing by young people. The program 'involves elders from the community caring for young people and re-establishing relationships within families' (p 10). The program requires a high level of commitment from all of those involved. It privileges a community-based Walpiri approach to dealing with substance abuse. This involves non-Indigenous and Indigenous people working together in a close partnership 'that is symbiotic, drawing together strength and experience from both cultures' (p 10). Healing in this context is a complex and multifaceted process that requires mutual understanding and action. This process encompasses the ability to listen to how the community understand the problem as well as respecting what they regard as the possible solutions.

For human service workers the skill of listening to an Aboriginal community is critical and means more than just acknowledging and respecting what is being said, but also hearing what is hard to understand and accept. This may involve hearing anger, hurt, sadness and a loss of hope. Understanding the basis of these feelings requires a cultural frame of reference that takes into consideration context, history, individual difference and trauma. This may challenge workers to stay engaged in messy, risky and hard spaces that are forever changing and to recognise that the community may not be cohesive or uniformly supportive of their work. These are all lessons that reinforce cultural safety and develop cultural courage.

When workers are engaging in a community it is important that they also become familiar with the community's protocols and understand how these might work in practice (Hurley, 2003). While it is not possible 'to know one mob, know them all' (Crawford et al, 2000: 190) a common protocol in many communities is to recognise and acknowledge the community's leaders and elders. This process will impact on how the workers' practice is integrated into and accepted by the community.

Providing Cultural Safety

Building on the foundations of working collaboratively is the process of providing cultural safety for Aboriginal and non-Aboriginal human service workers and the Aboriginal people and communities that they work in. The key factors here are an acknowledgment of the complexities of working with and across different cultural systems, being prepared to challenge racism and power imbalances, the development of supportive working relationships, the importance of accessing cultural supervision and the need to attend to self-care.

The concept of cultural safety has been variably defined as: 'What the cultural minority says it is' and as 'How safe clients and workers of the minority culture feel to express their cultural identity within the service or work environment' (Zon et al, 2004: 289). It is a concept that extends beyond the notion of cultural sensitivity by actively naming the racism and unequal power relationships that are inherent in bicultural helping relationships (p 290).

In human service contexts the concept of cultural safety can also be applied to how Aboriginal and non-Aboriginal staff work together to develop practices that confront racism both within the workplace and within the community. Zon et al (2004) examine these complex issues in the context of child protection work in Alice Springs. In this diverse Aboriginal community suspicion about the welfare system is historically entrenched, the experience of social disadvantage is pervasive and the expectations of non-Aboriginal people about what child protection workers should be doing to solve all of the problems is high.

For non-Aboriginal workers the challenge in this context is to confront racism. This process can be both personally draining and professionally risky because it often requires an acknowledgment that their own values and practices may be perpetuating the problems. Being willing to name and challenge practices, including those of management, should however not be a solo effort or campaign. Human service workers need to gain strength and resources from a network of supportive Aboriginal and non-Aboriginal colleagues and organisations. The key challenge for workers is to find a balance between offering assistance and support to others and considering their own needs for self-care and support (Crawford et al, 2000).

A useful first step is to recognise that Aboriginal co-workers can be mentors but can also be learners and decision-makers. For non-Aboriginal workers this may lead to opportunities to break down some of the traditional hierarchies of supervision, as long as their Aboriginal colleagues are also given the opportunity to seek support and guidance from a range of people. Engaging in cultural supervision can open up different possibilities in practice including the development of a deeper understanding of cultural norms and expectations. Accessing cultural supervision and developing supportive practice networks are key strategies in the self-care of non-Aboriginal workers. The challenges that these issues pose for Aboriginal workers is the focus of the final section of this chapter.

Issues for Aboriginal Workers

Although there are many issues that challenge Aboriginal workers in the human services field, this section will explore the key concepts of identity in the workplace and the community, the role of an Aboriginal worker and the concept of dumping.

Aboriginal Identity — Who Am I?

O'Shane (1995: 151) states that:

> We are the most ancient people in the most ancient land on Earth. Yet, we question who we are, what we are doing here, where we belong. [The psychological impacts of colonial experiences] strike at the very core of our sense of being and identity. Many of our people assume any other identity than that of Aboriginal. [This is] the denial of self. (cited in Atkinson, 2002: 256)

The traditional process of story telling and yarning is understood by many Aboriginal communities as a means of sharing and disseminating knowledge about relationships, obligations, Law and spirituality. In so doing the rules for living across generations are confirmed and affirmed (Atkinson, 2002: 33).

Overlapping circles of extended families also lie at the heart of the lives of most Aboriginal Australians. Networks of family relationship determine day-to-day activities and shape the course of destinies. From an early age Aboriginal Australians learn who belongs to whom, where they come from and how they should behave across a wide universe of kin. These are highly valued and integral components of Aboriginal cultural knowledge (Haebich, 2003: 13).

What does this mean for the generation of Aboriginal people and those workers who have grown up without these stories, ceremonies and kinship networks? For some of these individuals their sense of identity is fractured and fragmented, their sense of self appears lost, complex or unclear and they may not feel culturally connected to their community. This may also explain why many young fair skinned Aboriginal people say they feel 'lost' or have no 'identity' as an Aboriginal person. The denial of the self is linked to colonisation, but now has become part of the problem.

A lack of cultural connection can mean that workers may struggle with Aboriginal and non-Aboriginal people for the right to be recognised as an Aboriginal person. Who an Aboriginal person is, how they identify themselves and where they fit in the community and their culture are integral points of working with any Aboriginal group. For some, these questions are easily answered, but if, for example, the worker moves country or community, then they may have to face these questions. Certainly, professionally this question will arise when workers face the dilemma of family as clients.

Most Aboriginal workers go through a phase of finding their own identity in the field (personally and professionally). Workers need to work out where they fit in the community and how they belong. Choices need to be made; lines need to be drawn such as who you can see or how much you will talk about that certain issue at community events such as the football. The worker needs to get to know who they are in this new context and then decide how this can be best utilised in their/the local community.

In the human services, the work done by Aboriginal people as well as their cultural and therefore personal identities are often challenged by Aboriginal and non-Aboriginal people. In order to develop the courage to deal with these challenges knowledge of the self in relation to identity is important. Like any worker, integrating values, weaknesses and strengths into the role is necessary for this work, but Aboriginal people have the added components of identity, culture and spirituality to add into this mix. For any worker it is also essential to have strong support and supervision in the human services area. It may benefit Aboriginal workers to seek a supervisor who has cultural and/or professional knowledge to meet their needs. Seeking this form of support can facilitate not only their capacity to work with their communities but also their retention in these positions.

As an Aboriginal Worker – What is My Role?

There are some concepts that Aboriginal workers may find frustrating in certain human services systems. These include rules and regulations that seem to block access for minority groups, for example, a lack of support for home visiting and the adherence to strict appointment schedules. Concepts such as the sense of the self as a priority also do not resonate with many Aboriginal workers. In addition, strong personal and professional boundaries can exclude workers from sharing their professional identity with family, and confidentiality can exclude family and elders. Often Aboriginal workers are forced to challenge agency practices such as assessments and appointment policies to help others gain an understanding of cultural sensitivities. Employing people for their Aboriginal heritage and then imposing an agency or organisational culture (such as supervision, expectations and boundary issues) can make it difficult to work in culturally appropriate ways or be accepted by the community in which they work.

At times employers will hire Aboriginal workers to solve all the problems in the community, or worse, because of feelings of obligation or to meet service criteria or policies:

> The employment of minority workers to work with minority groups is undertaken for a number of reasons, but the attempt to make over people in the image of White is surely defeating the aims of diverse responses to diverse needs. (Young 2004: 8)

A good example of what we will term dumping is being hired as an identified worker and being expected to conform to the non-cultural standards. Often there is a secret rule that the worker keep quiet in this assimilation or speak up without anger or hostility. 'Dumping without also providing adequate resources to address the circumstances is merely exacerbating the problem' (Young, 2004: 8). Aboriginal workers need to be careful that everyone's responsibility for the problems is not ignored. This can take tenacity, training, complaining, advocating and networking to educate others in the service.

Sometimes people from other cultures, although trying hard to be respectful, engage in activities which inadvertently shame the worker. Shaming occurs when communication with an Aboriginal person is conducted in a culturally disrespectful way. This may occur when persistent eye contact is used with a person who interprets this as a form of 'telling off' especially when used by an older person to a younger one or across genders. One example is being told off in front of a group of peers. Being embarrassed in front of anyone – 'you should have known that, don't you know them and so on' – is very shaming for Aboriginal people. The experience of being shamed by non-Aboriginal and Aboriginal people is how traumatic responses can be compounded.

Being an Aboriginal human services worker is a challenging role and identity. It requires the development of skills and knowledge that facilitate the development of confidence about how they will work in the Aboriginal and non-Aboriginal community. It also requires the ability to be culturally courageous in the development of collaborative working relationships as a co-worker, learner and mentor. Finally, Aboriginal human services workers need to be given the support and opportunity to practice in ways that work across and between cultures.

Final Thoughts

> There are no magical solutions or "best" methods of working with Aboriginal people. A critical starting point for any practitioner is to look inward, to take responsibility for gaining cultural awareness and sensitivity not only toward people of another cultural group, but also toward their own culture. (Dudgeon, 2000: 249)

One of the key challenges for human services workers in Australia is how to forge truly meaningful and culturally courageous and collaborative working relationships with Aboriginal people. Such relationships need to acknowledge the history of dispossession of Indigenous Australians, the privilege of whiteness and the problems as community owned and not just Aboriginal issues. The key is not to be immobilised and disempowered by these challenges, but to acknowledge their potency on a deep personal and professional level. This is an ongoing process and one which needs commitment, energy and hope.

Summary

The purpose of this chapter has been to provide Aboriginal and non-Aboriginal human services workers who are working with Aboriginal people and their communities with a conceptual framework for developing culturally courageous and collaborative practice. This framework is based on a sound knowledge of the history of Aboriginal Australia, a recognition that the challenges experienced by Aboriginal people impact on all Australians. A key skill that human service workers need to develop is the capacity to reflect on the personal and professional meaning of this work.

How the Reference Group Worked

At the beginning of the chapter's development the authors made the decision to request collaboration and assistance from a number of Aboriginal human service workers and academics in order to ensure that the ideas developed and expressed in this chapter were culturally sound and respectful. The reference group comprised of Violet Bacon (Yamatji, Western Australia), Sue Green (Waradjuri, New South Wales), Christine King (Larrakia, Northern Territory), and Ginibi Robinson (Bunjalung, New South Wales). Members of the reference group were contacted on the criteria of: professional background, representation across Australia, and previous contact and collaboration with the authors. Once members were identified, emails were sent and phone calls made in order to gain interest and commitment. Once a commitment was given, an initial chapter draft of first ideas was sent to the reference group. The process of making contact and gathering ideas required the commitment of one dedicated organised person to be the 'meat' in the sandwich. Joanna fulfilled this role by meeting with most members of the group throughout the process to gather their ideas and comments. The final draft was sent to reference group members and their feedback was integrated into the chapter. This means that the rights to the chapter have been shared with the group.

Acknowledgments

The authors would like to express their thanks to the members of reference group for sharing with them their ideas, experiences and commitment. Their involvement was crucial in ensuring that the ideas presented in the chapter reflected the contemporary experiences of a range of Aboriginal people and communities. The authors would also like to thank Dr Sue Young and Dr Morag McArthur for their helpful editorial comments and Lorraine Thomson for her invaluable research assistance. Bindi would also like to acknowledge the contribution of her sister, Sian Bennett, for her editorial work.

Review Questions

1. Why is it important for human service workers to understand the history of Aboriginal Australia?
2. How does the history of Australian colonisation impact on the contemporary experiences of Aboriginal Australians?
3. What does the term cultural courage mean?
4. What does it mean to be collaborative?
5. How can non-Indigenous human services workers keep hopeful and safe in their practice?
6. What are some of the complexities experienced by Aboriginal workers in their practice?
7. Why is the process of understanding who you are and what you believe in fundamental to your work with Aboriginal people?

Useful Websites

Australian Indigenous Health*InfoNet*	http://www.healthinfonet.ecu.edu.au/
Australian Institute of Aboriginal and Torres Strait Islander Studies	http://www.aiatsis.gov.au/
Aboriginal Centres	http://www.faira.org.au/linkscon.html
Indigenous Links	http://www.abc.net.au/message/links.htm
National Aboriginal and Torres Strait Islander Education Website	http://www.natsiew.nexus.edu.au/

References

Atkinson, J (2002) *Trauma Trails: Recreating Song Lines: The Transgenerational Effects of Trauma in Indigenous Australians*, Melbourne: Spinifex.

Atkinson, G and Pease, B (2001) 'The changing role of Indigenous men in community and family life: A conversation between Graham Atkinson and Bob Pease', in B Pease and P Camilleri (eds) *Working with Men in the Human Services* (pp 174-187), Sydney: Allen & Unwin.

Australian Institute of Health and Welfare (AIHW) and Australian Bureau of Statistics (ABS) (2003) *The Health and Welfare of Australian Aboriginal and Torres Strait Islander Peoples*, Canberra: Commonwealth of Australia.

Baldry, E and Green, S (2002) 'Welfare provisions for Indigenous Peoples in Australia', *Journal of Societal and Social Policy*, 1(1), 1-14.

Bennett, B and Zubrzycki, J (2003) 'Hearing the stories of Australian Aboriginal and Torres Strait Islander social workers: Challenging and educating the system', *Australian Social Work*, 56(1), 61-70.

Campbell, L and Stojanovski, A (2001) 'Walpiri elders work with petrol sniffers, *Indigenous Law Bulletin*, 5(9), 8-11.

Crawford, F, Dudgeon, P, Garvey, G and Pickett, H (2000) 'Interacting with Aboriginal communities', in P Dudgeon, D Garvey and H Pickett (eds) *Working with Indigenous Australians: A Handbook for Psychologists* (pp 185-202), Perth: Gunada Press.

Dodson, P (1998) *Will the Circle be Unbroken? Cycles of Survival for Indigenous Australians* (Discussion Paper No 12), Canberra: North Australia Research Unit, Australian National University.

Dudgeon, P (2000) 'Counselling with Aboriginal people', in P Dudgeon, D Garvey and H Pickett (eds) *Working with Indigenous Australians: A Handbook for Psychologists* (pp 249-70), Perth: Gunada Press.

Frankenburg, R (1993) *White Women, Race Matters: The Social Construction of Whiteness*, London: Routledge.

Gilbert, S (2001) 'Social work with Indigenous Australians', in J McKinnon and M Alston (eds) *Social Work: Fields of Practice* (pp 46-57), Oxford: Oxford University Press.

Haebich, A (2003) *Broken Circles: Fragmenting Indigenous Families 1800-2000*, Fremantle, WA: Fremantle Arts Press.

Hermann, J (1992) *Trauma and Recovery*, New York: Basic Books.

Horton, D (ed) (1994) *The Encyclopaedia of Aboriginal Australia*, Canberra: Aboriginal Studies Press for the Australian Institute of Aboriginal and Torres Strait Islander Studies.

Human Rights and Equal Opportunity Commission (HREOC) (1997) *Bringing Them Home: Report of the National Inquiry into the Separation of Aboriginal and Torres Strait Islander Children from their Families*, Sydney: HREOC.

Hunter, E (2001) 'Best intentions lives on: Untoward health outcomes of some contemporary initiatives in Indigenous affairs', *Australian and New Zealand Journal of Psychiatry*, 36(5), 575-584.

Hurley, A (2003) *Respect, Acknowledge, Listen: Practical Protocols for Working with the Indigenous Community of Western Sydney*, Sydney: Community Cultural Development.

Ife, J (2001) *Human Rights and Social Work: Towards a Rights Based Practice*, Cambridge: Cambridge University Press.

King, C (2003) *Indigenous Issues and Social Justice from an Indigenous Social Work Framework*, Unpublished paper.

Markus, A (1994) *Australian Race Relations 1788–1993*, Sydney: Allen & Unwin.

Muirhead, T (2001) 'Interview', *Aboriginal Independent Newspaper*, Perth, January.

O'Shane, P (1995) 'The psychological impact of White colonialism on Aboriginal People', *Australasian Psychiatry*, 3(3), 149-153.

Reynolds, H (2000) *Why Weren't We Told?: A Personal Search for the Truth about our History*, Melbourne: Penguin.

Royal Commission into Aboriginal Deaths in Custody (1991) *National Report* (E Johnston, Commissioner), Canberra: Australian Government Publishing.

Taylor, J, Cheers, B, Weetara, C and Gentle, I (2004) 'Supporting community solutions to family violence', *Australian Social Work*, 57(1), 71-83.

Western Australian Aboriginal Child Health Survey (WAACHS) (2005) *Summary Booklet: The Social and Emotional Wellbeing of Aboriginal Children and Young People*, Perth: Telethon Institute for Child Health Research.

Young, S (2004) 'Social work theory and practice: The invisibility of Whiteness', in A Moreton-Robinson (ed), *Whitening Race: Essays in Social and Cultural Criticism* (pp 104-118), Canberra: Aboriginal Studies Press.

Zon, A, Lindeman, M, Williams, A, Hayes, C, Ross, D and Furber, M (2004) 'Cultural safety in child protection: Application to the workplace environment and casework practice', *Australian Social Work*, 57(3), 288-298.

Zubrzycki, J (2004) *The Construction of Personal and Professional Boundaries in Australian Social Work: A Qualitative Exploration of the Self in Practice*, Unpublished PhD thesis, Curtin University.

Legislation Cited

Native Title Act 1993 (Cth)

Chapter 11

Migrants and Refugees

Jennifer Martin

Introduction

In many ways working with migrants and refugees is no different to social work practice in general. It calls upon the same commitment to social justice, values and knowledge and is responsive to a range of factors including race, ethnicity and culture, gender, class, age, sexuality and spirituality. It is respectful of difference and facilitates access to resources in an empowering manner. Social work activities include the provision of essential goods and services such as food and housing, counselling, family work, group work, community work, policy development, advocacy and social action including media campaigns, management, education, research and evaluation. Interventions are made on the basis of a social work assessment of need for service. This is 'best practice'. In this chapter the diverse backgrounds of migrants and refugees are explored. This is followed by a discussion of changing legislative frameworks and issues and dilemmas related to resettlement and adjustment. Theory and practice considerations are discussed from a critical theoretical perspective. These include critical reflection, the naming of discriminatory practices, organisational considerations and the special needs of refugees and asylum seekers.

Migrants, Refugees and Migration

Migration is a natural and ongoing phenomenon that has occurred since the beginning of time by many species, humans included. Migrants and refugees come from extremely diverse backgrounds and circumstances. Migration generally occurs at times of environmental, political, economic or social change, with the migrant seeking a better way of life. This may be local, national or international migration. People migrate for various reasons with both 'push' and 'pull' factors influencing a person's decision, or imposition, to migrate (Cox, 1987). The circumstances of a person's migration will necessarily affect resettlement and adjustment to life in the country, or countries of migration, with some people migrating more than once. Some will choose to migrate and others will follow them yet for a number of people there is no choice at all. The experience of migration, personal and material resources and supportive networks, or lack thereof, will all impact on the migration process.

Pull factors include the freedom to choose a life that offers certain advantages such as employment, business opportunities, investment, family reunion, education in English and lifestyle. Push factors include discriminatory policies and practices that adversely affect minority ethnic groups. There are those who do not necessarily choose to migrate and may not choose the country of destination either. This latter group includes migrants forced to flee their country due to war, political unrest and fear of persecution and usually migrate as refugees or asylum seekers. Table 11.1 shows the estimated number of asylum seekers, refugees and others of concern to the United Nations High Commissioner for Refugees (UNHCR).

Table 11.1 Estimated Number of Asylum Seekers, Refugees and Others of Concern to UNHCR – 1 January 2004

Asia	6,187,800
Africa	4,285,100
Europe	4,242,300
Latin America and Caribbean	1,316,400
Northern America	978,100
Oceania	74,400
TOTAL	**17,084, 100**

Source: *UNHCR Basic Facts* (see http://www.unhcr.ch/cgi-bin/texis/vtx/basics)

A person seeking 'asylum' is not a refugee until he or she is assessed as being so. Refugees are a broadly definable group with numerous sub-groupings. This diversity is reflected in the United Nations definition of the term 'refugee'. Article 1A(2) of the Convention and Protocol Relating to the Status of Refugees applies to any person who 'owing to well-founded fear of being persecuted for reasons of race, religion, nationality, membership of a particular social group or political opinion, is outside the country of his [or her] nationality and is unable or, owing to such fear, is unwilling to avail himself [or herself] of the protection of that country; or who, not having a nationality and being outside the country of his [or her] former habitual residence, is unable or, owing to such fear, is unwilling to return to it' (United Nations, 1951).

Due to the changing nature of the world there will be ongoing groups of people applying for asylum. These people will also have diverse racial, ethnic, cultural and religious backgrounds. This diversity is reflected in three recent examples of refugee immigrants to Australia. A Chinese woman was granted refugee status in Australia because of persecution due to her personal and religious beliefs due to her practice of Falun Gong (V04/17079 cited in Roberts, 2005a). The grounds for refugee status for a man from Afghanistan were fear of persecution from the Taliban. This man claimed that he did not have any contact with anyone in Afghanistan and had lost contact with friends and family. He argued that he would be killed if he returned (V04/16981 cited in Roberts, 2005b). A man from Bangladesh was recently granted refugee status because he feared returning to Bangladesh because of his homosexuality. He argued that he had been arrested, physically assaulted and imprisoned for promoting safe sex practices among homosexual men (V04/16981 cited in Roberts, 2005a). The needs of these three people are quite different. However, the main need that they share, shared also by other refugees, is for a place to stay permanently, and to remain away from the place of persecution.

Refugees and migrants have common and distinct features. Some of the commonalities of refugees and migrants are the desire for a sense of 'normality' as soon as possible and to be able to partake in the freedoms associated with a 'free society'. These include freedom of speech, movement, property, religion, income, education and employment. For many refugees limitations are placed on these liberties that they long for, particularly for those placed in 'mandatory detention' where many of these basic freedoms are denied. Section 196 of the *Migration Act 1958* (Cth) allows for the indefinite imprisonment of asylum seekers without access to a hearing until their claim for asylum is determined. The election of the Howard Federal Liberal Coalition Government in 1996 has seen the extension of this policy and its continuance today despite public outcry and protests at the inhumane treatment and violation of human rights by both local and international groups. This has not deterred the Howard Government's approach. A main platform for their 2004 re-election campaign was around the protection and security of Australia. This was a campaign based on fear that saw the Howard government re-elected with a great majority despite serious claims of breaches of human rights.

A fundamental difference between refugees and migrants is the circumstances of their migration and their status in the country of migration. Migrants generally choose to migrate and have relative freedom of movement. They have a legal right to remain in the country of migration and generally have permanent resident visas or eligibility for citizenship. On the other hand refugees migrate due to 'well-founded fears' of persecution in their countries of origin and cannot return safely. They do not necessarily have a choice in whether or not they migrate or their destination. Often refugees have fled in circumstances that have not allowed time for adequate preparation, arriving in the country of migration with few or no belongings. Most migrants will experience varying degrees of disorientation, with this often referred to as 'culture shock'. However, this is often greater for refugees and asylum seekers who have arrived with few resources, and those who have experienced torture and trauma, prior to and during, migration and resettlement. The experience of loss and grief is often immense with many refugees having lost family and close friends and witnessed human rights atrocities.

Responses to Migration: Conventions, Legislation, Polices and Practices

Patterns of migration are reflected in government legislation and immigration policies. Historically government responses to migration all over the world tend to fit into one of five broadly defined categories of extermination, exclusion, assimilation, integration or multiculturalism. These categories are not mutually exclusive. For instance a policy of assimilation may result in a practice of extermination. The exercise of these policies will be influenced by dominant values and beliefs. Many Australians are unwittingly ethnocentric because they have been brought up in a society that is based on a class structure that privileges 'whiteness' and proficiency in the English language embedded in legislation policies and practices. Programs of racial extermination, such as Hitler's attempted extermination of the Jews during the Second World War, were based on the fallacy of cultural superiority. This false belief has also been the basis of policies of exclusion aimed at maintaining the character and institutions of the dominant culture, with the White Australia Policy an example of this.

Exclusion was the main argument in the 1850s for a 'White Australia', to maintain the British institutions and character in the Australian colonies (Willard, 1974). The *Immigration Restriction Act* (Cth) introduced in 1901 established the White Australia Policy. The White Australia Policy was formally enshrined in national legislation in 1901. This development was facilitated by continued British review of Australia's position on immigration. By the end of the century it found expression in Australian nationalism. Its restrictions were covert in their discrimination against non-Europeans. Under the 1901 *Immigration Restriction Act* any intending migrant could be rejected on grounds of failing to pass a dictation test that could be conducted in any European language. This provision in the Act remained until 1958. In 1925 an amendment to the *Immigration Act* granted the Federal Government the right to exclude anyone, 'deemed unlikely to be assimilated' (Lippman, 1979: 1).

Assimilation is when governments expect immigrants and Indigenous peoples to discard their own cultures and take on the way of life of the dominant culture. Assimilation was the aim of Australia's immigration policies from the late 1940s to the mid-1960s. This expectation, based on British influences, found expression in the commonly used term at that time, 'New Australian'. It was not expected that Anglo-Australians would adopt any part of a migrant culture. English classes were provided to assist with assimilation. The policy was based on the assumption of cultural superiority. Assimilation was largely a response to the demands of industry for an expanding labour force not met by local supply and the widespread opposition to mass migration of people from non-British backgrounds. Both major political parties did not officially drop the White Australia Policy and the policy of assimilation until the mid-1960s. The three main assumptions of assimilation are related to national identity. First, that the dominant culture is homogeneous, with this reflected in its institutions and values. Secondly, that local Indigenous populations and migrants from different cultures will upset this assumed homogeneity. And finally, that mass immigration by people from very diverse cultures would threaten this. It was under the policy of assimilation that Indigenous children in Australia were forcibly removed from their families and communities, by government and church officials – including social workers – to be raised on missions and reserves or by white families (Briskman, 2004). Ultimately the aim of policies of assimilation is the eradication of minority cultures with them subsumed by the dominant culture.

Integration acknowledges the desire of people to retain their culture with support for activities to assist with this. However, this is done in a way that supports the dominant culture. Integration gained popularity in Australia in the late 1960s when the Australian Government came to realise that most migrant groups did not support assimilation. After 1972 federal funding was provided for projects aimed at the preservation of the identity of different ethnic groups, with ethnic radio an example of this. While people of non-European background would be allowed to enter Australia, the entry criteria were to be much stricter than for Europeans. This was to preserve the homogeneity of the Australian population. Multiculturalism is based on tolerance and respect for cultural differences with the rights of different ethnic groups promoted. These include the right to separate organisations, cultural expression, media outlets and educational curricula.

Multiculturalism was introduced as a concept in 1973 by Al Grassby (1973), the then Labor Party Minister for Immigration. Efforts were made by the Labor Government to consider migrant needs in the formulation of social policy. In that same year amendments to the *Migration Act* introduced a structured assessment system for the selection of migrants. An emphasis was placed on educational qualifications and capital. The concept of multiculturalism was supported and further developed by the Liberal Government, who officially launched it in 1978 following the release of the Galbally Report in Victoria in that same year. Cultural differences were welcomed in the Report.

Multiculturalism was introduced in a policy context that saw Australia's future politically and economically in the Asia-Pacific region, with strong connections between economic and foreign policy. While multiculturalism remains the immigration policy of the incumbent Liberal

Coalition Government there has been a noticeable shift in the alignment of immigration policy with defence. Australian policy has taken on a more offensive approach aligned with the British Blair Government and the Bush administration of the United States of America rather than with the Asia-Pacific region (Fitzgerald, 1997). A strong focus of current immigration policy is business migration. Depending on its application this can be a celebration of cultural diversity or simply an extension of integration. Clear understanding of current national and international human rights laws, conventions, agreements and polices is required. These include United Nations Conventions, particularly the 1951 United Nations Convention Relating to the Status of Refugees and the 1967 United Nations Refugee Protocol (the 'Refugees Convention') (Kenny, Fiske and Ife, 2002).

Conventions, legislation and policies governing other areas will also be relevant such as international conventions on political, economic, social and cultural rights as well as those relating to inhumane treatment including torture and trauma. Migration legislation will determine migration status with different types and categories of migration, determining eligibility for services. However, other areas of legislation will also be relevant, such as social security, education, human services, employment and industrial relations. These will govern the amount and type of income support, entitlements to heath and welfare services, recognition of overseas qualifications, eligibility for English language classes, enrolment as a local student and ability to legally participate in paid employment.

Visas are not automatically granted unless, and until, the relevant government provides so. Protection or Temporary Protection Visas are required for people seeking refugee status and asylum in Australia. An application for a Bridging Visa must be lodged within 45 days of their arrival to be eligible for access to universal healthcare (Medicare), to study and to work. Without a Bridging Visa access to income support and community services is limited, with financial and other assistance provided by aid organisations such as the Red Cross, church and welfare agencies. Often these latter organisations are not clearly mandated to provide the level of service and support required and these people live in poverty reliant upon charity (Dixon and Macarov, 1998; Fincher and Nieuwenhuysen, 1998).

Resettlement, Adjustment and Identity

Cultural differences and understandings develop within the context of a dominant culture. However, similarities exist in the experience of people whose culture have been subjugated through colonisation, where Indigenous peoples are forced to adapt to the imposed dominant culture, and made to feel their culture is inferior. The histories of these people are denied and distorted. While they are told to adapt to the dominant culture they are relegated inferior status and denied the privileges of this group (Hage, 1998). This is also the experience of immigrant groups whose cultures are different to that of the dominant culture. Social workers and other workers in the human services live in a dominant culture and are educated and work within its institutions. The cultural backgrounds and understandings of these workers will influence the power they have and the way they work with others whose cultures are different to their own.

Generally in the early stages of resettlement a focus is on the provision of services and information on language classes, income, education, employment, access to basic health needs, clothing and safe, clean and affordable housing. The focus then shifts to adaptation to a new culture, social activities, parenting, intergenerational conflict, counselling and mediation.

Most immigrants want to have a sense of belonging and be able to call the country they have migrated to home, establish a better future for their children and contribute to the community (Martin and Hess, 2001). However, the reality for many migrants from groups different to the dominant culture is to identify yet feel alienated. They can find themselves not knowing who they are or where they belong. Often people make judgments based on appearances. Families who have lived in Australia for many generations may still not be viewed as 'Australian' due to their physical appearance and lack of assimilation. Citizenship is one way of formally becoming an Australian. While officially they are now 'Australians', often they are not viewed as such, particularly if they do not have Anglo-Saxon features or are of Asian or African descent. This is illustrated in the following exchange:

> The day I got Australian citizenship and I told the people in the factory I was Australian and was very proud. One said, 'No you're not'.
>
> I said, 'What am I'?
>
> He said, 'You're Chinese'.
>
> I said, 'No I'm not, I'm Australian'. (see Martin, 1999a)

Some people retain the identity of more than one culture even though they might not have dual citizenship as reflected in the following comment: 'I am Australian although I am Malaysian. I still think of Malaysia as my home' (Martin, 1999b). There are others, however, who belong to a more global community and who will travel and live in different countries depending on networks and opportunities available to them. Mak and Chan (1995) use the term 'astronauts' to describe people in these circumstances. Some people will identify and belong according to where they are at the time. The following comment by a man who was a citizen of Malaysia with permanent residency in Australia reflects the complexity of this: 'If I'm overseas I would say I'm Australian. If I'm in Australia I would say I'm Chinese' (Martin, 1999b).

For those whose cultures are deemed inferior there is the actual pain of cultural exclusion and domination (Tamanese and Waldergrave, 1994). This has caused personal hardship as well as family breakdown when members of the younger generation adopt the values and practices of the dominant culture and also begin to see their culture as 'backward' or 'inferior'. This can result in a cultural void where the young person rejects her or his own culture yet is not fully accepted into the dominant culture or is relegated a lower status. Emotional responses may vary from denial to anger and frustration and ultimately resignation or rejection. Young people who fare best demonstrate flexibility and adaptability in responding to changing cultural contexts. This reflects an embodiment of a variety of cultural responses appropriate to different particular social contexts.

As social workers and workers in the human services we are generally referred problems to manage or resolve. The concept of problem ownership is useful to consider when working with migrants and refugees. Who has decided there is a problem and why? Do those referred for assistance share the same view or is this simply a cultural misunderstanding? Ultimately you want to consider if a problem exists and if so whose problem is it? If immigrants are construed as social problems the contributions they make are often overlooked or ignored. This is implied in the term adjustment. It is generally expected that immigrants will adjust to the dominant culture without any expectation that the dominant culture will adapt to other cultures. The social problem view promotes activity aimed at assimilation or 'fitting in' rather than immigrants viewed as active and contributing community members. Past social work research has also contributed to problematic images of migrants and refugees (Singh and Johnson, 1998; Tsang, 2001). For example, Singh and Johnson (1998) point out how 'cultural conflict' in families has been a significant focus of social work research and has contributed to the image of 'problem' migrant families. Similarly, Tsang (2001) demonstrates how ethnicity has been deployed in a problematic manner in social work research in terms of a tendency to promote homogenised depictions of ethnic minority groups.

Social work and human service workers need to engage in practices that extend beyond securing rights and entitlements to facilitating and supporting active participation and involvement in leadership positions in the community and in government by members of minority groups. This includes helping people respond to, and deal with, both overt and covert discrimination. This discrimination can arise due to stereotypes and resultant expectations. For instance, some social workers find it difficult to work with refugees from wealthy backgrounds, as they do not fit their preconceived ideas of poverty and hardship. This was particularly evident when refugees fled Bosnia, formerly Yugoslavia, aboard airline passenger flights. Comments were made in the press questioning their refugee status due to the expensive clothing, mobile telephones and apparent wealth of many of them. Clearly they did not fit with community, media and human services stereotypes. Discrimination can also occur in the form of a community backlash when immigrants have been successful in advocating for themselves and meeting their own needs.

Your formulation of the problem, or assessment of the situation, will be influenced by your own dominant perspectives that may or may not be culturally appropriate. How then do you deal with practices that are acceptable and encouraged within a particular culture that are deemed disrespectful or inappropriate in the dominant culture? Likewise, how do you respond to practices by the dominant culture that are disrespectful to other cultures? Consideration of these questions requires personal reflection as well as consideration of the role of social workers as agents of social control. Child protection is an area where families are often referred because of cultural differences in child rearing practices. Some cultural groups have complained about child protection practices being dis- respectful and culturally inappropriate (Martin, 1999a). Critical theory is useful for considering such practice dilemmas and developing practices that are culturally respectful and affirming.

Critical Theory

A number of theories are included under the umbrella of 'critical theory'. These theories include: structural, feminist, anti-oppressive and anti- discriminatory and postmodern. Main features common to these theories include a commitment to social justice, human rights and empowerment. These theories are particularly relevant to cross-cultural practice in addressing issues of oppression and disadvantage faced by many migrant and refugee families. When discussing theories used in social work it is worth noting that the main theories used in contemporary social work are predominantly from the social sciences and psychology. Most of these theories have been developed by members of the dominant cultures in countries that have either colonised other parts of the world, or where there is a past history of colonisation. Major influences in thinking in social science and psychology have come from Britain, Canada and the United States of America. Much of this theory is culture bound and is one way of approaching and explaining events – predominantly through a Western lens. Increasingly social workers are being exposed to literature and research conducted in different cultural contexts by those who are not members of dominant cultural groups. This literature opens our eyes to different cultural interpretations and possibilities and increases our lear- ning and understandings of cultural experiences and diversity. Critical theoretical perspectives are useful in examining both the personal and political dimensions of social work practice (Martin, 2003). They demon- strate the collective power of individuals in like circumstances while also reminding social workers to recognise and respond to the uniqueness of individual experiences.

Structural theory encourages critical reflection on the personal and political aspects of migration and resettlement. This includes consi- deration of how migrants and refugees are viewed and subsequently treated (Mullaly, 1997). It provides an analysis of power and privilege by looking at who benefits and who suffers from the categorisation of certain migrants and refugees as 'undesirable' or as 'social problems'. A structural approach recognises the importance of responding to a person's immediate needs, with this particularly important for asylum seekers without income support. The power dimensions of relationships are highlighted with consideration of how services are delivered. A main focus is on social, political and economic change, to improve the lives of migrants and refugees that recognises and celebrates diversity. Human services workers are called upon to enact such changes both personally and professionally.

'Feminist theory' also focuses on both the personal and political dimensions of power and privilege. However, this is from a gender analysis (Dominelli and McLeod, 1989). Issues of oppression and discrimination are examined from a gender perspective that is respectful of cultural difference. Service responses are designed specifically to meet the needs of women from different cultural backgrounds, recognising individual and collective needs. Campaigns are aimed at developing gender appropriate organisational structures and service responses (Burke and Harrison, 1998).

Anti-oppressive and anti-discriminatory theories challenge social inequalities arising from racial, ethnic and cultural differences (Quinn, 2003). An emphasis is on addressing discrimination as a means of alleviating oppression (Dominelli, 1998; Thompson, 1998). Self and cultural knowledge that values difference is a central feature of anti-oppressive and anti-discriminatory practice. Activities include the development and implementation of culturally inclusive policies and practices. The engagement of social workers with civil libertarian and social justice lawyers can assist in reducing the oppressive aspects of the law as well as maximising people's rights. Openly naming and challenging discriminatory practices is required.

'Postmodern theory' highlights the uniqueness of individual experience and the notion of multiple truths and realities. Postmodernism highlights the exploitation, cultural destruction, devastation, genocide and impoverishment that has occurred as a result of what has been viewed as progress under the guise of colonialism, imperialism and economic development (Foucault, 1972). It stresses the relationship between power and knowledge and the contradictions of emancipation and domination. From a postmodern perspective multiple views and realities connect with, and inform, the broader political, economic and social structures (Leonard, 1993). People whose cultures have been subjugated by the dominated culture need to have their stories and experiences listened to, acknowledged and respected. Those who have experienced the pain of domination are best placed to speak of what they have lost on a personal, family and societal level. This is not a search for truth but rather the validation of personal experiences of exclusion and their place in a history that excludes them or places them in an inferior position. It also provides an opportunity for greater understanding of cultural behaviours and practices rejected by the dominant group. Critical theories inform practices that are culturally relevant and empowering.

Cross-cultural Practice

A 'critical approach' to cross-cultural practice embodies emancipatory practices that examine the social construction of reality. This requires self-knowledge and personal reflection on the dominant social discourses that impact on migration, resettlement and adjustment. Change is brought about by resisting and challenging discourses that lead to discriminatory and oppressive practices. A lack of cultural understanding can result in the imposition of dominant cultural views that displace or deny different cultural understandings and problem solving approaches. In this process workers can unwittingly perpetuate the pain of subjugation. Different cultural perspectives and understandings are important. A study of the heath and welfare needs of the Chinese communities of Melbourne found that problem solving approaches were preferable to non-directive interventions (Martin and Hess, 2001). Problem solving approaches recognise and value each person's own resources and skills and abilities in decision-making. These are central features of social work practice, particularly strengths-based approaches (Glicken, 2003).

Strengths perspectives focus on potential, not limitations, social interactions, strengths and capacities. Narratives are valuable for challenging the status quo by exploring alternative discourses, allowing for the development of different conceptualisations and understandings. Both strengths and narratives perspectives value the uniqueness of individual experiences and meanings, and identify and respond to the impacts of dominant discourses.

Cross-cultural working relationships take time to develop and are impeded by a brusque businesslike approach. Respect, sincerity, honesty and a trustworthy approach are central to developing culturally appropriate service responses. Shame and loss of face will prevent some people from seeking services and does not necessarily mean that services are not needed. Respect for privacy, cultural preferred ways of communicating and traditional health and problem solving practices is required as well as acknowledgment of different cultural meanings. For instance in some cultures lack of eye contact is a sign of respect, yet in others it is considered disrespectful. Indirectness and agreement are respectful ways of communicating in some cultures, yet in others are seen as confusing and possibly insincere. For some people 'yes' may mean they are listening, not that they are agreeing. Where possible it is best to avoid language that does not have a direct translation or shared cultural meanings.

'Critical questioning' is useful for deconstructing negative views and stereotypes. It provided opportunities to look at people and their situations from different perspectives by exploring expectations and behaviours within relevant social contexts. Critical reflection is the fist step towards developing culturally sensitive practices.

Critical Reflection

As social workers and workers in the human services we need to develop reflective practices that examine our personal responses to people who are different to ourselves due to racial, ethnic and cultural differences (Fook, 1999). While theory and research can assist in gaining understanding of main issues, it is through personal interaction and listening to accounts of people's experiences that empathy begins to develop. This requires substantial self-reflection and self-knowledge as well as meaningful exposure and interaction with people whose cultural background is different to your own. 'Self-reflexive practice' is crucial for the avoidance of processes of domination. This requires personal reflection in examining your own values and assumption claims to knowledge, power and authority, personal, cultural and social background as well as an understanding of your own personality and emotions. An understanding of 'internalised oppression' is useful in examining ways in which dominant social ideas and prejudices have impacted on your own self-esteem and sense of powerlessness. This may be associated with race, ethnicity or culture, or it may be oppression of another kind such as gender, class or age. 'Internalised domination' requires personal scrutiny, at times uncomfortable, for members of the dominant culture about their acceptance of prejudices emanating from a view of cultural superiority. Examination of exercise of power and authority is central to this analysis (Allan, 2003). How comfortable do you feel to name discriminatory practices?

Naming Discriminatory Practices

It is often claimed by academics that 'Everyone is racist'. Yet while some people exercise this, others do not. This adds the dimension of 'power' to relationships resulting in actions that treat people as inferior due to their racial background. Often this exercise of power is due to an unfounded fear of difference and possible subjugation. An often unspoken fear is that those who have been dominated will, if given the opportunity, in turn dominate their oppressors (Tamanese and Waldergrave, 1994). This fear can lead to discriminatory practices under the guise of protection with immigrants construed as social problems. The 'objectification' of people results in them being stereotyped and seen as strange or different and to feared, or as passive objects to be managed, or looked after, by government and human service organisations. This view serves to reinforce and promote the dominant culture (Hage, 1998). The example of the unfounded claim by the Howard Liberal Government in Australia of refugees throwing their children overboard is an example of objectification, with these people being seen as engaging in practices that were inhumane and abhorrent to the general community (Burnside, 2004).

Challenging discrimination and oppression calls upon workers to identify and name discriminatory discourses and practices. While this sounds simple enough it implies there is, or will be, some agreement that discrimination has occurred. This may be quite straightforward as in the case of overt acts such as violence, graffiti or name calling, perhaps telling a person to 'go home'. The irony of this last example is that generally they are in fact at home. Yet it is the more subtle covert forms of discrimination that are extremely difficult to deal with. These are often based on exclusion and the person is left wondering why they have been treated badly for no apparent reason. This might take the form of being made to wait in a shop while other customers are given priority even though you were there before them. It might be that your child has met a friend at school and wants them to come over to play and the response is simply, 'I don't think so'. You may begin to wonder: is this discrimination, or is it bordering on paranoia? How do you know the intention of another person's behaviour if in fact they do not openly declare it? Is it better to give people the benefit of the doubt and move on or is this a passive response that reinforces the discriminatory practices? On the other hand, do you accuse them of being a racist? This is an accusation that is often vehemently denied.

Calling someone a racist can have the effect of further reinforcing polarised views and closing down possibilities of dialogue. Yet how can a covert discriminatory practice be named in a way that is assertive and not confrontational or aggressive? Here is a situation I learnt from recently.

> I was teaching a class on cross-cultural practice to a group of social work students. As part of this class I had invited a friend and colleague to talk with the students about his life as a refugee immigrant to Australia, his practice of Cambodian culture in Australia and his work with the Cambodian community. Not long after the class started a student walked out. I followed and asked if there was a problem. He replied telling me that he could not understand a word the speaker was saying, that he had no intention of working with Cambodian people and that the class was a terrible waste of his time. I sensed that he was annoyed with me for this. He advised me that he was going to the library so that his morning was not totally wasted and that he would read about cross-cultural practice.

> This was a tense moment with my emotions ranging from annoyance to frustration to anger, arising in response to what the student was saying as well as the fact that I was now also missing the class. My dilemma was that I wanted this student to engage with developing his cross-cultural understandings and capacities that in this brief encounter seemed to be lacking. While I did not agree with his views I did not want to upset and alienate him, however, I wanted a quick resolution. My aim was to engage him in a dialogue in a manner that was respectful and not threatening. I reframed his 'waste of time' with 'very

important and worthwhile'. I tried to generate some interest and enthusiasm by speaking positively about the speaker and the class and requested he return. He was not convinced and again stated his intention of going to the library. At this point I referred to the assessment for the course and my concerns that this missed class might jeopardise his grades. He agreed to return to the class, yet I felt very uncomfortable with this exercise of power and it seemed that this feeling was mutual. Here I was dominating him as a student in a class that was about addressing issues of power and domination of another kind.

When I returned to the class I began to question my judgment in inviting the speaker and wondered if others could understand him. I then felt guilty for having these doubts about him. After the class I overheard this student say to another student, now familiar words to me, that the class was a total waste of time and that he could not understand a word that the speaker had said. Fortunately the other student replied that she really enjoyed the class and found it very interesting. She went on to say that she also had difficulty understanding the speaker at first and that she had to really concentrate on what he was saying until she got used to his accent. The student did not reply. However, in class after the lecture he was quite engaged in the discussion of anti-racist practice.

This example illustrates issues of power and domination operating in different contexts as well as the range of emotions that can arise in situations where there is a perception of discrimination by another party. It shows how this can lead to polarisation of views and a lack of engagement. It demonstrates how meaningful engagement did occur in this situation through connection by a peer. This was done in a respectful way that validated this student's view yet allowed for it to be open to scrutiny without him feeling attacked or dominated. It demonstrated a considered response rather than a reactive one. This engagement was continued in a group context with the further sharing of ideas and perspectives. The above example also illustrates that simply telling people what to do and what not to do is not enough and does not necessarily translate into action. It demonstrates the importance of meaningful engagement for effective cross-cultural understandings and communication to occur. The greatest challenge for organisations is not how to develop culturally inclusive polices and procedures but rather how to enact these.

Organisational Considerations

How do you create a culture within an organisation that is respectful and affirming of all cultures? Workers in the human services need to be careful not to perpetuate the dominant social discourse that sees migrants as social problems. Reframing of this problem focus is required with a focus on strengths and contributions. However, it is important for workers to recognise the diverse nature of migrants and refugees and ways they can be of assistance. A particularly challenging dilemma is organisations that have beautifully presented glossy publications on cross-cultural practice that say all the right things, yet workplace practices implementing these policy statements are hard to find and are at best superficial tokenism. How then do organisations move from a veneer of cross-cultural practice to one that is meaningfully integrated into all dimensions of organisational life? This begins with open dialogue and communication about meaningful cross-cultural practices with the development of a mission statement that articulates a commitment to cultural diversity and organisational policies and practices that acknowledge and affirm this. Culturally sensitive practices are important for all workers in human service agencies, especially for frontline staff whose staff development needs in this area are often overlooked. In human service organisations it is generally assumed that all workers, managers included, embrace cross-cultural approaches and understandings. The reality, however, is that workers will bring their experiences of domination and subjugation to the workplace and may wittingly or unwittingly develop and impose policies and practices that reflect this. It is not appropriate to expect people from different cultures to necessarily fit into a model of service delivery designed by, and for, people from the dominant cultural group.

Most students of social work and social work practitioners are from the dominant cultural groups and need to be equipped to work across a range of culturally diverse settings. Ethno-specific workers are small in number and often experience ongoing discrimination and exclusion in the same way as those they are working with. This is reflected in the poor funding arrangements and infrastructure of ethno-specific services. There is a danger of perpetuating practices of exclusion by referring people to ethno-specific workers and agencies rather than endeavouring to create culturally appropriate responses in mainstream services. While at times it is appropriate to refer to bilingual workers it is not appropriate to expect bilingual workers to be expert on all matters and provide all services.

Interpreters need to be made available with all staff trained to work with them (Rodopolous, 2002). Older migrants often have difficulty learning another language and it is not appropriate to expect them to do so, especially if they have never received any formal education. Working with interpreters takes time and can be costly, particularly for intensive service provision in the community. It is often easier to refer people to workers who speak the person's language and this may be desirable and appropriate. However, it may not be and the person may be denied access to services they need from your agency because of this.

Funding constraints of human service organisations mean that people are often being required to do more for less. This means that short cuts are taken with use of interpreters. Two agencies I have worked in had insufficient budget allocations for payment of interpreters. In one agency workers were actively encouraged to use family and friends as interpreters. As a social worker on a psychiatric community crisis response team I recall visiting a man who did not speak English, three times daily initially. I relied solely on what I could see visually, what his friends who were looking after him told me, some limited conversation with him interpreted by whoever was at the house caring for him at the times I visited, and conversations with his general practitioner. In this instance the outcomes were positive and his friends very supportive. However, is this a model of service delivery that is generally acceptable within the human services? In many instances the use of family and friends to interpret is not appropriate, particularly where sensitive and private matters are being discussed in a counselling situation. Confidentiality cannot be guaranteed and the interpretation cannot always be relied upon. In some cultures, a family member or close friend, due to bad karma, will not communicate bad news and will in fact change the message as illustrated in the following comment: 'If my mum got cancer and I was interpreter for her I wouldn't tell her she got cancer. I'd tell her something else' (Martin, 1999c).

The reliance upon children as interpreters is particularly problematic when they are being asked to assume responsibility that is not appropriate to their age and position in the family. They can become privy to information they would not otherwise know. Role reversal can occur with the child assuming a position of authority in the family due to their language proficiency with their parents reliant upon them. Sometimes workers will ask bilingual workers to interpret for them. This is often inappropriate, as while it may seem convenient, it is an imposition and could be seen as disrespectful. It is more appropriate to work collaboratively and together decide how best to proceed.

Many immigrant groups are small in number and people might not want their problems to be shared within the community. For others, however, this may be preferred. Some people argue for workers of the same cultural backgrounds as those they are working with. This is due to greater cultural knowledge and understandings. However, some people may prefer to see workers outside of their culture for reasons of confidentiality or possible bias (Hess, 1992; 1997).

Culturally inclusive practices are those where mainstream services employ bilingual and bi-cultural workers and forge partnerships and strong networks with community leaders and workers in ethno-specific agencies. This way those seeking services get the benefit of the range of services provided. Workers also gain from increased cross-cultural knowledge and understandings and networks. Personal contact is the most effective means of communication. Working with different ethnic communities and providing information in community languages is central to developing culturally inclusive practices. This is often achieved through networking with ethnic community leaders and using a range of ethno-specific media such as newspapers, radio, television and notices in shops.

Workers need to continually critically reflect on whose needs they are serving and the values and ethics of the social work profession. Are these needs personal, organisational or those of the person seeking a service? In reality all three areas of need will play some part in how workers respond. However, if personal and organisational needs dominate the service responses will be distorted and inappropriate. Ultimately the organisational culture will be reflected in the type of services and manner in which they are provided.

Responding to Special Needs of Refugees and Asylum Seekers

The gross denial of human rights experienced by refugees and asylum seekers does not mean that social workers cannot assist (Ife, 2001). Social workers play an important role in assessing needs and identifying obstacles and developing other pathways to meet these needs. This requires critical awareness and sensitivity to the values and ethics espoused by social workers and the commitment to human rights and social justice. It requires an ability to work effectively in a context where government policies are often hostile and contravene the values and ethics of social work (Ife, 1997). This involves political awareness and ethical practice with interventions that are responsive to both the personal and political dimensions of the person's situation. This involves both service provision as well as community work and advocacy for policy improvements and legislative change directed at a more humane approach. Due to the range, diversity and intensity of needs collaborative community-based responses are required across a range of services and workers, including refugee legal centres (Kenny et al, 2002).

Issues of trust and respect are particularly important. Trusting relationships will take time and may be difficult to establish due to past experiences of abuse that may be ongoing. For those who have survived torture and trauma the aftermath can be post-traumatic stress, flashbacks, ongoing nightmares and fear of authorities (Victorian Foundation for Survivors of Torture, 1998). Many refugees and asylum seekers suffer from significant psychological distress due to separation from family members and often not knowing where they are, or what has happened to them. Then there are others who are already living in poverty, who may be sending money back to support their relatives overseas. This financial strain impacts on relationships and quality of life. For many, experiences in refugee camps and detention centres have resulted in further human rights violations. A particular challenge for social workers is how to respond to both the personal and political dimensions of mandatory detention. On a personal level it may be arranging for visits and commu-nication via newspapers or other reading materials in the person's own language, telephone, email, letters, conversation, friendship and instilling a sense of hope. It may be in advocacy and assistance in pursuing applications for asylum and appropriate representation through legal and other sources. It may be in social action campaigns targeted at the abolition of mandatory detention with representations to key ministers in government for a more humane approach.

Summary

Best practice with migrants and refugees calls upon the same commitment to social justice, values, self-knowledge, theoretical understandings and practice skills as any other area of social work practice. It calls upon a commitment to learning about different cultures as well as your own. Critical theoretical perspectives are useful in highlighting issues of power and domination and the political, social and economic dimensions related to resettlement and adjustment. The dominant values of a society will influence policy and decision-making and will determine the way migrants and refugees are viewed and subsequently treated. It is necessary for human service workers to challenge and move beyond a familiar view that sees migrants and refugees as 'social problems'. Respect is required for different needs at different stages of resettlement with appropriate service responses. This includes recognition of special needs of people who have migrated as refugees who may have experienced torture or trauma and the loss of loved ones. Such responses acknowledge and respect the strengths and contributions migrants and refugees make culturally, socially, economically and politically as well as human rights obligations. Best practices are those that are welcoming, culturally inclusive and celebrate diversity of all kinds.

Review Questions

1. What are the dominant cultural influences in your life?

2. What contact do you have with people whose cultures are different from your own?

3. How would your friends and family react if you married a person whose culture is different from your own?

4. At what stage are people accepted on an equal basis into the dominant culture? Is this influenced by birthplace, citizenship or assimilation due to language ability and physical attributes similar to the dominant social group, or other factors?

5. As a worker in the human services how can you respond to policies and practices that do not actively support culturally sensitive practices?

Useful Websites

Australasian Legal Information Institute	http://www.austlii.edu.au/
Association for Services to Torture and Trauma Survivors	http://www.asetts.org.au/
Department of Immigration and Multicultural and Indigenous Affairs	http://www.immi.gov.au/
Australian Human Rights and Equal Opportunity Commission	http://www.hreoc.gov.au/
Immigration and Advice Rights Centre	http://www.iarc.asn.au/
Migration Institute of Australia	http://mia.org.au/
United Nations High Commission for Human Rights	http://www.unhcr.org/cgi-bin/texis/vtx/home

References

Allan, J (2003) 'Practising critical social work', in J Allan, B Pease and L Briskman (eds) *Critical Social Work: An Introduction to Theories and Practices* (pp 52-74), Sydney: Allen & Unwin.

Briskman, L (2003) *The Black Grapevine: Aboriginal Activism and the Stolen Generations*, Sydney: The Federation Press.

Burke, B and Harrison, P (1998) 'Anti-oppressive practice', in R Adams, L Dominelli and M Payne (eds), *Social Work: Themes, Issues and Critical Debates* (pp 229-239), London: Macmillan.

Burnside, J (ed) (2004) *From Nothing to Zero: Letters from Refugees in Australia's Detention Centres*, Melbourne: Lonely Planet.

Cox, D (1987) *Migration from Malaysia to Australia*, Melbourne: Department of Social Work, University of Melbourne.

Dixon, J and Macarov, D (1998) *Poverty: A Persistent Global Reality*, London: Routledge.

Dominelli, L (1998) 'Anti-oppressive practice in context', in R Adams, L Dominelli and M Payne (eds) *Social Work: Themes, Issues and Critical Debates* (pp 3-22), London: Macmillan.

Dominelli, L and McLeod E (1989) *Feminist Social Work*, London: Macmillan.

Fincher, R and Nieuwenhuysen, J (1998) *Australian Poverty Then and Now*, Melbourne: Melbourne University Press.

Fitzgerald, S (1997) *Is Australia an Asian Country?: Can Australia Survive in an East Asian Future?*, Sydney: Allen & Unwin.

Fook, J (1999) 'Critical reflectivity in education and practice', in B Pease and J Fook (eds) *Transforming Social Work Practice: Postmodern Critical Perspectives* (pp 195-209), Sydney: Allen & Unwin.

Foucault, M (1972) *The Archaeology of Knowledge*, London: Tavistock.

Galbally Report, (1978) *Review of Post Arrival Programs and Services for Migrants*, Canberra: Australian Government Publishing Press.

Glicken, M (2003) *Using the Strengths Perspective in Social Work Practice: A Positive Approach for the Helping Professions*, Boston: Pearson Education.

Grassby, A (1973) *A Multicultural Society for the Future*, Canberra: Australian Government Publishing Press.

Hage, G (1998) *White Nation: Fantasies of White Supremacy in a Multicultural Society*, Sydney: Pluto Press.

Hess, L (1992) 'Working within a multi-cultural setting', Paper presented at the *Australian Association of Social Workers, Victorian Branch State Conference*, Melbourne.

Ife, J (2001) *Human Rights and Social Work: Towards Rights-based Practice*, Cambridge: Cambridge University Press.

Kenny, M, Fiske, L and Ife, J (2002) 'Refugees, asylum seekers and the law', in P Swain (ed) *In the Shadow of the Law: The Legal Context of Social Work Practice* (2nd ed) (pp 244-253), Sydney: The Federation Press.

Leonard, P (1993) 'Knowledge/power and postmodernism: Implications for the practice of a critical social work education', Extended version of a paper presented at the *Annual Conference of the Canadian Association of Schools of Social Work*, Ottawa.

Lippman, L (1979) *Current Attitudes to Asian Immigration Into Australia*, Melbourne: Clearing House on Migrant Issues.

Mak, A and Chan, H (1995) 'Chinese family values in Australia', in R Hartley (ed) *Families and Cultural Diversity in Australia* (pp 70-95), Sydney: Allen & Unwin.

Martin, J (1999a) *Issues for Cross Cultural Practice with Australians of Chinese Vietnamese Background*, Melbourne: Ecumenical Migration Centre.

Martin, J (1999b) *Issues for Cross Cultural Practice with Australians of Chinese Malaysian Background*, Melbourne: Ecumenical Migration Centre.

Martin, J (1999c) *Issues for Cross Cultural Practice with Australians of Chinese Cambodian Background*, Melbourne: Ecumenical Migration Centre.

Martin, J (2003) 'Historical development of critical social work practice', in J Allan, B Pease and L Briskman (eds) *Critical Social Work: An Introduction to Theories and Practices* (pp 17-31), Sydney: Allen & Unwin.

Martin, J and Hess, L (2001) 'Cross cultural communication with Chinese communities', Paper presented at the *27th National Conference of the Australian Association of Social Workers*, Melbourne.

Mullaly, R (1997) *Structural Social Work: Ideology, Theory and Practice* (2nd ed), Toronto: Oxford University Press.

Quinn, M (2003) 'Immigrants and refugees: Towards anti-racist and culturally affirming practices', in J Allan, B Pease and L Briskman (eds) *Critical Social Work: An Introduction to Theories and Practices* (pp 75-91), Sydney: Allen & Unwin.

Roberts, L (ed) (2005a) *Refugee Review Tribunal Bulletin* (Issue No 2/2005), Canberra: Refugee Review Tribunal.

Roberts, L (ed) (2005b) *Refugee Review Tribunal Bulletin* (Issue No 4/2005), Canberra: Refugee Review Tribunal.

Rodopolous, L (2002) 'Culture and linguistic entanglement', in P Swain (ed) *In the Shadow of the Law: The Legal Context of Social Work Practice* (2nd ed) (pp 16-27), Sydney: The Federation Press.

Singh, G and Johnson, MRD (1998) 'Research with ethnic minority groups in health and social welfare', in C Williams, H Soydan and MRD Johnson (eds) *Social Work and Minorities: European Perspectives* (pp 231-246), London: Routledge.

Tamanese, K and Waldergrave, C (1994) 'Cultural and gender accountability in the "Just Therapy" approach', *Dulwich Center Newsletter Nos 2 & 3*, Lower Hutt, New Zealand: The Family Centre.

Thompson, N (1998) *Promoting Equality: Challenging Discrimination and Oppression in the Human Services*, London: Macmillan.

Tsang, AKT (2001) 'Representation of ethnic identity in North American social work literature: A dossier of the Chinese people', *Social Work*, 46(3), 229-243.

United Nations (1951) *Convention and Protocol Relating to the Status of Refugees*. Available at: <http://www.unhcr.org/cgi-bin/texis/vtx/protect/opendoc.pdf?tbl=PROTECTION&id=3b66c2aa10>.

Victorian Foundation for Survivors of Torture (VFST) (1998) *Rebuilding Shattered Lives*, Melbourne: VFST.

Willard, M (1974) *History of the White Australia Policy*, Melbourne: Melbourne University Press.

Legislation Cited

Immigration Restriction Act 1901 (Cth)
Migration Act 1958 (Cth)

Index